Cheiro
THE
WONDERFUL

ACKNOWLEDGEMENTS

My thanks to Adelais Farnell Sharp for her comments and edits on early drafts of this book, and for joining me on a pilgrimage to Bray where we visited Cheiro's birthplace.

I am grateful to the members of the Cheiro Project Facebook Group for feedback and discussions while research was ongoing, especially Yasmin Boland, Adam Fronteras, Philip Graves, Liz Hathway, Sharon Knight, Olga Morales and Muriel Pécastaing-Boissière.

Thanks to Teegan Morris for her assistance with the cover design.

And thanks also to Trish Marin for proofreading the final version of this book. I'm sure it was a lot more words than she'd expected.

DEDICATION

This is a book for Matthew Edwards. I hope he likes it.

CONTENTS

If Fate were naught—and we were wise,
How calmly we would plan the earth!
There'd be no sorrow, tears or dearth;
Nothing but joy would fill our eyes
If Fate were naught—and we were wise.

If: Cheiro

Undated cabinet card, about 1892-3. Getty Images.

CHAPTER

ONE

I entertain only the most sublime feelings of pity and regret for those who let their chance of seeing this great man pass them by like a sunbeam.[1]

CHEIRO WAS GORGEOUS. For what follows to make sense, you must understand this more than anything.

He was drop dead, tongue hanging out of your mouth stunningly handsome. Everyone said so. He had 'the figure of an athlete, with a strong head set upon a neck like a Greek god's'.[2] Taller than average, with a mass of dark, curly hair and regular features, he made 'as pleasing a presence as one might wish to see'.[3]

People gasped at 'his marvellous clairvoyant eyes' surrounded by long and luxurious lashes.[4] The press fought amongst themselves to define their colour—they were grey, dark blue, hazel or bright green. But they agreed that his 'eyes when you looked at him seemed to look right through you' and 'He can hold you with a single glance of his dark, searching eyes.'[5]

As if that weren't enough, Cheiro possessed an excess of charisma. Suave and softly spoken with a hint of an Irish accent, he 'has earned the right to be called a savant, and his easy, affable manner bespeaks his wide experience and breeding'.[6]

Men and women swooned in his presence. 'The personal magnetism of the man is irresistible… You dare not tell him an untruth.'[7] 'He is possessed of unusual gifts… a man of high courage who never refuses any adventure'.[8]

His gorgeousness is an essential facet of Cheiro's story. And yet it goes unmentioned in accounts that describe in puzzlement how rapidly he achieved and embraced fame. Obviously, he wasn't perfect; he took advantage of his gorgeousness on more than one occasion: 'I adored Cheiro, but there were times when he was very cruel,' said one of his friends.[9]

Cheiro was destined to become the most renowned seer of modern times; the best palmist ever known, mixing with the good and the great of high society. He told tall tales about being in places he never visited and spending time with people he never met. And yet, some of his wilder claims were true—he really did know a princess who married a lion tamer. Some of his untruths are based on what he saw as fact—he appeared to genuinely believe he had an aristocratic heritage. Other stories he hugged to himself, but his footsteps through time have left traces, and it is those traces we shall follow.

He was at the height of his fame when the press called him 'Cheiro the Wonderful'.[10] To his friends, he was 'Louis'.

Where did this paragon of Irish manhood come from?

Louis's father was William Warner, born about 1830. He was the son of John Warner, a gardener from Delgany—a village now part of Greystones, two miles south of Bray, a coastal town in County Wicklow, twelve miles from the centre of Dublin. Gaps in Irish records mean it's impossible to trace the family lineage with any certainty.

Does this matter? you may cry. *I'm interested in His Gorgeousness and it would only be a footnote.*

It matters because William Warner was an amateur genealogist—it was a hugely popular hobby at the time. Middle-class enthusiasts spent many happy hours searching for their aristocratic ancestors. Their task was infinitely easier after 1826 when John Burke, an Anglo-Irish poet and journalist, published *A Genealogical and Heraldic Dictionary of the Peerage and Baronetage of the United Kingdom*.

Unlike previous similar texts, which used hard-to-follow genealogical tables, Burke's *Peerage* listed its pedigrees alphabetically. It was a roaring success and was followed in 1833 by *A Genealogical and Heraldic History of the Commoners of Great Britain and Ireland* and other related titles. Burke's catalogues are still referenced today, and for many years they were the most widely available resource.

A tiny problem was that much of it was made up. Oscar Wilde stated in 1893, 'You should study the Peerage... It is the best thing in fiction the

English have ever done.'[11] Famously, one of its editors, Leslie Pine said, 'If everybody who claims to have come over with the Conqueror were right, William must have landed with 200,000 men-at-arms instead of about 12,000.'[12]

In the 1894 edition, errors were corrected and many fantasies removed. But the version William Warner read included them in all their glory. He believed he was entitled to the name 'Le Warner' and could trace his family back to the Hamons of Normandy. This is a simplified version of the story:

A man called Helier fled Belgium, and on finding Normandy too lively, he arrived in Jersey. After multiple attacks by Vikings, Saxons or Vandals (depending which version of the story you read), hardly anyone lived on the island, so Helier settled down to a holy life in a cave. From his vantage point, Helier could see the sails of approaching attackers and signal the locals so they could run off into the marshes.

Then Hamon the Sea King and his pirates arrived. Hamon became rather cross when Helier preached the Gospel to him and his men – especially when he told them they should give up their lives of pillage and murder. After all, Hamon and his company enjoyed charging around the seas and invading places. So Hamon raised his axe and with one blow he killed Helier. Later, Helier's friend Romard discovered his body on the beach still clutching his head in his hands. And later still, Helier became Jersey's patron saint and gave his name to its main town.

'Historical records show that this incident took place on July 17th, a.d. 526,' Louis said confidently.[13]

Louis believed he was descended from one of Hamon's descendants, Rollo, who also liked conquering places. After being driven from Norway by the King of Denmark, Rollo tried to conquer England but was repulsed by King Alfred. He was more successful when he invaded Normandy and in 912 became the first Duke of Normandy.

Rollo married Gilbette, daughter of King Charles the Simple of France, and had two sons—William the Long Sword, an ancestor of William the Conqueror, and Robert, the first Earl of Corboile and ancestor of Hamon Dentatus.[i]

It gets confusing here. A seventeenth-century pedigree of the Granville family says that Hamon Dentatus' sons included Robert Fitz Hamon (the oldest), Richard de Granville, and Hamon—called in the

---

i So-named because he either was born with teeth or had prominent teeth.

Domesday Book 'Dapifer' for having received the office of Lord Steward for the King. Other sources describe Robert and Richard as Hamon Danetus' grandsons and sons of Hamon the Dapifer.

Robert and Richard fought alongside William the Conqueror at the Battle of Hastings. After William the Conqueror died, Robert set out to conquer Wales. He took twelve knights with him, including Richard, and efficiently took over Glamorganshire, obliging the rest of Wales to pay tribute to the King of England. He later built Cardiff castle, and so increased the wealth and importance of Tewkesbury Abbey in Gloucestershire that he was regarded as its second founder. Robert returned to France in 1105 where someone stuck a pike in his head leading to brain damage. He died in 1107 and was buried at Tewkesbury.[ii]

At some point, this family became attached to the Venables family. Reputedly descended from Rollo's younger brother Thibault, Gilbert de Venables was born in 1085 in Venables, Normandy.[iii] In 1096 he married Isabel, the daughter of Hugh de Crepi; their son Hamon de Leigh was born in Cheshire in 1112. Gilbert died in 1118 and Isabel married William de Warinne the Earl of Surrey.[iv]

The Lee-Warner family, reputedly descended from Robert Fitz Hamon, was based in Bray. The precise family connection William Warner believed in is impossible to work out. But he thought he had the right to a forgotten title.[v]

As if this weren't exciting enough, Louis later described William Warner as Spanish or French, occasionally Greek. Sometimes he said his mother was of Greek extraction, at other times, Spanish.[14] Or she was descended from French Huguenots and a distant relative of the novelist Alexander Dumas. *Who's Who* later described Louis as the son of Count William de Hamon and Mlle Dumas. There is absolutely no evidence to support these claims, and even Louis gradually stopped mentioning them.

---

ii Although he held the lordship of Gloucester, no charter has been identified in which he is accorded the comital title. According to tradition, Robert Fitz Hamon had four daughters, Cecily, Hawyse (or Isabella), Amice and Mabel (or Maud) who married Robert de Courcil (or Fitzroy or de Caen) in 1107, the illegitimate but acknowledged son of Henry I, who became the Earl of Gloucester in 1122.

iii Sometimes rendered Theobald.

iv Sometimes rendered Warenne or Warner. The author Jane Austen's mother was related to this family.

v To complicate matters further, the name Hamon was also brought to Ireland by two brothers, Hector and Isaac, who settled at Portarlington in Laoise in the eighteenth century, but this is another line entirely, so we'll ignore it.

I'd wonder how he kept track, except the contradictory accounts make it clear he didn't.

That doesn't mean everyone was convinced. It was 'not on the face of it what the S.P.R. [Society for Psychical Research] would call "veridical" as a title, though the sound is not unfamiliar in the French of Stratford-atte-Bow.'[15]

Back to reality: In preparation for his future career, William Warner passed his algebra exams with flying colours in June 1860. He was now a teacher and married Margaret Thompson, the daughter of William Thompson, a collections clerk from Bray. Their wedding took place in Bray on 1 August 1861, the same month that William's poem 'A Vision of Love' was published.

By no stretch of the imagination was Louis brought up in an Irish village as often stated. To be fair, he never suggested this himself. Far from being filled with country bumpkins, Bray had been a favoured summer resort for wealthier Dubliners since the early nineteenth century. The Romantic movement had made nature attractive, and Wicklow's wild landscape was considered vital to the soul, rather than hostile or threatening as it had been before. As well as enjoying stunning scenery and visiting ancient buildings such as the castle, visitors could stroll along the mile-long seafront and avail themselves of opportunities to take tea in local cafés. It was also a popular location for weddings.

On 10 July 1854 the railway line was opened from Dublin to Bray. With improved access, more people not only visited Bray, they lived there while working in Dublin. William Dargan, the railway entrepreneur and creator of the Great Industrial Exhibition of 1853, worked with John Quin, the owner of Quin's Hotel (now the Royal Hotel) who owned most of the land in the area to develop Bray as a seaside resort. They laid out roads and built terraces, and in 1859 Dargan paid for the first effort at constructing the Esplanade. Hotels and guesthouses sprang up at an alarming rate, ideally placed both next to the railway line and near the seafront. Kiosks and bandstands sprouted nearby, and a range of churches appeared to cater to the expanded population. Efforts were made to improve street lighting, the water supply and paving. There were even Turkish baths built in 1859, although that was a step too far for locals. It closed in the early 1860s and the building was later converted to concert rooms.

Bray was known as the 'Brighton of Ireland'—the town it had been modelled on.[16] As the only southern Irish seaside resort town, its popularity increased still further when swimming became an acceptable public pursuit and it became swamped by tourists and day-trippers.

Margaret and William Warner taught at Bray Bridge School, a co-educational Church of Ireland infant school, on Belton Terrace, Castle Street. Later records also describe William Warner as a parish clerk and an organist.[17] The schoolhouse where they lived was converted to private residences in 1906 after Bray Bridge School finally closed.

Their daughter Mary Jane was born in 1863 and Sarah Elizabeth in 1864. Sadly, Sarah only lived for a few months. Louis was born William John Warner on 1 November 1866.[vi] Numerous later accounts describe this as his 'real' name and many say he was called 'John' or 'Jack' Warner.[18] Perhaps he was as a young child.

It isn't clear how long the family stayed at Bray Bridge School, but in March 1875 William Warner's application for a dog licence—he had a brown bull terrier, in case you're wondering—makes it clear they'd moved to Delgany by then. And it was now that Louis learned palmistry.

> On my tenth birthday my mother passed over to me her little library and jotted down in her notebook the following: 'My son has in his left and right hands the sign of the "Mystic Cross". For this reason I have given over to him all the books on occultism I possess… He is certain to become a writer, and will, from what I foresee in his hand, make a name for himself in connection with those subjects.'[19]

Learning palmistry from your mum's books doesn't sound thrilling. No wonder Louis later came up with a different story.

> I had made myself famous as a juvenile fortune-teller, and a band of gypsies who happened to pass through the country induced me to visit their camp and read their dusky palms. After that I used to hang around their encampment, and while doing so one evening I caught my foot in a tree root and sprained it… The Romany folks took me into their tents and carried me off with them the next morning. I became so proficient in reading hands while with them that I was put forward as the expert palmist of the band. After fifteen months I returned home and went to school.[20]

---

vi At 10:50 am, according to his own account.

The details differed on retellings—they kept him with them for eighteen months, fourteen months or a year. Louis ran away and ended up as an outlaw in Mexico—or perhaps these gypsies took him to Mexico and he ran away from them there. Nobody bothered to ask why Irish gypsies were travelling back and forth from Mexico. Maybe some of them had a quiet word with him because Louis gradually dropped this story.

Louis's claim that he wrote a pamphlet on palmistry when eleven or twelve and read hands for locals is more believable. It may even be true he was spanked by his father after going into the local pub and foretelling the future for a group of farmers.

And absolutely none of this may be true.

Louis says he was sent away to a church school where he worked hard and passed his exams.[vii] He'd hardly say otherwise. More excitingly, he had a dream in which he was due to receive a prize but at the last minute he was handed a sealed letter—containing a message of doom. At prize giving day, he did receive a letter from his father saying he'd lost all his money through a land speculation and Louis had to return home. In other accounts, he had to go home because his father had died. To Louis, he had. This was a truth Louis never mentioned.

In about December 1882 William Warner was committed to Maryborough Lunatic Asylum in Port Laoise with 'mania'. He spent the rest of his life there.

---

vii All Irish schools were associated with one church or another, so this doesn't mean what it would nowadays.

From the Sketch *1893*

CHAPTER

TWO

You only have to look at Cheiro… to feel the romance that is wreathed all round his striking personality.[1]

'SO DO TELL ME,' asked one journalist after another when Cheiro had become the talk of the town, 'What did you do before you arrived in London and became a palmist?'

'I worked as a bellboy in a Belfast hotel and wrote bad poetry,' is what he should have said, but didn't.

Instead, he waxed lyrical about how he'd travelled to Rome from London to delve through works in the Vatican before sailing to Egypt. Then he'd gone to India to spend four months, or perhaps two or four years, learning palmistry. Or he'd reached India via New York after tiring of his wild life in Mexico. Or he might have gone to Egypt *after* India.

He could have been fourteen, sixteen, seventeen or eighteen when he reached India. Usually, he claimed to have left Ireland in 1883 or 1884. In some accounts his father gave him fifty pounds to set himself on his way, in others he was obliged to seek his fortune.

As time went on, Louis realised he didn't have to claim he'd visited so many mystical places in one go, so he dropped the Vatican and Egypt stories, extending the amount of time he claimed to be in India.

There is no evidence he ever visited either Egypt or India, although he did visit the Vatican later. It's possible he spent some time overseas, but not as long as he claimed. But these tales, especially that of his stay in India, were part of Cheiro's identity. They surrounded him for the rest of his life and gave him a cachet other palmists lacked. And they are *really* good ripping yarns.

Let's start with the India story.

A short time after arriving in London, Cheiro was taking a stroll along the Thames when he reached Tilbury docks—said no one, ever. Although the nearest port for travel to India if you lived in London, Tilbury is in Essex, more than twenty miles away. If he'd said, 'I decided to take a long and arduous walk and stumbled through stinking mud and filth, constantly losing my footing, to reach the docks exhausted,' you might have said, *Why? There was a bus or a train you could have caught*, but if you didn't live in the vicinity, you might also have thought he was strange enough to have done this. Londoners knew reality had little to do with his story.

A shabby-looking steamer was about to leave so Cheiro approached the captain and told him he wanted to go to sea. '"Go to hell!" he said, and turned his back on me.'[2] Unable to take a hint, Cheiro waited until everyone's attention was diverted, sneaked on board and sat down on a pile of wet rope in a useless fashion.

> Night was coming rapidly on, the river was widening to the sea, the sigh of the wind against the mast reached me like a cry of pain. Green and red lights flashed from the fast-fading shore, flakes of spray lashed across my face. My wish had indeed been granted—I was at sea—but—alone.[3]

Not for long. Bored with staring out to sea, Cheiro decided to take a nose around the ship. Looking through a porthole, he saw the captain staring at books and papers on a table while munching on a sandwich. Because he felt in a helpful mood, Cheiro walked into the captain's cabin. The captain, instead of giving him a swift slapping and setting him to work on something useful, asked Cheiro to help him do his accounts and gave him a sandwich. Later, Cheiro read the sailors' palms and taught them introductory freemasonry, which was nice of him: 'I told them what I knew of the great Architect of the Universe who had planned all.'[4]

Eventually, they arrived in Mumbai, at the port of Apollo Bunder. 'I will not attempt to describe the great city that stretched in the distance before me. Histories of India and guide books have already painted the picture better, perhaps, than I could do.'[5]

Fretting because he wasn't carrying a letter of introduction, Cheiro watched the crowds and wondered what to do next. Then an old Brahmin priest made a beeline for him and launched into a nice chat about palmistry.ⁱ The man told Cheiro he was a descendant of the Joshi caste, who had kept palmistry and astrology alive.ⁱⁱ

> He suddenly turned and said: 'You have been reading hands for years. Read mine. I would like to see your European palmistry.' I was... nervous and disinclined to show my little knowledge before such... an adept, but he seemed so kind, so sympathetic, that I resolved to do my best and went into the task with all the earnestness I possessed... He then quietly said: 'Your hand reading is good. Will you come away from the noise and clamor of this petty world around us to solitude, peace and study, amid the mysteries of India and of nature?'⁶

'Why not?' said Cheiro.

They set off for the Western Glats, a range of low mountains north of the city, on a four-day journey. Once they arrived, Cheiro had to undergo an initiation which entailed entering a trance—a process so dangerous that he might not survive. After fasting for several days, Cheiro went deep into the mountains, and when they arrived at a large white slab of rock, the Brahmins poured on it some dark fluid around which they formed a circle with the tips of their fingers touching. Soon, pictures began to form on the liquid showing not only his family but also Cheiro's pet dog.

Then it was time for the trance. This took place in a cave temple which contained a magnificently carved white marble statue of Siva. The cave was illuminated by a light that appeared to radiate from the statue, but actually came from an opening above. Cheiro lay at the foot of the statue in a trance for seven days. Weakened and blind when he came around, he had to be nursed back to health. 'At last... little by little light seemed to break in on the darkness, and then colour, and lastly sight, only by moments at first, but, oh, such moments of delight; no words of mine could picture those moments to you...'⁷

An alternative version of events describes how Cheiro had to hide to watch a mystical rite. It was midnight when seven naked Brahmin sat naked in a circle around a man lying on the ground. They wriggled and the man at the centre of the circle began to writhe in agony.

---

i A *Brahmin* is someone belonging to the highest ranking of India's four *varnas* or social classes—it doesn't correlate to the European term *caste*.
ii *Joshi* or *Jyoshi* is a Brahmin caste and a modern surname. It's derived from the Sanskrit word jyotisha, which refers to astrology and astronomy. In modern English, it's often rendered as *jyotish* or 'Vedic astrology'.

The eyes started from their sockets. There was a gurgle, a sob, a sigh. The writhing ceased. His head fell back motionless. The spirit had been freed from the body and was sent back to the outer world to obey the wishes and the will of these men.[8]

After some serious chanting from the priests, a tiger roared and approached the Brahmin. He lay on top of the apparently dead man while the mystical chanting continued until the Brahmin leapt to their feet, jumping around in a frenzy. Suddenly, one of them:

...sprang forward, rolled the body of the tiger over, and plunging a knife into the carcass below the neck with one stroke ripped it in two. Quick as a flash, the intestines were torn out and thrown, quivering with life, into the flames. The body of the man was forced into the body of the tiger, the skin drawn together, and louder, wilder, fiercer than before I could hear the chant rising higher and higher.[9]

Cheiro lost consciousness.

The next day, the man was released from the tiger's body in possession of a range of mystical powers, including being unhurt by fire.

While in India, Cheiro witnessed many 'wonderful séances and occult mysteries'.[10] At one point he witnessed a Yogi in a trance buried alive and afterwards disinterred and resuscitated. He also saw the rope trick performed where a rope appeared to be suspended from an invisible point in space. When a boy climbed the rope and disappeared, there were calls for him to descend and he shouted his refusal. A man with a knife climbed after him and, after cries from above, portions of the boy's mutilated body fell to the ground. Then the man reappeared and a moment later the boy appeared on the edge of the crowd smiling and unhurt. And everyone clapped appreciatively. Cheiro reckoned this was achieved by hypnotism.

This is the classic Indian rope trick as defined by magicians. There are ancient accounts of similar tricks but the performance described above dates back no further than 1890 and originates with an article John Elbert Wilkie wrote for the *Chicago Tribune*.[11] The article was soon picked up by newspapers throughout the US and UK and translated into nearly every European language. Before long, people claimed to have remembered seeing the trick as far back as the 1850s. Despite a retraction published by the *Tribune* four months later, the story persisted. Fortunately, Wilkie didn't get into any bother; he later became head of the US Secret Service.

And magicians continued to try to perfect the trick, failing every time. Cheiro first wrote about it in the early 1890s, long after Wilkie's article had entered popular culture. It was only one of many marvels Cheiro claimed to have witnessed. Perhaps more of them were caused by hypnotism.

Much more important to Cheiro than any such display was a book he came across:

> This book was one of the greatest treasures of the few Brahmans who possessed and understood it, and was jealously guarded in one of those old cave temples that belong to the ruins of ancient Hindustan. This strange book was made of human skin, pieced and put together in the most ingenious manner. It was of enormous size, and contained hundreds of well-drawn illustrations, with records of how, when, and where this or that mark was proved correct. One of the greatest features in connection with it was that it was written in some red liquid which age had failed to spoil or fade. The effect of those vivid red letters on the pages of dull yellow skin was most remarkable. By some compound, probably made of herbs, each page was glazed, as it were, by varnish: but whatever this compound may have been, it seemed to defy time, as the outer covers alone showed the signs of wear and decay...[12]

There is a type of book called *nadi* or *naadi* in South India. They comprise bound palm leaves written on in red ink which are glazed and bound with threads. Usually, they're associated with astrology but many also refer to palmistry. And these books circulated amongst European collectors in the nineteenth century. Whether Cheiro based his account on an inaccurate description or simply got over-excited is debatable. But Indian palmists don't and didn't write books on human skin. As Hindus cremate their dead, it's hard to imagine where they'd find enough human skin to make such books in the exceedingly doubtful circumstances they suddenly decided to.

Cheiro's understanding of India in any form continued to be shaky, He later said, 'Brahmin priests will find new translations of Buddha's precepts to meet the demands of the new age', and he consistently described Hindus as Buddhists. [13] To be fair, although the West was beginning to learn about Eastern religions, most people's knowledge was vague at the best. What he did know, Louis was likely to have learned from the Theosophical Society's mixture of Western occultism and Hindu mysticism.

But surviving on a diet of fruit and rice had to end:

One curious Britisher from a passing regiment strayed to our monastery—and recognized me. He had known me in Dublin. He told me an aunt had died and left me money. I returned to Ireland and was wealthy again.[14]

In later years, palmists commonly claimed to have travelled to India and shared Cheiro's experiences. Let's take Countess Sobinska, the London palmist charged with telling fortunes in 1902. She was still active in Scotland until at least the First World War. The Countess described an ancient palmistry book made of human skin that contained hundreds of illustrations. And Californian Professor de Long claimed in 1912 to have studied palmistry in a temple with Joshi priests. His book was written on silver and gold plates, although he mentioned four maps of the hand on human skin. Madam Seera from Chicago gave the same account as de Long word for word in 1907 (marked as copyrighted in 1903), and added: 'the most celebrated palmists in Europe, such as the well-known Cheiro and others, have perfected their knowledge in this temple.'[15] There were many others.

In any event, Cheiro ended up back in London. At this point, he either spent his time amassing handprints to study, visiting prisons, asylums and hospitals, or he got bored and decided to travel:

An expedition was going to Egypt, so I went along, paying my own expenses. All went well there for a long time, but then a check I had given a Cairo hotel was returned, unhonoured. The man I had left in charge of my estate in Ireland had been playing the stock market, had ruined himself and me and had killed himself. I had been studying palmistry all the time, but had never practiced it for profit. I had to do so then to pay my hotel bill.'[16]

What a nuisance!

In another version of this story, the guide betrayed Cheiro and locked him in an ancient temple to die of hunger. He was close to death when he used the power of mental concentration (which he'd learned in India) to communicate telepathically with someone in his hotel who came and saved his life.

At some point, Cheiro ended up in possession of a 's hand, that of Tutankhamen's sister-in-law. This is long before Tutankhamen's tomb was discovered. The hand was given to Cheiro by an Egyptian he'd cured of malaria. 'It was the Egyptian's greatest treasure. He gave it to me because he swore I had saved his life. He claimed to be a descendant of an ancient family of priests...'[17] On the hand was a ring with three stones that represented the world, creative force and eternity. This is the ring Cheiro wore for the rest of his life.

Anyway, Cheiro beavered away working as a palmist from his hotel room, presumably wearing a nice ring, until eventually he made his way back home.

While his alter-ego was gallivanting around the world, Louis, along with his mother and sister Mary, had moved to Belfast, where they had family—the Hartys. William Harty was the son of a Dublin solicitor, John Harty who originally came from Limerick. He'd met Annie Hamilton Richards when he was giving an organ recital at a church in Greystones and she was part of the choir. Annie came from Greystones near Bray and was the daughter of Joseph Hamilton Richards, a soldier and later a member of the Royal Irish Constabulary, also from Bray. They moved to Hillsborough, a village in County Down about twelve miles from Belfast, in 1879 when William Harty was offered a job as church organist.

The Hartys had ten children, their fourth being the musician and conductor (Herbert) Hamilton Harty. He was Louis's second cousin— they shared a great-grandparent, although it isn't clear whether the relationship was from Louis's mother's or father's family.

The Hartys had close links to Bray and one of Hamilton Harty's first jobs was as a church organist in Bray while he was still a teenager. In later years, Margaret Warner moved to Hillsborough where the Hartys lived.

William Harty maintained that his ancestors were of noble blood and he was entitled to a dormant baronetcy. This could be a massive coincidence, but there surely must have been a limited number of families from Bray who claimed such a heritage? Harty was also an early spiritualist. Although no formal spiritualist organisation existed in Ireland at this time, William was known locally for hosting séances.

In 1887 the Warners were living at 9 Eia Street, Belfast. We know this because Mary died of consumption on 22 August. She was buried three days later in a family grave owned by William V Warner, suggesting Louis's father came from a Belfast family. Later newspaper reports say Louis worked as a bellboy in a Belfast hotel.[iii]

Later, Louis said he continued to study palmistry in the 1880s. This

---

iii It appears that these reports come from someone close to his family as the same reports refer to Louis as 'Jack'.

was easy as many popular palmistry books were available. Edward Heron-Allen's *Chiromancy, or the Science of Palmistry* written with Henry Frith appeared in 1883, followed by *Science of the Hand,* a translation of Casimir D'Arpentigny's eighteenth century French work in 1886—the same year Heron-Allen undertook a highly successful tour of the United States. *The Handbook of Palmistry* by Rosa Baughan was also published in 1883. There were many more, along with articles in newspapers and magazines.

Louis also consistently said he wrote poetry, and this claim lends the lie to his assertion that he moved to London 1888-9. Louis didn't only write poetry, he entered it for competitions. The *Belfast News-Letter* reports that his submissions (as Louis Warner) were 'highly commended' several times from 1887 to 1889. In October 1888, his prize-winning poem written to celebrate the opening of the Belfast free library appeared:

There are within the human breast
 Strange, longing thoughts that will not rest,
     Nor quiet be;
Strange thoughts. like bubbling springs that rise,
Whose hand oft stains with tears our eyes-
     Then, bid us see
The visions and the saddening dreams
Of fettered genius without means
     To reach its goal.
It may be that some poor man's heart
Longs after books and learning's art,
     And tells his soul
His longings. On its silent wings
That soul slips forth, and wondrous things
     Straightaway appear;
For surely 'tis not wrong to think
That souls are fettered by one link
     Of kinship dear,
That in our midst strange things are wrought
By influence of kindred thought,
     Whose mystic power
Has raised within our town to-day
A Library, whose wondrous sway
     May ever shower
O'er cities, towns, and lands afar
A halo, like a heaven-lit star,

Whose radiant light,
Reflecting some sweet scene Above,
Some mystery of Jesu's love,
    Leads thro' the night
To where Life's destinies are wrought,
Where springs the flowing fount of thought,
Where saints with holy angels roam,
Where God is King and Heaven home.
Belfast.[18]

There's no doubt that Louis had literary pretensions. He was a member of the City Literary Society which met at the YMCA for which he read a paper on poetry in March 1889—there was 'free admission open to ladies' on that occasion.[19] He diligently gave feedback on papers throughout 1889 and occasionally chaired meetings. And he was particularly taken with a debate in January 1890 entitled 'Is marriage a failure', voting for it to continue the following week. But despite becoming Vice-President of the Society in April 1890, Louis wanted more. According to an 1890 street directory, Louis was a 'manager' living at Connaught Terrace, Lawrence Street, off University Street and close to the station.[20] But he wanted to live where there were:

Gin palaces, music halls, saloons, beef and mutton and mutton and beef on every side. Men and women fighting each other to live. The juggernaut car of money dragged through the streets while virtue and innocence fall under its wheels.[21]

He wanted to live in London.

Programme for Arrah-na-Pogue *where Louis appears as L Warner. Author's collection.*

CHAPTER
THREE

Among the minor social crazes with which the less occupied part of the world amuses itself from time to time, few perhaps have attained greater popularity than palmistry.[1]

*L*OUIS CLAIMED THAT HE ARRIVED in London in late 1888 and took up palmistry immediately. Why not? It was all the rage. Articles on the subject appeared frequently in magazines, books describing how to perform the art were easily available, and members of high society raved about it. Every bazaar or garden party worth its salt had a palmist. Reading palms was also a great way to make friends.

But we already know he was living in Belfast until 1890, so how could he have moved to London two years earlier? Perhaps Louis had muddled his dates—an easy mistake when writing about events years after they happened. Or perhaps he was lying? Maybe, but the explanation might be simpler. Belfast is a seaport, after all, and there were regular ships from Queenstown to Liverpool. Louis could easily have spent time in London before moving there. In an early account, he talks about spending a few months in London and lodging in a room off the Strand.[2] The different versions of his story are confusing and contradictory, but there's no reason to assume he hadn't visited London before moving there permanently.

Whatever the truth, palmistry was a feature of his arrival in London.

While waiting in Liverpool for the London train, my eyes caught sight of a book with a hand drawn on the cover, which I immediately bought. It was a translation of one of those books on palmistry that had been printed at the same time that the Bible was first printed with movable type; it was called in German 'Die

Kunst Ciromanta'... The only other occupant of the carriage was a gentleman who sat opposite with his back to the engine, and had wrapped round his shoulders a heavy rug that almost concealed his face. When, however, my book was finished, as I laid it down I noticed that his sharp eyes were fixed intently on the drawing of the hand that adorned the cover. As I put it aside, in a genial but rather bantering way he said: 'So you evidently believe in hand-reading.'[3]

Of course, Louis had to read the man's hand. And he predicted that his downfall would be:

'A woman, without a doubt... You see yourself how the Line of Heart breaks the Line of Destiny just below that point where it fades out.' Taking his hand away, the stranger laughed—a low, quiet laugh—the laugh of a man who was sure of himself.[4]

As they arrived in Euston, the man handed Cheiro his card—he was the Irish politician Charles Stewart Parnell who in 1890 was involved in a scandalous divorce case after fathering three children with his married lover Katherine O'Shea. Parnell died in October 1891—long before Cheiro published this account. It's an unlikely encounter and *Die Kunst Ciromantia* wasn't translated into English until 1923.[5] Even then, it wasn't the sort of book to be found at a railway bookstall. But maybe that isn't the point.

By his own admission, things weren't great when Louis first arrived in London. 'I soon began to feel keenly what it is to be alone in the heart of a great city, without friends and without prospects of making any,' he said miserably.[6]

He tried to be positive, but it's clear his early days in London were spent in the nineteenth-century equivalent of student accomodation.

Those who have never lived the 'simple life' will not, perhaps, realise the pleasures that one can find in a top room of a seven-story house looking over the Embankment—the subdued dull roar of the great city at one's feet; the sob and sigh of the river of life as its tides ebb at night, and flow again with the coming of the day. In the distance one may see the Thames with its gliding craft and its long stretch of silver and blue and green, as it gleams under the skies of June or becomes grey and grim with a November night, or hides itself in the folds of some yellow fog—yellow as the wrappings of the mummies that hold the past of Egypt in their deathless sleep. In a room on the top of a seven-story house one's anxieties are also less—one never sees one's enemies, and one's friends may be few, but they must be real if they ever reach one's door. From such a point of vantage one does not see the horrors of life, the daily brutality of the streets, the starving faces that rise in the crowd and disappear again, like the bubbles that float on some muddy stream—all these things one does not see, and so a seventh-floor abode has often considerable advantages.[7]

It took Louis a while to get the hang of living independently:

My breakfast, with the regularity of clockwork, appeared on the table at 9; but, as it often happened that I slept till 10, it just as often... disappeared at the appointed hour for its clearance, and hungry, but not daring to remonstrate, I repaired morning after morning to a chophouse nearby.[8]

Breakfast was at nine, his landlady insisted when Louis asked if he could have it a little later to avoid paying for two breakfasts. He didn't think it was his fault for waking up late because a ghost kept him awake at nights. After investigating, Louis discovered there were ghosts in the cellar. The local priest sent him on his way when Louis sought help, but luckily he bumped into a more obliging priest when he was taking a walk in the park. Louis invited few friends over and at midnight the priest conducted a short service, which allowed Louis to have dream-free nights. Several weeks later, a skeleton was discovered in the cellar. Louis doesn't mention if he then got up in time for breakfast.

In some versions of Cheiro's story, he ran away to India at this point. In others, he launched into becoming a professional palmist and was a roaring success from the start. But in his earliest accounts, he said he'd come to London to be a writer. That failed when he went to see the 'Rev. Dr. Richardson', editor of *Great Thoughts*, and was gently told his writing wasn't up to standard. The publication Louis probably meant was *Great Thoughts from Master Minds*, a literary magazine that printed stories, essays and reviews. And 'Richardson' was probably Franklin Thomas Grant Richards who was later an editor for W T Stead's *Review of Reviews* and who launched his own publishing house in 1896 at the age of twenty-four. Richards was a contributor to Great Thoughts, rather than its editor, but this is a minor error. If an interview did take place, it's likely it was only one of many knockbacks.

Cheiro said it was a miserable October morning when he began to trudge home in dejection. And to his surprise he bumped into someone he recognised—'a man of decidedly Jewish appearance'—who called out to him.[9] This man reminded him they'd met in Egypt when Louis had read his palm. And he suggested that palmistry would be an ideal way for Louis to make money.

The man was some sort of government official and talked Louis into a contract where he'd act as his manager and take fifty per cent of Louis's earnings for the next twelve years. Finding this agreeable, Louis set out to rent suitable rooms, an onerous task as 'In those days the Study of the Hand was an unknown and unheard-of quantity in London'.[10] It certainly wasn't.

He finally succeeded in renting from a Scottish woman who cannily demanded double the usual rent for the bother of having someone so dodgy on her premises. But that wasn't enough—she also sprinkled holy water night and morning at his bedroom door, and when he moved out, she charged him for damage done to the carpet.

A suitable name was necessary for his new career, and after long discussion, Louis rejected the suggestion of 'Solomon' in favour of 'Cheiro'. An hour after Louis had erected a brass plate with his name on it, his first client arrived—Arthur Balfour, President of the Society for Psychical Research and later Prime Minister. The impressed Balfour invited Cheiro to a dinner party and recommended him to his friends and Cheiro was soon swamped with clients. At about the same time, the Jewish man realised palmistry was more dodgy than it had first appeared. As he didn't want legal problems, he released Cheiro from his contract—leaving him to become rich and famous on his own.

Maybe Louis did try and fail to succeed as a writer. Maybe someone did try to help him set up in business and it went wrong. But he neither adopted the name of 'Cheiro' at this point or became renowned as a palmist—or as anything.

In this version of reality, Cheiro met famous people immediately after arriving in London in 1888, including Nellie Melba, the Australian soprano who was then performing regularly at Covent Garden but who wasn't to achieve true fame for a few years to come. And Lord Kitchener, the military leader who would later become Secretary of State and whose most renowned military successes were also yet to come.

One of the most famous of his encounters which might not have happened (at least, not how Louis described it) was with Helena

Blavatsky, co-founder of the Theosophical Society, in late March 1889 at the Society's headquarters in Avenue Road, St John's Wood.

In case you haven't heard of Madame Blavatsky, checking on Wikipedia won't give you much of a sense of how famous and influential she was at the time. Blavatsky combined religion with science and modern thought through occultism, offering a new way to follow a spiritual path. She claimed to have developed her ideas through contact with spiritual adepts, Masters of the ancient wisdom. Her followers saw her as enlightened. To others, she was a charlatan who faked paranormal phenomena. Controversy followed here wherever she went. Whatever you thought of Blavatsky, her influence was undeniable. She brought Eastern religion and philosophy to the West, paving the way for practices such as transcendental meditation and yoga and popularising belief in concepts such as reincarnation. Theosophy's influence permeated our culture to such an extent that today its ideas are accepted by people who have no idea Blavatsky even existed – the New Age that emerged in the 1970s was a legacy of theosophical thought. When Cheiro said he'd met her, everyone had heard of Blavatsky.

> I arrived, and was immediately shown into a large *salon* by an elderly woman servant. After a wait of perhaps ten minutes, heavy velvet curtains at the end of the room were drawn and disclosed the celebrated woman I had called to see, half reclining on a couch at the farther end of the inner *salon*.
>
> 'Cheiro,' she said, in a soft melodious voice, 'I am happy to receive you. I have heard of your success from many quarters, but as you are so young I fear your head will be turned by so much adulation. Do you realize from what source you derive your powers of prediction?'
>
> 'No, Madame,' I answered, 'I fear I can only give the credit to long years of study and my most earnest desire to help those who come to consult me.'[11]

Blavatsky informed Cheiro that he was the reincarnation of the glamorous Count Cagliostro, the eighteenth century occultist Giuseppe (Joseph) Balsamo. The greatest magician ever, or the biggest con merchant for centuries depending on your point of view, Cagliostro's history was surrounded by rumour and debate. He was highly popular amongst nineteenth-century occultists, who craved to be reincarnated from him (Aleister Crowley believed that he was). Instead of ending his days in a dungeon, he'd escaped imprisonment by swallowing an elixir that enabled him to fake death. And then Blavatsky added:

> You are only half way through you first season in London and yet you have already made your name. You will also make friends of kings; you will also become rich; you will also cure the sick.[12]

She invited him to come back the next day so Louis could predict when she was going to die.

> 'The series of fours and eights hold the secrets of your life, Madame,' I replied.... Taking her pencil I jotted down 31st July. 'Add the 3 and 1, you will find the final digit of four. Add the year of your birth – 1831 – 13 or again 4 for the last figure. The opposition in the Zodiac to 31st July is the House of Saturn, called the "House of the 8". Your marriage in your seventeenth year also produced an 8, a most unhappy indication. The year 1849, if added together, makes 22, with its final digit of 4.
>
> 'On your hand the Line of Fate runs from the wrist to the base of the second finger, called the Mount of Saturn. The Line of Health cuts the Line of Life about your sixty-second year, but in your fifty-eighth year, governed by the number 4, you will have reached the fadic number of your birth sign, but your indomitable will power may carry you a little beyond that age, especially as at your date of birth your Sun, the Giver of Life, was then entering the House of Mercury negative.'[13]

Cheiro refused to join the Theosophical Society, saying he'd resolved to stay independent. And his prediction turned out to be correct—Blavatsky died in May 1891 at the age of fifty-nine. OK, almost correct but parts of his story don't make sense. For example, Blavatsky didn't live at Avenue Road until July 1890. It isn't *impossible* that Louis met Blavatsky—lots of people did, so it wouldn't have been a great achievement—but it's worth noting Louis didn't make this claim until towards the end of his life.

However, this does give us a good idea of what Cheiro offered in a reading and what Louis wanted us to think he was capable of. It wasn't just about the shape of a hand or how the lines criss-crossed it; a palm reading included numerology and astrology. This blurring of lines still pervades—many an astrologer has been irritated by a demand to look at a palm. And this might be the place to point out that what we call a 'reading' was often referred to as a 'séance'. Although the modern definition refers to people gathering to receive messages from the departed or listen to a medium communicate with spirits or produce phenomena, back then it was commonly used for any gathering where people might sit down and do something related to the occult or fortune telling. It could even be used in more general terms. After all, it's the French word for 'session' and many people Cheiro mixed with would have at least a smattering of French.

It would be dull, and long-winded, to list Cheiro's claimed encounters and argue whether they did or didn't happen or in what way they might have happened. So I won't. However, it is worth mentioning one meeting that's been accepted by numerous sources and couldn't have occurred.

Cheiro didn't travel to Philadelphia in 1890 with Major Ricarde Seaver to see the inventor John Keeley's work where playing a violin started a motor. Keely claimed he'd discovered a new motive power, an etheric force based on musical vibrations, and on the basis of this the Keely Motor Company was formed in New York. He also invented a vaporic gun and an etheric generator. Keely's work attracted huge amounts of interest and plenty of investors. Unsurprisingly, many people wanted to see his claims proved or disproved, and Ricarde Seaver did indeed visit him—but this took place in 1885 and many of the details Cheiro gives are stolen from theosophical writings.[14]

The earliest independent record of Louis being in London appears in later newspaper reports that say he met Edith Keighley, who was later to become a professional palmist, in late 1890.[15] It's as if Louis was trying to hide what he'd done before taking up palmistry as a profession.

According to the census, Louis was living in Hunter Street, Bloomsbury in April 1891 as a lodger with George and Harriet Hewitt. Although his year of birth is incorrect and his place of birth is given as Tipperary, it's clearly him. Most importantly, he's described as an actor.

His earliest performance I have been able to trace was 9 June 1891 in *Matrimonial* at the Novelty Theatre (later the Great Queen Street Theatre), in Holborn. The plot centred around a matrimonial newspaper, misunderstandings, past lovers and general running around London. After a minor conflict and tears from the heroine, the police stick a few people in the cellar, everyone else arrives, and it ends happily. Louis played the starring role of Percy Prattlewell, a barrister, in the three-act comedy performed for copyright purposes.[i]

---

i Plays weren't granted copyright like books, they needed to be performed—though 'per-

Only a few weeks later, on 7 July, Louis appeared in a short play as part of a fund-raising variety show presented by Mlle Gratienne's company at West Southwark Liberal and Radical Club. This was a small touring repertory company that lived hand to mouth, teetering on the verge of bankruptcy. The performance went down well, being 'one of the best this company has given at this club' and Louis 'left nothing to be desired in his characteristic impersonation'.[16]

Later newspaper reports describe Louis working as a stagehand at the Princess's theatre in Oxford Street before taking on acting roles there.

While making his living as an actor, Louis read palms and was gaining a reputation for his talent. Amongst those whose palm he read was that of the American actor and comedian Marshall P Wilder, primarily known for his comic monologues. He was also a hunchbacked dwarf. Unusually for this era, Wilder had shunned offers to appear as a 'freak' and had established himself as a mainstream entertainer. After travelling to London in 1883, he'd become a favourite of the royal family and, although forgotten today, he was a major celebrity at the time. History mainly remembers him for the line 'Fate handed me a lemon—but I have made lemonade of it.' There's no proof the line originated with Wilder, but it might as well have done.[ii]

Wilder was also a clairvoyant with a strong interest in the occult, especially palmistry. He'd helped Edward Heron-Allen out in his first American tour of 1886 by introducing him to people. And he met Louis in the summer of 1891.[iii]

> Several of my friends were at the Victoria Hotel in London while I was also stopping there, and among them was Miss Loie Fuller, who usually held an informal reception after theatre hours the Thespian's only 'recess'. One evening, on returning from an entertainment I had given, I went into Miss Fuller's parlor and found the hostess and her friends clustered about a gentleman whom I did not know. He had dark hair and eyes and was extremely good looking, a perfect type of Irish manhood. He was

formed' is too grand a word for what took place. The cast read the script to twenty-five people who would rather have been elsewhere.

ii In later years, Wilder made films and helped develop smart bombs in World War II.

iii Although Wilder said this conversation took place in 1892, it had to be in 1891. Wilder was in London that summer and he worked with actress Loie Fuller at that time. This was also when Louis landed his first proper role at the Princess's Theatre—he was no longer there by summer 1892.

reading a lady's palm, and the others were listening with great interest. Soon Miss Fuller said:

'I want you to read Marshall's palm.'

'Oh, yes,' said the others; 'let's hear what Marshall's luck will be.'

We were introduced; his name was Louis Warner, and on looking at my hand he began to tell my characteristics with an accuracy which was startling. I had no opportunity for conversation with him that evening, so I invited him to lunch with me the next day. He came and we had a very interesting chat about palmistry. I asked him if he made a business of it and he said he did not he was an actor, and playing at the Princess Theatre.

'Do you ever think of taking up palmistry as a business?' I asked.

'No,' he answered, 'but I may some day.'...

I told him I thought there was a great deal of money in it, to which he assented.

Louis wasn't going to consider becoming a professional palmist at this point because he'd just landed his first proper role. Sidney Herberte-Basing, who ran the Princess's company, had decided to revive *Arrah-na-Pogue or the Wicklow Wedding* by Dion Boucicault, first performed at the Princess's in 1864. Audiences were down and he hoped a few old favourites would turn things around. Herberte-Basing decided to try out new performers alongside more experienced actors. It helped that Louis had precisely the right accent, and he played Lanagan from 28 August to 7 November 1891. Presumably to create a good atmosphere, the theatre was scented with White Lilac perfume, a bottle of which you could buy from the attendants.[18]

Arrah na Pogue (Arrah of the Kiss) is set during the Irish rebellion of 1798 and takes place over a forty-eight hour period. It has everything you'd want from an Irish melodrama—romance, adventure, evil landlords, rebels, love triangles, mistaken identity, betrayal, wild chases, an excess of scenery and a happy ending. Louis only had a handful of lines and stood around for most of the time he was on stage, except when he got to grab the landlord by his collar and throw him out, but you have to start somewhere. And he no doubt got to join in the singing and dancing. The opening night played to a full house which included several theatrical celebrities and received positive reviews.

Inspired by his success, Herberte-Basing decided to produce another of Boucicault's plays, *After Dark: A Tale of London Life*, in which he starred. He took advantage of a music hall scene to insert a number of performers, turning part of the play into a variety show. Singing, dancing and acrobatics forced those who fancied a melodrama to wait patiently while trying to remember the plot.

After Dark was an adaptation of Adolphe Dennery's 1854 play *Les oiseaux de proie* (*Birds of Prey*). Marvellously, it plagiarised the scene from Augustin Daly's melodrama *Under the Gaslight* in which a character is placed across a railroad track and rescued at the last moment from an oncoming train.[iv] When the play was first produced, this was its main attraction. The plot centres on a baronet's son who marries a barmaid to receive his inheritance. Along the way we meet a corrupt lawyer who turns out to be a wanted Australian criminal and who gangs up with a woman who runs a gambling house, an aristocrat who's forged his father's signature and is blackmailed, a wronged soldier and his abandoned daughter, and an heiress who has joined the Salvation Army.

Louis was 'amusing as Jem, the kerbstone vocalist and Elysium artist'.[19] He barely had time to draw breath as *After Dark* ran from 9 November to 19 December 1891 for forty-five performances including matinees. Before it ended, he was rehearsing for a revival of Robert Buchanan and Harriet Jay's *Alone in London* which opened 21 December.[v] It's unclear whether like other members of the company Louis also appeared in *The Swiss Express*, the pantomime which took the matinee slot.

In *Alone in London*, a crook tries to make a thief of a boss's son and ties a flower girl to a canal's lock gates, leading to an impressive sluice scene instead of an exciting train scene. Louis was 'decidedly good' in his role as Robert, a policeman.[20] The production ran until 16 January 1892, making Louis an up-and-coming actor.

At the end of January Louis began rehearsals for *The Great Metropolis* which opened 6 February, a rewrite by the actors William Terris and Henry Neville of the American *Shadows of a Great City*. The plot concerns a hero who has to prove his identity after living abroad because a scoundrel has replaced him in his father's affections. Most of the action takes place in or near the sea (anyone expecting a detailed depiction of a metropolis would have been severely disappointed) and Louis played an Irishman

---

iv Produced 1867. This is the origin of the scene popularly believed to have appeared in silent movies—it didn't.
v First produced in 1885.

who kept a sailors' lodging-house. The sensational scene this time was of a shipwreck. In some unclear way, rocket apparatus borrowed from the Board of Trade by Herberte-Basing also participated. And there were plenty of thunder and lightning effects. Louis 'carefully played' his role.[21]

And then it went wrong.

Louis was playing Dr Grieg in the new play *Strathlogan* by Charles Overton and Brian Moss, an Irish melodrama in which a lord returns to Ireland after a long absence to find his estate mal-administered by an evil bailiff who's in love with one of the heroines.

> Maurice O'Mara, a friend of the Earl of Strathlogan, an unpopular Irish landlord, has, become at an early age a sworn member of a homicidal society, and finds, soon after his return from South Africa, that he is 'told off' to murder his friend, the earl, with the alternative of being himself shot from behind a hedge by one of his associates if he refuses...
>
> Most Irish dramas have a gentleman landlord, a scheming and agonising agent, a sympathetic heroine, and a mechanical sensation. Messrs Charles Overton and Hugh Moss apparently determined to 'see' Boucicault, and 'go him one better'. They have two aristocratic landlords, two remorseful schemers, two heroines, a bendable tree, and a whirlpool in motion. They also have two Irish detectives, and a large number of minor personages, all of whom have something to do with the story...[22]

Expectations were high. A thousand pounds (over £100,000 in today's terms) was spent on the scenery alone; renowned scenic artist W T Hemsley had been engaged along with Hugh Moss as stage manager. Herberte-Basing was so confident of success that he'd invested everything he had in the production—along with money he didn't have. Rehearsals began in May and went on for three weeks. As costs rapidly mounted, Herberte-Basing made cuts by letting the theatre and hiring a hall for rehearsals.

Hemsley was paid half of what he was owed and was then told to stop work and asked to return his payment. After some bickering, a new contract was finally signed. Hugh Moss demanded that the production be postponed twice as the cast weren't ready, meaning they lost the increased audience expected during the Whitsun holiday.

It's no wonder they weren't ready. Focused on getting the best cast, Herberte-Basing was still looking for actors while rehearsals were under way, and there was never a rehearsal with a complete company. Finally, on 9 June the first performance, lasting four hours, took place in front of a tiny audience. *Strathlogan* ran for four embarrassing nights.

> The verbosity of the new and original modern Irish drama is so stupendous that it completely overshadows all idea of mastering the details of the plot, even if anyone dared to risk such a feat. The words of the play, to speak, knock the audience in the eye, and induce incipient headaches at an early hour. Plot, story, and characterisation are talked out of court, and conveniently dull the intellectual faculties. Each character talks worse and at greater length than his predecessor... the audience feels inclined to shriek in order to break in on the maddening monotony of vapid and uninteresting conversation, and, as usually happens on such occasions, the orchestra emphasizes the misery of the occasion by wailing and whining out tones of which the most venerable heifer must have died.[23]

But the strongest reaction was reserved for the special effects. One reviewer said, 'I laughed until tears ran into my boots.'[24] He wasn't alone.

> The management decided to represent a whirlpool; but the whirlpool knew that it was quite irrelevant and behaved badly – very badly. At first it stood still—which is obviously rank suicide for a whirlpool—then it pulled itself together and made a start, but it went like an omnibus in the season and kept stopping frequently. After this it got tired and took a rest. However, it had a conscience, so it made another effort, during which it groaned and creaked horribly. Still, to be just, when one of the heroines was thrown in it rose to the occasion and whirled her round till she must have had a decided 'mal au coeur'... However, it is unkind to criticise a whirlpool too harshly on its first appearance: doubtless when it is less nervous it will get along quite smoothly.[25]

> Never... has an Irish whirlpool so exactly resembled a huge revolving artichoke or whirling cauliflower. The luckless heroine once flung from the broken bridge, finds herself in the embraces of a fiendish octopus in the shape of vegetable matter. It is the green-girdled hasty pudding of despair. Round and round poor Miss Dorothy Dorr is whirled, her arms sticking out of this

curious viridescent compound, like the pigeon's legs in a parsley decorated pie.[26]

The small audience shrank even further on the second night. On Saturday, the orchestra refused to play unless someone paid them— Saturday being payday. The few people who'd turned up shouted for the curtain to rise. In desperation, one of the actresses offered to temporarily cover the orchestra's pay and the play went on. The cast were willing to stand by Herberte-Basing until they realised he had no money. On Monday night, actress Olga Brandon pleaded illness rather than go on stage again. On Tuesday a handful of people turned up to find the theatre doors locked. That same day, bailiffs arrived and started removing goods.

The argument about what had happened played out in the pages of *The Era*. Hugh Moss pointed out that publicity had been next to nothing and Herbert-Basing's lack of funds before the play opened meant that Moss had paid some of the tradesmen himself. There'd never been enough money for *Strathlogan*. Herberte-Basing decided to sue the press for libel, claiming he owed some rent but not as much as people were saying.

The disaster meant that Louis hadn't been paid for a month and was out of work. He couldn't even think of taking a holiday (assuming he had the money) as the world was in the midst of a cholera pandemic, and things had suddenly got much, much worse.

Outbreaks had been reported in India and Iran at the end of May. Cholera spread through the Iranian/Russian border and reached St Petersburg, leading to outbreaks in Italy and Germany. Passenger trains were suspended and travel was impossible in some areas. France denied from early June there were any cases, despite reported deaths, but finally had to admit cholera had reached Paris. It was made worse by Western Europe experiencing a heatwave.

That year, cholera claimed 267,890 lives in Russia, 120,000 in Spain, 90,000 in Japan and over 60,000 in Iran. In Hamburg alone, 8,600 people would die. The USA took precautions against travellers bringing cholera into the country, leading to a review of immigration policies. British subjects stuck overseas hurried to return home. But Americans who'd planned a summer adventure in Paris or Italy shifted direction to visit Britain and filled hotels on the south coast. And they were willing to pay for entertainment.

There was money to be made and Louis needed to make money.

It was only natural for Louis to discuss his predicament with fellow cast members, including American Dorothy Dorr—the unfortunate sufferer of the whirlpool. Dorr had made her English debut on 18 March 1891 at the Vaudeville Theatre in *Diamond Deane*, written by her friend and journalist Harry Jackson Wells Dam, who reputedly 'induced him [Louis] to give up play acting and go into palmistry as a profession'.[27]

Dam was from San Francisco and had ended up in London in early 1887 as correspondent for the *New York Times*. He'd been private secretary to Governor Stoneman of California and accused of selling releases to jailed criminals. As if that weren't enough, he'd also been having an affair with Stoneman's wife, for which the Governor threatened to kill him.

In 1888 Dam had moved to the *Star*, edited by T P O'Connor, the future MP, and someone Louis later claimed to have been friendly with. The *Star* focused on offering sensational news to working-class readers. Thomas Power O'Connor was a pioneer of New Journalism, the type of reporting that led to the likes of the *Daily Mail* and was becoming popular in America. Dam was happy to supply human interest stories, scandals and true crime reports. By February 1888 the *Star* was selling 125,000 copies a day. And Dam was to go down in history as the man who reported (if not created) Jack the Ripper. The *San Francisco Examiner* of 2 December 1890 credited Dam with being responsible for the 'Dear Boss' letter, received by the police on 25 September 1888 and signed 'Jack the Ripper'.

I'm not going to go down the Jack the Ripper rabbit hole as we'll never get out of it again. But it's worth mentioning for another reason—later, Louis was to say he achieved fame when in July 1891:

> A mysterious murder was committed in the East End of London. A blood-stained hand-mark on the white paint of a door attracted the attention of a detective; he had heard of me and asked me to see if I could make anything out of the impression of the hand. An examination of the lines in the dead man's hand convinced me that the print could not have been made by his hand, but as there was a similarity in some of the markings, I can to the conclusion that the crime was undoubtedly done by a close relative, most probably a son. This clue led to the arrest and subsequent confession of a son by a former marriage, who up to then had been the least suspected.[28]

There's no other record of this having taken place, but bloodstained hand prints at a murder site in the East End certainly brings to mind the Ripper murders.

On 18 July 1892 in Paris the cholera vaccine was invented by Waldemar Haffkine.

And on that same date in Eastbourne, Cheiro was born.

Cheiro's India room.

CHAPTER

FOUR

I think everyone should have their hands told once a month, so as to know what not to do. Of course, one does it all the same, but it is so pleasant to be warned.[1]

*T*HE CREATION OF CHEIRO was a carefully executed plan, essential in 'That Great City where Fate meets Ambition in equal combat,' as Louis described London.[2] It could be a complete coincidence that this plan involved people Harry Dam had known for years, along with clever manipulation of the press, but it's more likely he had a hand in it.

Dam was a networker. He was one of the founders of the Bohemian Club in 1872 in San Francisco, established for journalists, artists and musicians, although over the years, it began to accept businessmen and entrepreneurs. It still exists today with a membership of many local and global leaders, and every year, it hosts a camp at Bohemian Grove where guests partake in ceremonies and act in plays. In London, Dam was part of the Bohemian Savage Club, founded in 1887 at the suggestion of the Prince of Wales. Its members mainly comprised actors, musicians and singers and it was dedicated to the 'pursuit of happiness'. Again, this club still exists. Dam's club contacts coupled with his journalistic network meant he knew most people worth knowing.

The first step of the plan was to think up a suitable name. Being known as an actor wouldn't attract confidence. If people thought Louis was putting on a show like a stage magician, he'd never reach the clientele he wanted or make serious money. Plus, palmistry wasn't legal and it was foolish to draw too much attention to your true identity.

Louis *might* have had a vision that led him to his choice, but it would be a vision led by pragmatism. From the mid-1880s, palmists often described themselves as *cheiromancers*—a word derived from the Greek words *kheir* meaning 'hand' and *manteia* meaning 'divination'. The more scientific *cheirognomy* or *cheirosophy* might be indulged in by a *cheirosophist*, terms widely used in the press and advertisements. The name 'Cheiro' immediately signalled what was on offer and had an added bonus—being phonetically the same as 'Cairo' in English, it hinted at the mysteries of Egypt, as big a deal as the mysteries of India.

Reading palms at the seaside is one thing (it would pay urgent bills, at least) but more focused effort was needed to earn serious money. Creating a reputation with a famous client and making sure everyone knew about it was far more effective than hoping a transitory audience had enough friends to recommend. If you're going for big, you might as well go *really* big, so Cheiro read the palm of the French actress Sarah Bernhardt.

To call Bernhardt—or as Oscar Wilde called her 'the Incomparable One'—famous is a vast understatement. She played male and female characters and even achieved the male actor's classic ambition of playing Hamlet. British and American audiences flocked to see her perform in French, even if they didn't understand a word of the language—the sound of her voice and her gestures were enough. And she played to no-one's rules but her own. Bernhardt embraced her half-Jewish heritage while being a practising Catholic and was an unmarried mother and wildly promiscuous, conducting numerous affairs with high-status men. Oscar Wilde scattered lilies in her path and wrote a play in French, *Salomé*, especially for her. She sometimes slept in a coffin, wore a stuffed bat on her head, dripped with jewels, and filled her house with exotic pets, including tigers, leopards, monkeys and an alligator she slept with until it died of its diet of milk and champagne.

The divine Sarah knew how to handle the press. Although she sometimes complained that journalists abused her, she hired press agents to spread gossip about her such as the story of her playing croquet with human skulls.

In 1892 she was completing a world tour and arrived in London on 25 May accompanied by her family, six servants, a collection of pets, numerous trunks and 250 pairs of shoes. And from the middle of July the story that Cheiro had read her palm spread throughout the British press and was later picked up by the American press.

One evening, a gentleman asked if I would drive out with him and meet a lady whose hands he thought would be of great interest to me. I agreed, and together we went to a house standing in a large garden near St. John's Wood. I had been made to promise to ask no questions, but I must confess I was somewhat anxious when, after what appeared to me a considerable time, the door at the end of a corridor opened, and a lady, with a heavy black lace mantilla covering her head and face, came towards me and held her hands out under a shaded electric light. What hands they were! From my point of view—of lines and marks—they completely fascinated me.[3]

While being fascinated, Cheiro charged through a reading, saying that Bernhardt was marvellously brilliant but when she got older, she'd experience a tragedy and die—except he said it more nicely than that. He must have said it *really* nicely because:

The white hands were drawn away, great sobs came from under the veil, until suddenly it was thrown back, and those wonderful eyes of the great Sarah looked straight into mine... in the sweetest of voices my young ears had ever known, she murmured over and over again in French, 'It is the most wonderful thing I have ever known—wonderful, wonderful, wonderful.'[4]

Sensibly, he took a mould of her hand and made sure she signed his autograph book. Never one for understatement, Bernhardt wrote:

Since God has placed in our hands lines and marks which tell our past and future, I only regret that from these lines we cannot know the future of those dearest to us, so that we might warn them of coming troubles or sorrows, But God doeth all things well—so be it then. Amen.[5]

Newspaper reports added that Cheiro had already studied 10,000 hands—he knew what he was doing. The story didn't do Bernhardt any harm either; she had an eccentric reputation to keep up, after all.

There's no mention of Cheiro after this for several weeks—he may have been on the south coast; at that time of year no-one with real money was in London. But by the end of September he'd taken a suite of rooms at 106 New Bond Street. He didn't charge a fee but accepted gifts. Alternatively, he allocated two days a week to help those who couldn't afford to pay and the rest of the week was devoted to those who could. There was soon a flurry of society ladies queuing for his attention, and Cheiro happily accepted invitations to 'at homes' and garden parties.

But he needed access to the crème de la crème—people with money to spare and time to fill. And he found that through another palmist Dam was friendly with—Oscar Wilde.

Irish-born Wilde was a writer who was renowned for his great wit and flamboyant dress and was a leading member of society. He was an aesthete, part of an art movement that emphasised aesthetic value and effects in preference to socio-political themes and positions. Aesthetes considered that beauty came first—art for art's sake. Life should copy art according to aesthetes and they focused on suggestion rather than statement, sensuality and symbolism.

As a leading personality in London, Wilde knew many of the famous actresses of the time—Cheiro's ideal audience.[i] Contradictory reports give a variety of dates for their meeting but Wilde signed Cheiro's visitors' book on 23 October 1892.

Wilde had been fascinated by palmistry since the mid-1880s. His story 'Lord Arthur Savile's Crime: A Story of Cheiromancy' was written when palmistry was highly fashionable and details palmistry techniques.[6] Briefly, Lord Savile has murder written in his hand and has to fulfil his duty to murder before he can marry.

The palmistry craze had been created by the thoroughly marvellous Edward Heron-Allen, who we met briefly in the last chapter. Heron-Allen was a true polymath—in addition to reviving palmistry, he translated the works of Omar Khayyam, played and learned how to make a violin (he wrote a book on it that's still in print), learned to speak Turkish, qualified as a solicitor, became a historian, was a champion of the Boy Scout movement, and wrote on archaeology, Buddhism and asparagus (he was obsessed with asparagus for a while), as well writing novels, and several science fiction and horror stories under the pseudonym of Christopher Blayre. And he refused to wear colours—he had special permission from Baden-Powell to wear a black scout uniform.

It was also Heron-Allen who'd revived the ancient terms related to palmistry, starting with the Greek word *cheiro*. And he practised what he preached. In addition to writing about palmistry, he saw clients and conducted hundreds of readings.

---

i During the First World War he worked for the intelligence services.

Wilde was already a friend of his when 'Lord Arthur Savile's Crime' was published—at that time, Heron-Allen was in the midst of a wildly successful American tour. In 1885 he read Wilde's palm and later cast the horoscope of Wilde's son Cyril. Letters from Wilde in 1886 call Heron-Allen 'My dear Astrologer' and discuss his palmistry writings. Therefore, when Wilde met Louis, he knew plenty about the subject. Later newspaper rumours that he taught Louis palmistry and set him up by announcing him as an Indian seer weren't too far off the mark.

The meeting took place at the home of Blanche Roosevelt at 69 Oakley Street in Kensington, a short distance from where Wilde and his wife Constance lived. American-born Roosevelt was a highly successful opera singer who'd retired after marrying the Marquis d'Alligri and beginning a new career as a writer. As well as working for several newspapers, she produced successful novels such as *Stage-struck* and non-fiction books such as *The Life and Reminiscences of Gustave Doré* for which she was reportedly the first American woman honoured by the French Academy.[7] Her social circle comprised literary and artistic giants, including Giuseppe Verdi, Victorien Sardou, Wilkie Collins and Guy de Maupassant.

Louis said he'd met Roosevelt after she'd turned up anonymously for a reading and he'd told her she was in danger of being caught in a fire that evening. Because she didn't take his warning seriously, after she'd left a fretting Louis went outside and asked a cabbie where she'd gone. Then he followed her to her hotel and insisted on seeing her. After Louis became insistent, Roosevelt went to stay at a friend's house. 'No real fire took place,' said Louis. 'But her pet dog which she left behind in her bedroom was during the night asphyxiated by an escape of gas which occurred under the floor in this very room.'[8]

Oddly, Roosevelt regarded this as a successful prediction rather than realise that if she'd ignored Louis, she might have been able to rescue her dog. Anyway, Louis was more than taken with her.

If I could only sketch her you would perhaps understand it—the whitest teeth, the fairest skin, the bluest eyes and hair like beaten gold that any artist has ever imagined, a figure divinely tall with the bearing of a queen, the grace of a thoroughbred, and with it all the simplicity of a child... everyone loved her...[9]

Roosevelt invited Louis to a party at her home—a coup because this was where the best people in London hung out. He wasn't a guest though; Louis was the entertainment. He waited patiently while jewels and wit sparkled out of his reach. Finally, dinner was over, people trickled into the drawing room and Louis began work.

> It was arranged that I was to read hands through a curtain, so that I might not know who my consultants were. Undoubtedly the greatest 'hit' I made that memorable evening was with Oscar Wilde... I little thought when his rather fat hands were passed through the holes in the curtain that they belonged to the most-talked-of man in London... They were interesting hands, and I was impressed by the difference in the markings of the left from the tight... 'The left hand is the hand of a king,' I said, 'but the right hand is the hand of a king who will send himself into exile.'... 'At what date?' came the quiet query from the other side of the curtain. 'A few years from now,' I answered, studying the right hand intently. ' Between your forty-first and forty-second years.' Everyone laughed. They treated it as a huge joke. But in the most dramatic manner Wilde came from behind the curtain and turned to them: 'The left is the band of a king,' be repeated gravely, 'but the right is that of a king who will send himself into exile.' Without another word, then, he left the room.[10]

That night, Nellie Melba, the Duke of Newcastle, Prince Colonna of Rome and Lord Leighton were amongst the impressed guests. But when *Wilde* said a palmist was good, you knew they were *really* good. Blanche wasn't as impressed as she might have been—she told Louis he was too realistic for drawing room entertainment. Some accounts suggest that Wilde later read Louis's palm. Maybe he did, but Louis wasn't going to go on about that.

Wilde later had palm readings from Charlotte Robinson, 'the sybil of Mortimer Street', who took an impression of his hand a few months later—he also saw her in 1894 and 1895.[11][ii] She saw a brilliant life for Wilde 'up to a certain point. Then I see a wall. Beyond the wall I see nothing.'[12] And in 1895 a Miss Edwardes predicted sudden notoriety for Wilde after which he'd die. Wilde also saw an unnamed palmist in Paris in 1897 and Wilfred Chesson in 1898. Cheiro's was only one of many, many palm readings Wilde had, and they were all gloomy.

Approval from Wilde was enough to tip the balance and increase the number of high-society clients Cheiro received. Whether they were as thrilled as he claimed will never be known—partly because Cheiro tended

---

ii Robinson later became Winston Churchill's palmist and wrote a book on palmistry, *The Graven Palm*, in 1911.

to discuss their visits after they were dead. For example, he said he'd met the Poet Laureate Alfred Lord Tennyson who died 6 October 1892 and who mentioned how the number six appeared in all the main events of his life.

However, it's likely Cheiro did meet the Prince of Wales after an invitation from Lady Arthur Paget (she started life as New York heiress Minnie Stevens) as he claimed. Again, his client hid behind a curtain to protect his identity.

> Once or twice he asked questions, and occasionally withdrew his hands to make notes... Gradually I began to indicate the important years for certain changes and events which appeared to be beyond his control... Tuesdays, Thursdays, and Fridays, I said would be the most important days each week for him; his important numbers were sixes and nines; and the months representing these numbers, being March 21 to April 21, and April 21 to May 27, and October 21 to November 27, would contain the most important events affecting his life. 'Strange,' he said, 'but that is remarkably true.'
>
> At that moment he allowed his hands to rest too heavily on the curtain. The fastening pins came out, the curtain dropped at our feet—and I found myself face to face with the Prince of Wales![13]

The Prince told Cheiro not to worry, but to carry on.

Louis didn't sit at home twiddling his thumbs in the hope of receiving an invitation to read at a celebrity's supper party. If he dressed up and hung out in the right places, he'd bump into rich people who'd be delighted to test Cheiro's skills. One of his hunting grounds was the Savoy hotel.

The Savoy had been built by impresario Richard D'Oyly Carte with profits from his Gilbert and Sullivan opera productions and opened on 6 August 1889. This was the first luxury hotel in Britain, with electric lights throughout, electric lifts, private bathrooms, constant hot and cold running water and many other things we'd expect in a Premier Inn today but which at the time were signs of breathtaking luxury. And this is without considering the food and entertainment. Part of that entertainment was the dinner guests themselves.

Women didn't eat in public restaurants so D'Oyley Carte enlisted the actress Lilly Langtry (then the Prince of Wales' mistress) and the Countess de Gray (a professional beauty whose portrait was on sale and displayed in shop windows, although she went by the unfortunate name of 'Gladys') to eat at the Savoy and made dining out more respectable for women. When the Prince of Wales joined Langtry there for dinner,

dinner parties at restaurants became a popular London pastime. Maybe your address book didn't allow you to invite the crème de la crème to your own events, but you could sit only a table or two away from them. Oscar Wilde often entertained at the Savoy as did Nellie Melba.

On the last Sunday of October 1892, Melba hosted a supper party in her suite at the Savoy after her performance of *Aida*. She received her guests while still in her stage costume because it would have taken too long to remove her black make up. And she'd invited Cheiro to read her guests' palms. Apparently, the Duke of Newcastle's hair stood up on end when he heard his predictions.

Cheiro's version had Dame Melba stroll down Bond Street and pop in for a quick reading in November 1888, afterwards offering him a box at Covent Garden to watch her sing the next night. He attended, armed with a huge bouquet. And then she invited him to her party at the Savoy. Later it was discovered that someone had run off with her jewellery as Cheiro had predicted. But again, he was simply the hired entertainment.

Back in the real world, on 27 October Harry Dam married Dorothy Dorr at All Saints, Gordon Square, Saint Pancras. Maybe Louis was there. Dorr continued to act and Dam went on to write hit musicals such as 'The Shop Girl'. They had two sons and Dam became renowned as the author of articles about science and invention. He was one of a few journalists who interviewed Wilhelm Röntgen at his laboratory in Wurzburg, Bavaria about X-rays and also interviewed Marconi in 1897. But interesting though Dam is, he leaves Cheiro's story at this point.

Louis had plenty of competition, so he couldn't afford to slack. For example, Madame de la Tours was firmly established at 97 New Bond Street and taught classes as well as offering her *Treatise on Palmistry* for sale. She was available for 'at-homes' on request and advertised heavily in the *Morning Post*.

It would help if Louis looked the part. As well as ensuring he was well-dressed and there was a secretary at hand to see people in, Louis wore his mystical ring—the one he'd earlier said he'd brought back from Egypt. 'It is in shape a large maquire, set with three round stones, on which are carved the figures of a cock, a hog, and a beetle, signifying… the devil, material advantages, and eternity…'[14]

Sometimes Cheiro said he'd acquired the ring from a man who found it on a mummy after crossing the desert from Babylon to Nineveh and this man had left it to Cheiro in his will.[15] Or it had been given to him by a 'Hindoo prophet' and was 'over fourteen hundred years old'.[16] Wherever he'd got it from, it coordinated well with the skull and crossbones scarf pin he wore that he claimed a strange woman had given him on the streets of London.[17]

Decorating himself was all very well, but where Cheiro went to town was in decorating his rooms. Atmosphere is everything. The journalist who turned up to interview him for the *Sketch* in July 1893 was certainly impressed.

I have scarcely time to glance round the charming waiting-room, draped artistically from floor to ceiling with sage-green curtains, which form an effective background to the white, quaint furniture, when Cheiro himself noiselessly flings open the folding doors leading to his sanctum... As he crosses the room to move from a little exquisitely carved Indian table the cast of a hand he was studying, I seize the opportunity to examine the beautifully worked pieces of Indian drapery that cover the walls and ceiling... and also the rare skins which lie dotted about on the polished floor. A sacred Hindoo bull attracts my attention... Cheiro relates how it was looted during the Mutiny from an Indian temple, and presented to him by the officer who secured it, and then he calls my attention to many other curios, notably a real god, that stands a grim and silent witness to heathen mythology upon his writing-table. Here, also... his wonderful autograph book, crowded with the names of celebrities... some in whose veins flows the bluest of English blood.[18]

Cheiro had the look.

The final stage of the plan was to write a book, so he hastily completed Cheiro's *Book of the Hand* in late 1892, which was almost completely ignored on publication.

'It had been commonly rumoured in London that... Princess May... had been to see me,' Louis claimed, although he probably started that rumour himself.[19] Anyway, when it was announced that the Princess was going to marry the Duke of York, Louis sent a copy of his book bound in white calf with gold type as a wedding gift. Once he'd received a thank-you letter, he made sure any passing journalist heard about it. Gradually, reviews trickled in: 'Cheiro... has certainly written a very interesting volume, quaintly and prettily got up, easy to read and understand.'[20] 'There is an atmosphere of mystery and romance about it—cheap but substantial.'[21]

For a few months, things bounced along nicely, but one thing could ruin the plan.

During my first season in London, some of the newspapers began printing many articles about me; some were extremely flattering, but some were equally hostile and again called attention to the old Act of Parliament, making out that my profession was illegal, and calling on the authorities to have me suppressed... one Monday morning, I received the visit of a Police Inspector, who politely but firmly told me that no steps would be taken if on the following Saturday I closed my consulting-rooms.[22]

The legislation in question was the Vagrancy Act of 1824 of which Section 4 described as vagrants: 'Every person pretending or professing to tell fortunes, or using any subtle craft, means, or device, by palmistry or otherwise, to deceive and impose on any of his Majesty's subjects.' Palmists in seaside towns regularly fought prosecution, while those catering for society clients in Bond Street and its environs were largely ignored.

This was why people claimed that palmistry was a science and why Cheiro claimed he didn't ask a fee for readings. Some palmists sought to get around the Act by saying they only read character and didn't make predictions, and therefore couldn't be classed as fortune tellers. Prosecutions were actively sought by the constabulary and judiciary who often used paid informers. The penalty if found guilty was usually severe: a prison sentence of up to three months, accompanied or followed by hard labour. Plus, appeals weren't usually allowed. Although a few people regarded conviction as an occupational hazard, for others it was the end of their career.

A single threat was enough for Louis who said, 'I gave orders to my secretary to book no appointments beyond the end of that week, as on Saturday at six o'clock I intended to see my last client. I never worked harder or did better than during that week, and at six o'clock on Saturday, as far as my plans were concerned, I had finished my career as "Cheiro".'[23]

And then a woman turned up and asked how much it would cost for him to perform readings at a party she was hosting at home that evening. Louis said, '"Cheiro" has ceased to exist, but if you will allow me I will give you my services with pleasure.'[24]

Jean Palmer (wife of Walter Palmer, the director of the biscuit firm Huntley and Palmer and later an MP) wasn't concerned about the finer points of Louis's identity and told him to be at her house at 9:30. Amongst the guests Louis met were the actor Henry Irving, Herbert Gladstone and George Lewis, the lawyer so famous for disposing of skeletons in closets that he warranted a mention in Arthur Conan Doyle's Sherlock Holmes story 'The Adventure of the Illustrious Client'.

Louis finished his readings at three o'clock in the morning and undertook to return the next day to talk over his success and presumably collect his payment. When he did so, Jean said, 'You cannot possibly think of giving up this work,' and offered to get Lewis's opinion.[25] Apparently his conclusion was, 'You are working on such a totally different foundation from what this old Act was intended to apply to, that you do not come under it. You are to send his card to Scotland Yard and tell them to address any further communications to him.'[26]

That was OK, then. In any event, there were no further problems and the plan continued. Louis ensured he was the subject of lengthy magazine and newspaper articles that sang his praises.

'It requires no persistent questioning to elicit these incidents,' pointed out one journalist after describing how one society lady acted on Cheiro's advice to buck up and get her act together or she was doomed—apparently her life line grew a sixteenth of an inch when she did as instructed. And Cheiro persuaded a young girl to hand over her revolver and not shoot herself, which was nice of him. 'Cheiro's whole conversation is filled with adventures, anecdotes, and romantic escapades which time forbids me to enter into,' added the journalist.[27] Louis was more than prepared for interviews. He had a book to hand to offer as a gift, signed his autograph with a flourish and insisted on inflicting a short poem on the journalist.

In the days to come,
TO ONE Who stooped so low as e'en to touch my hand –
Who whispered soft,
Life is not always youth,
Nor is youth life.
Live, then, to make a stand,
It matters little where—be it for Truth.[28]

Louis still wanted to become a poet and he'd continue to inflict his poems on any captive audience he could find. He'd conquered London and the obvious next step was America. So he hired an American promoter and planned to make a lecture tour in the US at the end of July 1893—after which he was going to travel the world, he claimed recklessly.

And then things went wrong. Whether Louis was partying too much, caught a virus or had been working too hard is unknown. He claimed he'd collapsed with exhaustion after reading 6,000 hands in a year and had to spend three months in a nursing home in Devonshire Street. He was certainly ill enough to postpone his trip for several weeks and had to give up his and mope around his flat.

In September 1893, Louis stood on a platform at Waterloo station waiting for the boat train. Travelling under the name of 'Louis Cheiro', he was accompanied by two doctors (it isn't clear what they were doing there apart from offering a friendly wave), half a dozen of his best friends and Blanche Roosevelt.

'I was en route for the States without any letters of introduction, without knowing a person there, and knowing little or nothing about Americans,' he said, presumably with his fingers crossed behind his back.[29]

Also waiting for the boat train was Lillian Nordica, the American opera singer. Through a happy coincidence, she knew Blanche Roosevelt who hastily introduced her to Louis. Louis was en route to fame and fortune that would exceed even his wildest expectations.

A READING WITH CHEIRO

If you move in the right circles, you might meet Cheiro at a supper party after the theatre. It's probably well after midnight once the party has got going and your hostess announces Cheiro is ready to expose your secrets. He sits to one side and patiently waits for each guest to come forward and offer him a hand, which he studies carefully. When it's your turn, you sit with trepidation and he describes your past, your character and an amazing event that will occur to you in the upcoming months. Most of the guests will be hovering nearby, leaning forward to ensure they don't miss a word.

Or perhaps you attend a dinner party. He may be a guest at the table in which case he asks your birthday. You say that you were born in late June. Ah! You are under the sign of the crab and a water being and therefore emotional and sensitive, someone who needs to take great care near water. If the dinner party is small, he will be happy to describe the characters of your friends and family if you offer their birth dates.

More likely, you enjoy your meal and then your hostess suggests with a clap of her hands and a gleeful expression that she has a treat for you in the drawing room. Armed with a glass of something sparkling, you wait your turn to be told what life has to offer you. Those closest to your hostess will be ready and make sure they are first to gain attention from the great seer. You probably step into the room alone, or you might choose to take your closest friend with you. But this is false privacy—everyone will want to know what you were told the moment you leave the room. And everyone will join in—it would be rude to your hostess to turn your nose up at the entertainment, whatever your private thoughts on having a reading.

Or you might come across him at a ball or gala, sitting to one side once he'd had enough of dancing. No money would exchange hands—that would be far too vulgar. But you are no fool and would realise that your hostess (it would be a hostess, this is women's territory) would call on Cheiro the following morning with effusive thanks and an envelope containing money to represent her gratitude.

All such occasions allow for a cursory reading. If you want more, you have to attend an appointment at his rooms. But given Cheiro's popularity, such appointments can be hard to come by. It can take a week or two—maybe longer—until he has time to see you. Someone with the right social standing could persuade him to make adjustments to his diary so they can be seen sooner. If you're a particularly attractive young woman (seventeen or so), he may suggest you call at the end of the day. Although his business hours are between eleven and five, he could make an exception and offer you a six o'clock appointment. If all else fails, offering extra money will ensure he can fit you in at the end of the day.

But you may not move in any circles whatsoever. In this case you will need to book an appointment and sit in the waiting room until he is ready to see you. You sit on a comfortable modern chair, surrounded by artistically draped full length curtains. There is no need to give your real name to his secretary. Cheiro prefers not to know the identity of his clients. Indeed, if someone arrives who he knows well, he'll gently refuse to read for them. Should you be fretting about a loved one, you may have brought with you a print of their hand. It isn't ideal, of course, but when circumstances demand, Cheiro will perform such an analysis. A few well-prepared people arrange to have a plaster cast made of the hand of a dear one who is overseas and sit patiently with it wrapped in a bundle on their lap.

Finally, the door to his consulting room opens and he casts an eye around the waiting room. His secretary nods to indicate it's your turn. You have to attend alone. Unless you are young and with your mother, Cheiro won't allow anyone else to be present during the reading. Certainly not your husband or wife. It's too distracting.

The next half hour is all yours.

He waves you into his room. You'd heard he was good-looking but never expected him to be so handsome. A tall and athletic looking man, he brushes his hair from his eyes as he offers you a smile. There is a flash from the stones on his ornate ring. Somehow, he radiates vitality and his dark eyes tell you that he already knows your secrets. The idea of lying to him seems insane.

Cheiro waves you to sit down on a well-stuffed easy chair. The lights are shaded except for the single electric lamp over a small table with a red velvet cushion on it. Cheiro takes the chair opposite you and asks you to place your right hand on the cushion. He then picks up a gold instrument and begins to gently trace the lines on your hand. After a few moments of considering them, he drops his instrument and takes your hand by the wrist and glances at it before looking up and staring into nothing while he considers his words.

What do you want him to say? Like everyone, you hope for a little flattery and a peep into the future—as long as that future doesn't hold too many horrors.

He begins to speak in a soft Irish accent and asks you if you ever have breathing problems. Indeed, you do but why should he ask this. He tells you that you have narrower than usual nails.

Maybe you look worried because Cheiro hastily explains he rarely has to offer an unflattering reading of a hand—only in the most extreme circumstances such as when he is confronted with the hand of a murderer or other criminal. In that case, you will understand, he may be more severe. You can't help it, you pull back a little. Cheiro continues to explain that he rarely tells hands in full if he sees crimes committed in them. You now wonder if he thinks you are a criminal.

He again traces the lines in your hand with his instrument and you ask if it's possible to avert any danger or disaster he might see. He says, of course, but few people try to. And now he begins to talk about your health, how to guard against threatened lawsuits and other domestic worries. He explains the course you should pursue in life to gain fame and wealth. Gently, he outlines some of your faults and how you can act to avert the worst outcomes.

And while he does this, he explains how he has arrived at his conclusions. He points out the line of life, the heavy line that encircles the base of your thumb. Then he traces the line that runs parallel to it from the bottom of your palm to the base of your second finger. This is the line of fate. Methodically, he indicates the major lines on your hand, telling you what they signify. Perhaps your line of fate crosses the line of the head. This suggest you are firm willed. Your third and fourth fingers and the portion of the palm lying under them show your fortune in material terms and speak of your general well-being. The markings on your line of fate designate the times when certain events will happen. He notes there is a small cross under your first finger—this shows you will marry for love.

Each time he makes a new statement his eyes meet yours and he waits a split second for your reaction. Should you gasp or raise your eyebrows, he launches into a more detailed justification of what he has said.

You could be better informed than many and know Cheiro's interpretations differ from those suggested by the Chirological Society. For example, he suggests that the marriage line curving upwards means you will not have a successful marriage. The Society would never make such a definite prediction. But if you broach this subject, he will tell you that after reading thousands of hands he has learned what works. Theory is all very well, but he is a man of experience.

Once he has completed looking at your palm, he leans back in his chair and reaches for a pen and paper. He asks you for your date of birth and scribbles down a few calculations while you wait. Then he tells you that according to his calculation, the number 60 governs your life and it will be in your sixtieth year that you achieve the climax of your career.

And then he explains about the period within which you were born. These period aren't like calendar months but run to different dates. For example, the January period commences on 21 December and lasts until 20 January. And within that period the dates have different strengths. You must allow seven days at the start of the period for it to come into its full strength and seven days at the close for it to die out.

You tell him that you were born 3 March. Cheiro tells you that you therefore possess a natural understanding which you have not obtained from books or study. Knowledge is easy for you to acquire, especially of history. You are by nature generous, but may be inclined to be anxious about money matters. This is because you don't wish to be dependent on others. It is likely you are artistic, but your success in the arts relies on you being encouraged.

But your concern is love, you cry out. When will you find love and with whom?

Cheiro suggests you seek someone who has the same number as you for their birth date. That means you should focus on those born on the third day of the month or on any day when the two digits of that number add up to three. It may help you to wear certain colours, he suggests, and you have an interesting discussion about a suitable gemstone you could wear.

Finally, your reading is over so you get to your feet and ask his fee. He raises his eyebrows and tells you he isn't allowed to charge but then his eyes move to a small bowl on the table. Next to the bowl lies his autograph book, filled with the names of celebrities singing his praises. Unable to help yourself, you leaf through it. With a smile, Cheiro points out the autographs of two well-known London doctors who express their opinion that palmistry is a true science. Then you look at the bowl that contains a good many sovereigns (pound coins) and take the hint, discreetly dropping in some coins of your own.

Before you leave, you might take the opportunity to buy a copy of his latest book—a pile of them is lying prominently on a table near the door. On perusing it later, you find it an easy-to-understand guide, lavishly illustrated and straightforward. It might inspire you to attend his classes so you can become a palmist yourself. Should you mention this to him, he may offer you a discount if you flutter your eyelashes. It's rumoured that sometimes he drops the costs to half price.

Or you may do what many others do and make an appointment with the next palmist along the street to see what they have to say.

Cheiro in New York, 1894

CHAPTER

FIVE

Palm reading is an occupation requiring the utmost concentration of thought. It breaks down nerve tissue and there is danger to the reader unless he finds something to feed the nerves and thus replace the wasted energy. Nothing does this like Paine's celery compound... Before I took it I was depressed and nervous. My appetite failed and my sleep was broken. Now I am well and lively enough to make jokes.[1]

*L*OUIS HAD SEEN NORDICA AT SOCIETY EVENTS, but this was the first time they'd been introduced. Travelling first-class gave him—hopefully—enough *cachet* to socialise with her. 'Madame Nordica was extremely lovable and good-hearted,' Louis said, 'but not demonstrative or showy in her affections. She helped many young singers to realize their ambition for a musical career, but she never allowed the good she did to be advertised in the press.'[2]

American-born Lillian Norton, who'd adopted the name of 'Nordica' to sound more operatic, had trained in Italy and was one of the most prominent international prima donnas of her era, singing at the major opera houses on both sides of the Atlantic. Unfortunately, her marriage had been less successful. 'Her first husband was Mr. F. A. Gower of the Gower-Bell Telephone fame,' pointed out Louis. 'This marriage was not a happy one and its ending was peculiar. Her husband attempted to cross the Straits of Dover in a balloon and was never heard of again.'[3] She was in the process of divorcing Gower when he disappeared in 1885. Nordica married twice more, but this was yet to come.

They were travelling on the *SS Paris*, a luxury liner that had previously gained the 'Blue Ribband' for the fastest crossing on the Atlantic.[i] Its luxuries included hot and cold water, electric ventilation, and electric lighting. Travelling first class gave you access to magnificent rooms, such as the library with its writing tables and the smoking room, both fitted with walnut panels. The dining salon boasted an arched roof that provided natural light. On the inside was stained glass and between this glass and the outer roof were hundreds of incandescent lights. At night the outer roof was closed by iron shutters and the saloon brilliantly illuminated. The portholes had two slides, for the day of stained glass, and at night a mirror. In the library, the stained-glass slides over the portholes were inscribed with quotations and the panels between them decorated with the names of famous writers. Second-cabin passengers had their own rooms and separate kitchens.

Three days into the week-long voyage, Nordica asked Louis to visit her in her stateroom to have tea with her and Don Giovanni Perugini, the celebrated tenor. Born John Chatterson in New York, Perugini had launched his career in Europe—his name change occurred when he switched from popular music to opera.[ii] He'd also won a prize in P B Barnum's first baby show in New York as a four-year-old in 1855 and the press never forgot. And he might have wanted to forget he was a ballerina in the 1870s and believed to be a girl.[4]

At that time, he was feeling morose and, according to Cheiro, was considering withdrawing from the world to live in a monastery—unlikely, but he may have needed cheering up. In any event, Louis read Perugini's hand. 'I told him… that within a few months he would become engaged to a woman in his own profession, marry her in six months and be divorced inside of a year.'[5]

'A little rapid even for the States,' Nordica laughed.[6]

They soon arrived in New York and Louis rented a set of rooms that took up a whole floor at 432 Fifth Avenue. He focused on creating the

---

i Previously, it was the SS City of Paris.

ii His original name is often given as John Haley Augustin Chatterton and he is claimed to have been born in in New York or Michigan. However, newspaper reports discuss his earlier performances under the name of John Chatterson—for example, 'The Italo-American tenor known in his ballad days as John Chatterson and in his operatic career as Signor Giovanni Perugini', the *Evening Star* (Washington), 1 December 1883, p.3. His name change is also discussed in the British press. Under this name he appears in the 1861 and 1871 censuses in New Jersey where his birth year is given as 1851, not the often claimed 1855.

right environment for a celebrated seer—which he fully planned to be. Louis had brought little luggage with him, so it must have taken him some serious shopping and several weeks to complete his new India room. But it sounds as if it was worth it.

> The front room you enter is hung with dull, dark green cloth. This cloth covers every bit of the walls except a wide frieze of old gold. On two of the doors it is draped and looped like window curtains. Against this green background hang a few etchings and photographs.
>
> A large oriental carpet covers the centre of the polished floor, and some handsome leopard skins are scattered about. Tall, beautiful ferns are in white and gold wickerwork baskets upon wicker pedestals, and the mantel is draped with Oriental stuff, while a cover of the same is thrown over one of the easy chairs by the window... Two writing desks are to be seen, and at the larger sits a gentleman who takes the cards into Cheiro. When you are admitted to the mysterious presence you enter a small room on the right and find yourself in a distinctly East Indian apartment...
>
> The little room is draped with strange Oriental stuffs from ceiling to floor. On one side there is the head and forequarters of a large brazen bull. It is an East Indian idol which dates back 200 years before Christ... came from a temple near Bombay...
>
> Near the window was a little stand upon which rested a soft pillow covered with green silk. This is for my lady's hand to rest on while Cheiro traces with a long slender silver instrument the lines of the palm. You are placed in an armchair on one side, while the unfolder of mysteries takes the other.[7]

The room contained:

> Quaint white and gold furniture... a red marble statue of Buddha... a genuine Hindu idol... tall graceful palms and many photos... the walls are covered with Burmese curtains grotesquely embroidered by hand... on the ceiling is an Indian tapestry which contains an authentic written account written in Hindoostani of the history of the Hindoo gods... Above the door the palmist's Italian motto, "Che sara sara (What Will be Will be")
> wasrendered ghastly by the reflection of a Moorish lamp.[8]

> Lying about here and there are casts in plaster of a few of the noted palms which Cheiro has examined, first in interest being that of Sara Bernhardt...[9]

Less kind commentators referred to his collection of 'bric a brac'.[10]

There was one final item. Louis was carrying a revolver that he later maintained he'd accepted from a suicidal client in London in November 1892. The woman had told him that if things didn't get better as he'd promised, she'd come back for her pistol and shoot herself in his rooms. Happily, things did get better and she told Louis he might as well keep the gun now she'd changed her mind.

We may safely assume that Louis paid equal attention to his wardrobe—he certainly waved his jewelled ring around whenever possible. But none of this was of use without clients. Although he gained some attention from the press, suggesting, 'He has fashionable New York by the hand' was vastly over stated.[11] Most of New York had no idea who he was, despite his 'fine physique, regular features and gray eyes'.[12]

By good fortune, Louis knew someone in New York who'd offered to lend him a hand if he was ever there, so he engineered a meeting with Marshall Wilder.

> I was walking through the corridor of the Imperial Hotel (New York) when I was stopped by a gentleman, who said: 'You don't remember me, do you, Mr. Wilder?'
>
> 'Yes,' I answered, 'you are Louis Warner of London.'
>
> He laughed and said: 'You have a very good memory, Mr. Wilder, but I have taken another name. I wish to be known as Cheiro... You see, I have followed your advice, and taken up palmistry as a business.'[13]

Wilder introduced Louis to his friends and when a woman journalist asked him for suggestions of articles she could write, he referred her to his friends, suggesting she acquired casts of their hands and took them to Louis to interpret.

> Without knowing whose hands they were he read each and every one correctly. Among them was an impression of my own hand. He picked it up, and said immediately: 'This is the hand of my friend, Marshall Wilder.' To my mind, this was the greatest test of his powers.[14]

The article in question appeared in the *New York World* on 26 November 1893. Louis had analysed a dozen or so hands when impressions of a strange-looking pair of hands were offered.

> I was struck by the fact that the lines on the left were in every way normal while those on the right were as abnormal as possible...
>
> I summed up the impressions before me by stating: 'Judging from these hands, the owner of them undoubtedly commenced his career in a normal way...' I went on to describe how the man's entire nature slowly and steadily had changed under the continual urge to acquire wealth at any cost, until he was finally prepared even to commit murder for money... This man in his forty-fourth year will pass through some sensational trial, he will be condemned to die, yet his hands show that he will escape this fate and live on for years-but in prison.[15]

Louis's comment was actually, 'I refuse to read that hand to any one but the owner,' although it was true he recognised Wilder's hand.[16] The version above appeared years later.

The *World* disclosed that the print was of Henry Meyer who that week had been arrested on suspicion of poisoning wealthy patients for the insurance he'd taken out on them. German-born Meyer had been killing people since 1878. He'd married three times and killed two of his wives using poison which couldn't be detected at an autopsy. Despite being suspected several times, he wasn't charged until 20 July 1893 and was now awaiting trial.[iii]

It didn't matter that he had little to say about Meyer. Cheiro had successfully read the handprints of numerous leading lights and had appeared in a major newspaper. The article came out on Tuesday, and on the following Sunday, Louis was woken by his servant who said, 'Get up, sir, there are over a hundred people sitting on the stairs waiting to see you.'[17]

Louis loftily told them that Sunday was a day of rest and they should return the next day to book an appointment. On Monday, his secretary booked appointments for the next two months. But being busy didn't stop Louis from checking out the competition. He met a medium who he had a couple of private sittings with, afterwards passing along his clients to him.

---

iii Later, Cheiro claimed to have visited Meyer in Sing Sing prison before he was due to be executed (his sentence was reduced to a life sentence). He certainly obtained an impression of Meyer's palm in 1894.

A New York doctor, who had waited nearly twenty years to marry the one woman he had ever cared for, was at last able to wed this woman, only to lose her, ten days after, by death from double pneumonia…. [He] decided to commit suicide. One evening he and 'Cheiro' were walking in New York City, when the latter, as they were passing the rooms of a private medium known to him, suggested to the doctor that they should go in and get a sitting. This they did, and shortly afterwards the doctor was holding a clear and distinct conversation with his wife.[18]

Once Louis had made contacts, he clung onto them. He clearly stayed in touch with Nordica because she gave him a silver cigarette case lined with gold and engraved with his name for his birthday. Louis had got it into his head that Nordica was unknown in New York—in reality, she had a fully booked calendar and was due to appear at the Metropolitan Opera House in early December as part of the Italian Opera Company, alongside renowned names such as Emma Eames, Emma Calvé and Nellie Melba. Louis decided that as the other stars would doubtless receive plenty of bouquets, it would be a nice gesture to send Nordica a basket of flowers.

Buying flowers wasn't something Louis had much experience in. He went to a florist on Fifth Avenue and asked for the best roses. When pressed for details, he loftily told the salesgirl he'd leave it up to her and she should send him the bill. Louis was sitting in his box waiting for the production to begin when he was summoned to speak to Henry Abbey, the manager of the Metropolitan. Laughing, Abbey informed Louis that the basket of flowers he'd ordered had turned up and was too big to get through the front doors.

Looking through the glass doors we could see a lorry In the street, and a crowd of people gazing at what looked at first sight to be a small mountain of roses. It was, in fact, a basket about 16ft. high by perhaps 4ft. across, made entirely of those famous American Beauty roses, costing five dollars apiece. Mr. Abbey saw my look of dismay.

'All right,' he laughed, 'I'll have the scenic doors on the stage opened; It will be there when Nordica comes on.' The curtain went up on the temple scene of Aida. As the light gradually Increased, all eyes were attracted to the basket of flowers standing at the corner of the stage.

My 'Queen of Flowers' in the shop had indeed excelled herself. She had also known what giving her 'carte blanche' meant, and, further, she had not forgotten to festoon gracefully a small silk

Stars and Stripes to the handle of the basket. For a moment a hush of astonishment crept over the crowded house; then, realising the compliment paid to an American singer, the basket received an unstinted round of applause… The bill for the basket duly reached me the next morning… it taught me not to give 'carte blanche' to anyone in America again.[19]

An expensive gesture, but it got everyone talking. And then in January 1894, Perugini suddenly married the famous actress and singer Lillian Russell. He'd been her leading man in several productions and Russell was already twice married and divorced. The cracks in their relationship soon showed when Perugini started to insult his new wife while onstage, unheard by the audience but clear to the cast. He was so insulting that Marie Dressler, a member of the company and friend of Russell's, chased him out of the theatre and threatened him with a stage brace made of wood and iron. Perugini refused to perform until the management provided him with a bodyguard. Later, Russell claimed that Perugini had threatened to throw her out of a seventh-floor hotel window. The marriage only lasted six months although they didn't finally divorce until 1898.

For the last few months Cheiro was in New York, Perugini's statement in Cheiro's visitor's book that '"Cheiro's" remarkable predictions when crossing the Atlantic in September 1893… were not alone curious, but have been verified to the letter' provided him with an enormous boost.[20]

Life was moving along nicely but Louis hadn't broken into New York Society. He attended what events he could (for example, he was present at a high-profile suffragist meeting in May 1894) but he needed to improve his plan. His stay in New York was coming to an end when on 9 June 1894, at ten o'clock at night while he was busy working on a palmistry book, he was interrupted by his secretary who brought in a stranger who'd said his visit was of extreme urgency. 'He was a gentlemanly looking individual, neatly dressed in a frock coat, clean shaven, with hair turning grey at the temples. He had an anxious look on his face and a very nervous manner,' said Louis.[21] Later, Louis added that the man had a large mole with hairs growing from it on his left cheek—he got uglier with each retelling.

The man indicated the nearby open door on the other side of the room saying, 'That leads out to the stairs, does it not?'[22]

Louis agreed this was the case, and the man commented on his ring so Louis told him it was a protective charm. The man offered his left palm. Louis leaned forward to look at it and the man said, 'You devil, you will, will you,' reached into his coat, retrieved a dagger and stabbed at Louis's heart—straight into the silver cigarette case Lillian Nordica had given him.[23]

Louis fell back against his desk and as the man aimed his dagger a second time, he pulled out the revolver from the desk drawer. He hadn't moved fast enough. The knife pierced his side and Louis let off a wild shot as he fell to the ground. Or maybe he fired three times with the bullets landing all over his room—one in a statue of an Egyptian bull. It didn't matter, as he still missed. The dagger remained entangled in Louis's clothes.

Clearly not anticipating a fully-armed palmist, the man made a swift exit through the door he'd pointed out earlier. Cheiro's secretary rushed in to see what the commotion was about, but was too late to catch the man, so he ran outside to summon a policeman and an ambulance.

Policeman Wooden (yes, that was his name), who was hanging around on the street corner, rushed inside but said he hadn't heard any shots or seen anyone rush out of the building. No-one had heard a shot except Louis and his secretary.

Louis bravely refused the ambulance and summoned a doctor who stitched up his four-inch long cut that he said was wide enough to stick a pencil in, telling Louis to rest. Less sympathetic reports say Louis only needed to put a sticking plaster on his wound. The police arrived and after thorough questioning, they took away the cigarette case, the dagger and the revolver.

His assailant was never traced. Many years later, Louis said he'd discovered that the man was the spurned lover of one of his clients—spurned on Cheiro's advice because he was much older than the young woman who'd complained to Cheiro he was ruining her life.

The next day, a group of journalists gathered while Louis lay on a couch, showing off his wound. He airily said he'd been stabbed before so it was all in a day's work to him. And he'd dreamed about being stabbed directly before his would-be assassin arrived. That's why his gun was easy to hand and loaded. When the journalists asked the reason for the assault, Louis muttered, 'Les femmes, les femmes' (the women, the women).[24]

Eventually, the police returned the cigarette case, but Cheiro didn't get his revolver back. So he called at the police station and was summoned to a room to see Theodore Roosevelt, future President of the United States. Apparently, promising to return Cheiro's revolver at any minute, Roosevelt jotted down his date of birth and asked for a quick prediction. Cheiro quickly described the nature of a Scorpio and that did the trick. Roosevelt handed back his revolver and wished him a happy stay in New York.

Despite announcing he was about to embark on a world tour, spending an extended time in India as the guest of a Maharajah (he probably meant the Marahajah of Bikaner who Louis claimed to have met several times in London) who was going to lend him some books on cheiromancy, Louis sailed back to London. Press reports describe how Louis became a journalist at this time, reporting on the Sino-Japanese War. He certainly wrote lengthy articles for the Associated Press on his 'experiences' which were not only published that year but popped up at intervals over the next couple of decades when newspapers had a space to fill, bearing titles such as: 'Cheiro, the Palmist, Describes Life In a Hindoo Temple. A SPIRIT FREED FROM ITS BODY. When It Returned, It Was Invested With Supernatural Power.'[25]

And Louis wrote to S S McClure, who established the McClure syndicate, on 26 March 1894, enclosing a letter of introduction from Hillary Bell, the Belfast-born portrait painter who moved to America in the 1870s and became a theatre critic for the New York Press, and an article—'Palm Leaves by Cheiro the Palmist'. Later letters promised more articles and a copy of Louis's poem *The Burning of Hinckley*.

His ripping yarns had nothing to do with China or Japan.

Cheiro claimed in *True Ghost Stories* (in 1917) to have visited Japan in November 1894. He said a financier friend was unable to travel and had asked Louis to conduct his negotiations. Cheiro was in China when the Port Arthur massacre took place and was able to stop looting by the Japanese of a Chinese nobleman's home he was visiting. This led to learning lots of ancient Chinese occult secrets. He never mentions such a trip elsewhere.

Back in England, Cheiro received numerous eminent clients over the summer, most of whom allowed him to take an impression of their hand that he used as illustrations in his books. Many of these encounters are described in painstaking detail in Cheiro's writing. For example, he claimed he met politician Joseph Chamberlain in the House of Commons on 22 June 1894 and predicted a glowing career for his son Austen. Obligingly, Chamberlain made Cheiro an appointment to meet Cecil Rhodes the following day. And he saw Lord Kitchener on 21 July who, like many of Cheiro's more famous clients, claimed to have first visited him years before and received an accurate reading. Kitchener obligingly explained why he consulted Cheiro.

'Look here'—he [Kitchener] turned and pointed to a small blue vase about three inches high that was standing on his table—'can you tell me anything about that?'

Utterly taken aback, I [Louis] took the vase in my hands, looked it all over, and then put it down, saying, 'I am sorry, but I don't know one vase from another. I never had the inclination to study such things.'

'Just so' he laughed... 'I have never studied hands and you have. If a man makes a lifelong study of a thing, I expect him to know more about it than anyone else...'[26]

I then showed him... towards his sixty-sixth year, that his death would be by water, but most likely caused by storm at sea...[27]

In response, Kitchener pointed out he was a good swimmer.

Cheiro also saw royalty such as Nicholas II, the Czar of Russia, who Cheiro told that war would be fatal to him and his immediate family, celebrities such as the actress Constance Collier, a Gaiety Girl and then sixteen (who he took a strong liking to), and mystics such as Annie Besant who became President of the Theosophical Society.

One of Louis's most famous clients during this period was Mark Twain, who he saw in early August. Twain must have been impressed as he also saw Cheiro in New York in 1895 and again in London in 1897.

Cheiro the palmist told me that I should become very wealthy in my 68th year. I was a bankrupt and heavily in debt at the time and I properly thanked him. He said it again in London, two years afterward and I properly thanked him again. Shall I be able to complete my thanks next year? If not can I sue him for breach of promise?[28]

Twain's fortunes did change for the better in 1903 as predicted. However, his experiences with Cheiro didn't contribute towards his novel *Pudd'nhead Wilson*, which had a plot point based around fingerprint patterns, as often stated for the simple reason that this was written at the end of 1893.

But someone would have a greater effect on Cheiro's life than any of these—a young lawyer called Jehangier Cola.

CHEIRO'S PALMISTRY METHODS

Although many describe palmistry as a fad, it deserves far better and higher recognition. It isn't a belief to be adopted and abandoned tomorrow. It's a science, one in which the wise of the past were well versed.

Your palm and its lines reveal your past, present and future. Cheiro can't tell you what you're thinking and what you're going to do. But he can determine your characteristics. He can tell what line of work would be best for you, whether success or failure are within your grasp, and whether your life is to be a long or a short one—unless you have an unforeseen accident. Your palm can't reveal that.

First, Cheiro will look at the general make-up of your hand.

Your hands are divided in two hemispheres by the line of head. The upper hemisphere represents mind and the lower the material. Large hands show the power of completion. Small hands denote ideas too large for your power of execution.

If your palm is thin, hard and dry, you're probably timid and lack energy. A thick, clumsy palm tells of brute force and obstinacy. A hollow palm is very unfortunate. People with this, although working hard to obtain success, receive but the wages of disappointment.

And what of your fingers? Long fingers show a love of detail and that you're strict and proper, with a leaning towards affectation. Or perhaps you have short fingers. This shows you're quick and impulsive.

You follow your intuition; you can't be bothered with little things and are inclined to jump to conclusions. The conventions of society mean little to you. Hopefully, you don't have thick and heavy fingers. This shows you're cruel and selfish.

If your fingers are curved inwards or contracted, they denote timidity and shyness. Conversely, if they're supple and inclined to bend back, you're charming, clever, and inclined to extravagance. Pointed fingers show idealism and a desire for love—they indicate impressionable and impulsive people. Square fingers show a love for logic and exactness.

Your nails show the state of your health. Large nails that are bluish suggest bad circulation. Thin nails, especially if small, denote delicate health. Short-nailed people are bard to beat in debates; long-nailed people are more yielding, but are more enthusiastic at their work.

If your thumb is stiff and straight, it can be hard to fit in. Or perhaps your thumb turns backwards? This shows that you're suave but not always reliable.

But this is just background. Your life is written in your hand and told by its lines and here lie the details you seek. Those on your left hand show the traits you were born with. Those in your right hand show how you have cultivated or thwarted them.

The heavy line that encircles the base of your thumb is your line of life. The line that runs parallel to it from the bottom part of your palm to the base of your second finger is called the line of fate. The line that crosses your hand horizontally from the right of your palm, beginning at the end of the line of life, is the line of the head, and the other horizontal line beginning just below your little finger is the line of the heart.

When your life line is long, clear and of a good colour, you'll lead a long and healthy life. When it's linked or made up of little pieces, it's a sign of ill-health.

If your line of head is straight and clear, this denotes practical common sense and learning capacity. Or perhaps it slopes? That shows that you lean towards romance and bohemianism. If it's straight and goes to the side of your hand, you're blessed with great intellectual power. However, if it slopes to your wrist, you bow to your imagination. When it runs into or through a square, this shows critical moment in your life.

Firmness of will is shown when your line of fate crosses your line of the head. If your will is strong enough to overcome fate, your hand will show it by a strength in the line of the head and a corresponding weakness in the line of fate where those two lines cross. Cheiro will remind you that will and fate are symbolised by a cross, like religion.

If you want to know when an event will take place, remember that your line of fate crosses two horizontal lines, your head line and your line of the heart, which runs parallel to your line of the head and a short distance above. This line of fate describes the course of your life and is crossed by markings that designate when certain events will happen. Your line of fate crosses the line of the head at twenty years of age and the line of the heart at forty. If you divide the distance which separate the two lines, you can locate the thirty year point. This will help you to work out the exact time of events.

If you can see a cross under your first finger, you will marry for love. If the cross isn't clearly defined or is crossed by little lines, your marriage will take place only after you have surmounted many difficulties. An imperfect cross shows that your marriage will never take place. Two well-defined crosses in your hand signify you will marry twice and will only be a widow for a short time.

If your line of fate is clearly defined and your line of the head at the point of intersection is correspondingly weak, you tend to accept whatever comes to you, accepting what happens without complaint.

You don't need a strong and uncrossed line of fate to lead a happy and a prosperous life. An uncrossed line of fate is found only in those who have had not a single adverse moment from the day of their birth until the day of their death—impossible for an ordinary person.[i]

You hand will show trials and tribulations, happiness and sadness, success and failure. Everything is written there—you need only learn how to read it.

---

i Summarised from the *Buffalo Morning Express* and the *Illustrated Buffalo Express* (New York), 17 December 1893, p. 30 and *Buffalo Commercial* (New York), 19 May 1894, p. 10.

Portrait of Cheiro by Jean Selinger, June 1895.

CHAPTER

SIX

*Cheiro impresses me as having reduced gulling to a fine art. It's truly
beautiful the way he does it, and underlying this art is a profound
knowledge of human nature—a knowledge of both the tendencies and
destiny of human nature—which makes Cheiro's palmistry a jest at which
men wonder, the gods weep and the devil sulks with envy.*[1]

USUALLY THE IDENTITY OF CHEIRO'S SECRETARY
is obscured—they are no more than a cipher,
their sole purpose to help Cheiro be wonderful.
Londoner William J Masters may have been the 'athletic young
Englishman' who accompanied Louis on his first American trip.[2] He
claimed to be an ex-pupil of Cheiro's as well as his secretary for two years,
and was a palmist in New York from June 1901, later moving to Fall River,
Massachusetts. In 1916 he lectured on palmistry in Los Angeles—using
prints of the hands that comprised Cheiro's most famous clients.

J H D'Arville from Boston, who claimed he'd been Cheiro's secretary
for three years, travelled the US and Canada from 1895, spending a
year or two at each stop. D'Arville taught twenty-six ways of breathing
and controlled seven voices, which was enterprising of him. More than
once he was arrested for working as a clairvoyant. The policeman who
came to his office in Altoona, Pennsylvania in 1904 had to wait patiently
for three hours while D'Arville finished seeing his clients. Once it was
the policeman's turn, he promptly arrested D'Arville. At a hearing in
1905, D'Arville wore the judge and jury down by explaining the science

behind his abilities for over an hour and then trying to demonstrate his clairvoyant skills before being firmly told to stop it by the judge.

Jehangier Dossabhoy Cola was different.[i] He became renowned in his own right and was Louis's close friend and companion as well as his secretary.

Born in Mumbai, Cola was from a well-moneyed family of pioneers and reformers. His grand-uncle was Dadabhai Navoroji, a Liberal Party member of Parliament between 1892 and 1895, and a founding member of the Indian National Congress.

It was common for young Indians of a certain class to complete their education at a British university—girls as well as boys. Such qualifications were essential to obtain a job with the Indian government, for example, the Indian Civil Service exam was only held in London. Cola was a law student and was admitted to the Middle Temple in January 1890.[ii]

Jehangier wasn't alone in England. By the end of the nineteenth century, thousands of Indians had travelled to Britain, including his family. His father had followed the trend set by middle-class returning Britons of settling in a seaside town, making his home in Torquay in Devon. But unlike most Indians in Britain, Jehangier was part of the Parsi community, the diminishing ethno-religious group of Zoroastrians descended from Iranians who'd fled their homeland when it became Muslim to settle in India.

Traditionally, Zoroastrian rituals include shamanic elements involving spirit travel to an invisible realm and consuming the psychoactive *haoma*—a divine plant, the cognate of Vedic *soma*. Many nineteenth-century Zoroastrians were influenced by theosophy and Western schools of occult thought. Not all Parsi did or do go around being mystical— Freddie Mercury developed a reputation as a singer, for example. But they were and are a highly-educated and influential group.

Shortly after Louis returned to England, Jehangier called to see him. Smartly dressed and wearing wire-rimmed glasses while sporting a silky moustache, he told Louis he was interested in mysticism and the occult— especially telepathy and thought-transference—and thought they might have something in common. Louis was entranced with him and they were soon meeting regularly to conduct occult experiments. 'On several

---

i A multitude of spellings were used for his name, including 'Jehangir', 'Jehanghile', 'Jehangler' and 'Ichangier'.
ii The Middle Temple is one of the four London Inns of Court entitled to call their members to the English Bar as barristers.

occasions he spoke guardedly of a remarkable character living in London,' said Louis. 'I gathered he was a recluse, and my attention was stimulated when Jehangier let fall certain hints that this man was in reality a Mystic of the highest order.'³

This man was Edmond Savary d'Odiardi, a chronic over-achiever of strange things.ⁱⁱⁱ Born in 1834, d'Odiardi had been on crutches since an accident when he was twelve and began his professional life as a musician, winning a joint prize with Georges Bizet at the Conservatoire de Paris in 1852. He became Director of Music in the Cambridge Academy, Jersey where in the mid-1880s as President of the General Society for the Welfare of the Blind, he'd developed a music training system based on formulas that enabled students to read pieces while they were played. He also busied himself trying to improve the writing of languages, especially Hebrew and regularly gave concerts, performing his compositions and organ solos in England, often to raise money for the blind.

After his father's death, d'Odiardi claimed the title of the Duc de Rovigo, although it had been abolished in 1872. He moved to London to take up 'medical science', using electricity and magnetism as healing agents and founding the Pan Electric Institute in 1890, claiming he could cure consumption, nervous diseases, paralysis and women's diseases. D'Odiardi opened a hospital in Notting Hill and the French awarded him a number of gold medals for his work in this field.

D'Odiardi had invented 'auto conduction' where a patient sat within the coils of a gigantic electric magnet through which an alternating current of high frequency was sent. His work was investigated again and again and his conclusions denounced as nonsensical. 'For how long is pestilent rubbish of this kind to discredit the name of medical electricity?' asked the *British Medical Journal*.⁴

One evening, Jehangier escorted Louis to d'Odiardi's home in Hampstead.

> Together we went up the richly carpeted staircase to a magnificent set of rooms that occupied the whole of the first floor. Pushing aside some heavy dark purple curtains, we entered a fine salon, exquisitely furnished. Then passing through a smaller room, we came to another. To my surprise it contained an organ so large that it occupied the whole of one side of the room. In a window

---

iii Sometimes rendered as 'Édouard Savary d'Odiardi', 'Edmund Savory D'Odiardi' and 'Edmond Savary de Rovigo Odiardi' . His death certificate calls him 'Francis Edmond'.

recess overlooking the garden there stood a grand piano and an unusually beautiful harp.

Awaiting me was a medium-sized, but noble-looking individual. His high-domed head and piercing eyes proclaimed the man of intellect and conscious power; his quiet voice, though slightly foreign in accent, impressed me as belonging to one accustomed to being obeyed. His deep purple coat, flowing cravat of lighter hue, and ring that gleamed upon the forefinger of his slender left hand gave him a touch of the bizarre.[5]

According to Louis, d'Odiardi decided to test his palmistry skills and Jehangier politely excused himself. Louis successfully recited d'Odiardi's biography to him, then settled down to listen him play the organ 'to ascertain the vibrations that will unite our spirits in one harmonious bond and enable us to solve problems of interest to us both.'[6] After some mystical harp playing in the background, Louis agreed to help d'Odiardi out and they chatted about his work.

He so controlled electric forces that he was able not only to dissolve any metal, but he could direct the 'ions' of the dissolving metal into any organ or part of the body that he so desired. He knew to his finger-tips the effect that the 'ions of gold' must produce on various parts of the spinal column and so cured many of the worst cases of paralysis… In many cases he cured cancer where an operation would not have been possible.[7]

This was the first of many such visits. At one, d'Odiardi planned to change Louis's vibrations.

On a table at the side I noticed a helmet of copper with a copper band so constructed to go down the spine, with two arms from it to go round the body and terminate in a twelve-pointed magnet on the solar plexus. Connected to the centre of the helmet an insulated covered wire led through the open windows to a series of copper wires hanging from the edge of the high roof to a few feet from the ground. These in their turn were joined to an aerial of immense height over the house… the copper plate on which my feet would rest was connected with a wire which, passing through what he called 'a magnifier' at the other end of the room, terminated in an 'earth' zinc pole at the bottom of a well in the garden.[8]

Louis worried that the machine could kill him (or maybe turn him into a cyberman), but agreed to go ahead because he'd given his word. The helmet was placed on his head and d'Odiardi played his organ. Then a strange voice told Louis he was about to see a vision of Atlantis.

> The scene changed, the city became still more beautiful, the temple more magnificent. The wide space before the throne was filled with myriads of people, tall, straight, lordly, with the light of intelligence gleaming from their eyes, like gods or sons of gods they appeared.
> I noticed that all were drawn by some mysterious magnetic force to the Sign of the Zodiac under which they were born; every man, every woman and every child was robed in the same colour as their Sign and on each forehead was their own distinctive jewel.[9]

It was rather marvellous but Louis couldn't spend all his time messing about with his vibrations. His new book, *The Language of the Hand*, appeared in November 1894 under the name of 'Leigh Warner'.[5] The first edition of 5,000 copies sold out in four months. The second was expanded with additional handprints, and by summer 1897 thirty thousand copies had sold and a deluxe edition had appeared.

The book's content would be familiar to any modern reader interested in palmistry. In fact, it would have been familiar to any reader at the time who was interested in palmistry. No one would accuse Cheiro of being original.

> 'A Defense' comprising good 40 pages is nothing but the summary of 'Preface' and 'Introductory Argument' written by Edward Heron Allen in his book 'The Guide to Study Palmistry' published in 1885...[10]

The difference was that Cheiro's book was filled with satisfyingly flowery language, was easy to follow and was replete with illustrations. Not any old illustrations—Louis had commissioned the artist John Theodore Bentley, working under the name of 'Theo Doré', who was famous for his enormous painting of Christ which had toured the US in late 1893 before ending up back in England. To the less artistically minded, he was famous for marrying his dancing teacher Sophia Shepherd in 1887, then twice the age of twenty-six-year-old Bentley.

Reviews for *Language of the Hand* were generally positive. Those opposed to palmistry on the basis that it was silly, sinful or unscientific offered more scathing reviews. The concern was primarily about how unscientific palmistry was—important because of palmists' attempts to legitimise palmistry by claiming it as a science.

It is curious to note that he has not yet learned that the thumb differs from the fingers by containing only two phalanges instead of three...[11]

Cheiro's brilliant theory as to the part which the hairs on the back of the hand play in life... The theory is... is simply this, each hair is a small and attenuated volcano spouting out, like a miniature Vesuvius, the excess of electricity under the skin of the back of the hand little safety-valves, probably, to keep the entire skin from being blown off. [12]

With his book now published, Louis was ready to launch on an American tour and Jehangier eagerly agreed to accompany him. He arrived in New York on 17 November 1894 to prepare the way and by January 1895 Louis had joined him.

Mr. Cola is nothing if not enthusiastic on everything pertaining to the occult, and to Cheiro. So strong is his affection for him that he gave up his profession in his far-off native land to make a tour of the world with Cheiro...[13]

Louis and Jehangier rented an apartment at the Hotel Plaza where Louis offered readings and Jehangier acted as his secretary. Jehangier's presence puzzled the journalists Louis rounded up: 'Mr. Cola is evidently a man of high caste' one said valiantly—he wasn't of any caste, being Parsi, but he put up being called a 'Hindoo'.[14] Oddly, so did Louis. He never claimed to be other than Irish, but the press felt there was some confusion:

He claimed to be Hindoo or Egyptian, as the mood seized him, but... is an Irishman.[15]

He possesses a strong Irish brogue, with an entire absence of the air of the cad so often seen in an Englishman 'not long out.'[16]

He told journalists he was launching on a journey around the world with Jehangier and had vowed to bring India's knowledge to the West.

One might fancy Cheiro practices palmistry to make money. This is a mistake. He works under a vow made to the Yogi of India, who taught him the science, to carry the truths of palmistry over the world wherever the shadow of modern civilization obscures the minds and destiny of struggling human kind. If, incidentally, he is filling his pockets with our American dollars at the rate of $5 per twenty minutes of palmistry administered, how can Cheiro help that? Everybody knows our vulgar American way of throwing money to the winds.[17]

Louis fully intended to make money—as much as possible. Women made up the bulk of his clientele, and there was no point in pretending otherwise.

I always have many, and some are foolish enough to think me a fortune-teller. They come hoping to have their vanity flattered, no doubt, by the pretty things they expect me to say. Do I always tell what I see? Yes, invariably, noting first their sensitiveness… After a while in any new place I always get the men interested and the days are not half long enough to meet them.[18]

Jehangier happily promoted Louis as a man of mystery, saying, 'with a smile that scintillated with the interior illumination of a high-caste fakir' that 'Cheiro's name is known only to himself and three others in the world.'[19]

The main thing was, however, that Louis was still gorgeous. A multitude of sins could be forgiven once you looked into his eyes. Even those convinced he was a con merchant were smitten.

He was a surprise. Young, handsome, manly, his presence gave one a new sensation, that of pleasure at coming in contact with a unique personality. As a rule palmists are old, sorry-looking beings, askew from contact with the world, but here was a man brimfull of humanity…[20]

He smiles infrequently, and with a painful effort that disturbs only his upper lip. The rest of his face is Nirvanic in the depth and perpetuity of its calm. It is an elegant face for poker… He is a great man, but his magnetism is all negative and concealed. [21]

But being gorgeous wouldn't pay the bills.

At the conclusion of my first season in New York, I made up my mind to start off on a lecture tour and see as much as I could of the great continent of America… Knowing nothing of the routine of engaging halls, advertising, etc., I put myself into the hands of an enterprising American, who assured me that the correct thing to do was to make my debut before the public in that centre of culture and home of learning, otherwise known on the map of America as the City of Boston...

Bostonians give themselves such a superior air of learning, or at all events... I have heard it said that more men and women wear glasses in Boston than in any other city of the same size in the world![22]

Louis doesn't mention who 'the enterprising American' was, simply referring to him as his agent. However, he mentions a contract with New Yorker James Burton Pond (popularly called Major Pond) and it seems likely this is who he engaged—especially considering Louis's account of how his agent behaved.

America's premier booking agent Pond represented American and British explorers, preachers, politicians, scientists and writers on the lecture circuit from 1874 until he died in 1903. His illustrious clients included Arthur Conan Doyle, Oscar Wilde and Mark Twain. Winston Churchill, whose agent Pond was in 1900, called him a 'vulgar Yankee impresario'.[23] In return, Pond thought Churchill was 'disagreeable and ugly' and complained about the expenses he had to cover, including the pint of champagne Churchill had every morning with breakfast.[24] Twain observed that Pond was 'neither truthful nor sensible' and said, 'if you get half as much as Pond prophesied, be content and praise God—it has not happened to another'.[25]

Pond's approach worked because he was pragmatic to a fault. He was happy to book his speakers at private homes for even the smallest payment if it filled a gap in the calendar, and he sometimes sold lectures to a local organisation for a fixed sum so he didn't have to be on the spot and could remove the risk of financial loss if there was a poor attendance. He was very, very good at his job.

And Louis intended to be good at his, so he bought a stereopticon—a device that could project two images simultaneously, allowing for a 3-D effect or images to merge into each other. With some effort, it was possible to animate slides so they looked like a modern-day GIF (this was the nineteenth-century equivalent of PowerPoint). Meanwhile, Jehangier busily collected palm prints of Louis's socially prominent clients to use for the lectures.

Louis constantly sought better ways to keep records of the hands he examined. Evangeline Adams said, 'Cheiro was using lampblack, which was far from satisfactory... He even asked for my "secret method" of removing the ink stains... He then offered me five dollars for a small package of the mysterious production.'[26]

The mysterious substance was Gold Dust, a common cleaning agent. But sometimes, ink wasn't enough:

> Cheiro... makes a most carefully prepared model of the hand he wishes to study in modeler's clay or prepared wax. He then has the cast transferred to paper. This enables him to observe better the form and shape of the hand and the peculiarities of the fingers.[27]

Jehangier and Louis took the night train to Boston on 18 April. Louis had been booked to speak the next day at Chickering Hall, a room on the second floor of Chickering and Sons, the piano manufacturer's showrooms which often hosted fashionable musicals.

He was horrified to discover he was speaking on 'Cheiro's tour of the world'.[28] Hands weren't even mentioned. On being challenged, Pond grinned and said, 'Don't teach me my business... The less Bostonians know of the subject of a lecture, the more reason for them turning up to find out.'[29]

He was right—the talk was fully booked and Jehangier and Louis's suite at the Hotel Brunswick (hastily decorated with a hotch-potch of vaguely oriental items) was soon crowded with visitors.

> The smaller room—the inner sanctum—smacks of the Orient, and about the walls are draperies of Javanese stuffs, rich in coloring, strongly suggestive of mysticisms. In the centre of the room is a small table, on which is a red velvet cushion, where Miss Confidence and Mr. Cynical alike lay down their hands and hear their character exposed.[30]

It helped that 'Mr. Jehangier D. Cola... has an interesting history and is an altogether agreeable person to meet.'[31]

Louis saw up to twenty clients a day, all happy to pay $10 for twenty minutes of his attention—a small fortune at the time. Among them was poet and social activist Julia Ward Howe, known for writing the 'Battle Hymn of the Republic'. Jehangier had visited her shortly after his arrival, armed with one of his many letters of introduction, and both he and Louis frequently visited her home. By June 1895 Louis was so popular that local artist Jean (John) Selinger painted his portrait. In the evenings, he and Jehangier attended as many social events as possible.

After working hard for several months, it was time for a holiday. They spent July and August at Newport, a seaside town in Rhode Island, where wealthy families stayed for a summer social season.[32] Or he may have been in Saratoga where he was a great social success.[33] Perhaps both. Louis enjoyed himself, that's what matters.

Amongst those Jehangier had taken a palm print of in New York was Swami Vivekananda. Born Narendranath Datta, Vivekananda was a Hindu monk and the chief disciple of the Indian mystic and religious leader Ramakrishna. He introduced Vedanta and yoga to the West, popularising a modern interpretation of Indian tradition, and is credited with bringing Hinduism to the status of a major world religion. From 1888 he'd been a wandering monk, carrying only a *kamandalu* (water pot), staff and copies of the *Bhagavad Gita* and *The Imitation of Christ*. After travelling around India for five years, he'd reached the US by way of Japan and China, and in September 1893 had spoken at the Parliament of the World's Religions in Chicago. The opening of his speech, 'Sisters and brothers of America', had earned him a two-minute standing ovation from the crowd of seven thousand. Over the next two years, he travelled the eastern and central United States. Vivekananda had also become a fixture at Greenacre since its opening in 1894 when he'd spent two months there.

Greenacre was established by Sarah Farmer in Eliot, Maine on the banks of the Pistcaqua River. The Eliot Hotel had opened in 1891 and Farmer wanted to develop the property with a spiritual theme. When the hotel was failing in 1894, she approached investors with her plan to host lectures on religion and provide a base for discussion of intellectual, ethical and artistic matters. Greenacre became simultaneously a school, a summer hotel and a religious colony. (It later became the Greenacre Bahá'í School.) If you were short of money, you could pitch a tent rather than stay in the hotel. Although speakers offered their services for free, their accommodation and expenses were covered by donations.

> It is a quiet spot, with gently sloping banks, and off to the west lies a long meadow with its fringe of apple trees and birches reflected in the waters of the bay. There is a sense of space and distance, a limitless expanse of sky, a broad sweep of river and bay with the distant low-lying banks, and far beyond, ever changing in hue against the sunset sky, range the foothills of the White Mountains. With the going down of the sun a golden bridge spans the waters glowing and radiant at our feet.[34]

The hotel itself has some sixty rooms; the accommodations in all ways are excellent… Near by on the lawn is a large tent capable of seating 300 people. On a raised dais is a rug, a piano, a table for the speaker, chairs, etc., and the seating for the audience is by camp chairs. The lectures are given at 3 and 8 p.m. each day. They are free to all.[35]

Jehangier was invited to speak at Greenacre on 1 September—on 'Zoroaster and the Parsees'. He returned with Louis at the end of September who spoke on palmistry. They stayed for a while and listened to speakers such as Colonel Francis V. Parker on 'Conscious Good' and Alice S. Mitchell on 'The Spiritual Possibilities of Music' as well as Vivekananda.

And then it was time to get back to work.

Jehangier at Greenacre (in white).

TALL TALES

Restoration of a waif

In March 1893 Cheiro agreed to read the hand of a young girl in Waltham Cross, about twenty miles from London. He arrived at the station to be met by a man who led him across the fields until they reached a small house at the edge of the woods where he was greeted by a man and woman.

> The man, coarse and uneducated, utterly without conscience or principle, associated with a woman also uneducated, yet with an innate charm of manner that lent a certain grace and refinement to every word, to every action. A woman wily as a snake, unscrupulous in all her dealings, and yet one guided, governed, enslaved, by the superstitious fears that held her. She looked upon me as a being possessed by a supernatural power… She wanted that power used for her advantage.

The woman led Cheiro upstairs to the attic where lying on the floor was a half-naked little girl.

> Fixing her large frightened eyes on the woman as she entered, she crept away on all fours and crouched like a dog under a table that occupied a corner of the room.

Cheiro asked if she was frightened. 'Oh, she is always that way before strangers,' said the woman, adding, 'She is a great affliction to me, I can assure you, sir. She is so unlike other children that I can't let her out of the house. She's very delicate, too, and I've often thought, sir, that it would be better for her if God in his mercy took her from this world of misery.'

After further questions, the woman said she didn't know how old the little girl was, but she wanted Cheiro to read her hands and say how long the girl had to live. Cheiro came to the conclusion that it simply wasn't possible that the little girl was the couple's child. He coaxed the girl to show him her hands and noted she had no line of destiny. 'Is it possible that you have kept the child all these years from education of any kind?' he asked the woman.

Fear entered the woman's eyes and she said that she wasn't even sure if the child could speak. Cheiro could elicit no more than animal-like sounds from the child. 'Putting down the little hands, I quietly but firmly demanded of the woman the full history of the child.'

The woman turned white and closed the door so the man wouldn't hear what she was saying. She told Cheiro that in the past she had kept a baby farm in London. She'd been twice imprisoned for the suspicious deaths of infants in her care—she didn't even like children—and was about to give up the business when she received an offer from a woman to take charge of a child, as long as she did so away from London. The woman had been living with the man, a notorious poacher, for fourteen years with the child hidden in the attic.

But the money for the child's care had stopped arriving two years ago. The man wanted to kill the girl and bury her body in the woods. But the woman felt there was something uncanny about the child and she'd recently had a dream that the girl's palm would reveal she would die in the next few months. As she'd recently come into a little money, she could afford to send for Cheiro.

Cheiro felt that he had to rescue the girl. He didn't think it would be a problem persuading the woman, but the man would probably insist on the money that was due for her care. And he'd already promised not to go to the police. What he needed to do was trace the child's mother.

When he returned to London, Cheiro approached institutions that dealt with foundlings to be met with suspicion. He had no idea what to do next.

Then one day he was reading a client's palm when he noticed 'a peculiar knotted blue vein that stood out clear and distinct at the base of the little finger.' He struggled to remember where he'd seen a similar palm recently and asked his client if she had any questions for him. Indeed, she did.

You were right when you said that I had a child when 18. I was not married then, and my child was taken away from me in order to save my name. A year later a marriage was arranged by my father to a man I barely knew, and with him I went to reside in one of the British settlements in South Africa. After the death of my husband I returned to England, and after 14 years have learned that the child that I was led to believe had died is still alive, and up to two years she was supported by money sent by my father for the child's care. My father died suddenly of heart disease, and I can get no cue or trace of my little one. Look at my hand again, and for God's sake tell me if I may still hope on.'

Like a flash of light, I remembered that that knotted blue vein was also in the hand of the child. Such things run in families for generations. The story tallied with what I knew. Why say more? At the last moment I had found the mother of the poor little waif.

Wilkes-Barre News (Pennsylvania), 15 August 1894, p. 5.

Ghost hunting

Cheiro was about to join some friends at a theatre party at the Garrick when he received a note from his friend Max Markham asking him to meet him at eleven that night at Blackheath station—and to be sure to carry his revolver. They often went on ghost hunts together and Markham always carried a revolver.

'I slipped my British bulldog and some cartridges into my pocket,' said Cheiro, 'and started for the train.'

Markham was a member of the Society for Psychical Research and spent all his time testing mediums and exposing trickery. He was also a spiritualist and simply wanted to expose fraud. Markham also considered that Cheiro had clairvoyant powers, despite the fact that Cheiro had only demonstrated this once—one he sent a telegram to Markham telling him not to catch the train to Manchester but to wait. The train Markham had intended to catch crashed.

That night, Markham rushed Cheiro out of the station as they had two miles to go to their destination and needed to be there by midnight. The house that they were going to was reported to be haunted by the ghost of a monk from the ruins of a nearby abbey. But there was more as Markham explained.

Since it was built murder has followed murder, suicide followed suicide, but yet there was no talk about any ghost theory until within the last 12 months, and since then the old monk seems to have made himself master of the situation. The present owner a year ago while traveling in America one morning received the startling news that his father had hung himself in the cellar, so he hurried home with a newly made bride to take possession. His wife, a young and fearless American from some out of the way place in Texas, a woman who never heard of ghosts, was the first to see the apparition. Going into the nursery one night to look after her child, she found the nurse asleep and the form of an old monk leaning over the cradle. She screamed, fainted, and when people came to her assistance the monk had disappeared and the mark of a cross was found on the child's forehead. From that moment the monk visited them regularly. Even in the daylight he might be seen walking down the corridors and the stairways, and a strange noise commenced every night at 12 o'clock that seemed to shake the house to its foundations. The servants of course threw up their places and left, and the only one that remained, an old butler, a few days after was found hung in exactly the same place as the owner's father.

Markham had planned that they should spend the night at the house with Dr. Appleton who now lived there. 'To tell the truth,' said Cheiro, 'I did not quite fancy the idea.'

He was even less enthusiastic when they arrived and Appleton told them he'd seen the monk that day in broad daylight. 'Oh, bosh,' said Markham, 'It's too late now to turn back.' Ten minutes later, they were at the old abbey.

Cold and gaunt the ruins looked in the moonlight, like a skeleton of the past. At its back a wood of pines swayed in the night wind like an army of ghosts waiting for a leader, and a little farther on, surrounded by the shadow of the trees, stood a desolate looking house, with empty windows and broken panes...

They forced a window open to get into the house and they made their way to the dining room where they lit a candle and sat down on a couple of empty boxes. As a nearby clock struck twelve, they heard a sound. 'We sprang from our seats and stood looking at one another in consternation and dismay,' said Cheiro. 'It seemed as if on the very stroke of 12 the house had received some blow that shook it to its foundations. Every door seemed to open and creak and bang one after another as the wind moaned and swept on its way from room to room.' The door to the room had been flung open and as the moon emerged from a cloud, they saw the figure of a monk.

'I could hear my heart beat like a drum. I was almost sinking with fright when suddenly, with a hollow, grating laugh, the figure disappeared,' said Cheiro.

They grabbed their things, opened the window and ran as fast as they could back to Appleton's house. That was enough investigating for one night and they decided to go to bed.

The next morning, they returned to the house. Everything looked the same as they'd left it. Appleton thought the apparition was a punishment because he'd neglected the house. Markham fretted about the awful laugh he'd heard. They decided to search the house and made their way into the cellars.

When we... got accustomed to the darkness, a grewsome sight met our eyes, which startled us nearly as much as did the apparition of the previous night. Hanging from a beam in the ceiling was the rope and noose by which the unfortunate butler had hung himself. There it had remained, white with mold, swinging softly in the draft…

Cheiro and Markham decided to go home and return for a further investigation that evening. This time, they were accompanied by a detective from Scotland Yard, named Mitchell, who often joined in their ghost hunts. Back at the haunted house, they sat in the moonlight until they heard the clock strike twelve. Nothing happened.

'Why, Mr Markham,' said Mitchell. 'we never had a "sell" like this before. We haven't had even as much as some table rapping. The ghost hasn't given us a fair run for our money.'

They decided to investigate the cellar again. Groping their way along tha passages that led there, they were surprised to find the cellar door closed. Mitchell looked through the keyhole and said there seemed to be something peculiar swinging in the centre of the room. Markham took a look and turned white as a sheet. Mitchell was about to burst the door open when it suddenly swung back.

Swinging in the noose of death hung the figure of the monk. His face, ghastly and horrible, seemed, to grin at us in agony, a white and awful contrast to the darkness of the vault. Spellbound, we seemed rooted to the spot, but we suddenly became conscious of a new terror, and one rapidly approaching. There were steps coming behind us.

Seeing a figure approaching, they threw themselves into a room to their right and shut the door. They heard the sound of someone entering the room where the rope hung and then it fell silent. After a few minutes, Mitchell opened the door and peeped out. There was nothing in sight, and even the swinging body of the monk had disappeared. Mitchell led them outside and they returned to Appleton's house.

Three months later, Cheiro picked up a newspaper to read: 'Startling discovery at Blackheath. Supposed haunted house the resort of coiners.' The article said that the police had raided the house and found 'a desperate gang of coiners'.

The terrible noise had been produced every night by their letting fall in the basement a tremendous iron weight upon the foundation stone of the house. The body of the monk that we had seen hanging by the neck in the cellar was nothing more than a well made dummy, with its clothes steeped in phosphorus. And such was the end of the Blackheath mystery.

Little Falls Weekly Transcript (Minnesota), 17 August 1894, p. 12.

CHAPTER

SEVEN

A man who is thoroughly acquainted with nature if not at all times with the requirements of poetry.[1]

FTER RENTING AN APARTMENT at 423 Boylston Street, a major thoroughfare, Louis and Jehangier were soon part of the Boston social whirl. Notices appeared regularly in the press saying one or both of them had attended lunch or a dinner party, sometimes with Cheiro as the main attraction. Many of these gatherings imitated Louis's interior decorating tastes.

> Mrs Charles Henry Bond gave a luncheon Tuesday... when her new oriental room was open for the enjoyment, as well as admiration of her guests... The oriental room is perfectly appointed... All the paintings on the walls are oriental scenes... An Egyptian-tiled fireplace in the colors of the draperies adds much to the effectiveness. Articles of rare value... occupy places on the various pieces of eastern furniture.[2]

Louis also gave lectures for charity, where the event was 'crowded with women all eager to hear this picturesque young man' who gave talks in 'his rather dramatic style which is without exaggeration and always refined.'[3]

Proud of his achievements, Louis invited his mum for a visit and Margaret Warner arrived in Boston in October 1895. He still yearned to be a poet and in late 1895 published *If We Only Knew and Other Poems*. The title poem appeared in newspapers from October.[4] 'I had to correct the proofs by telegraph,' said Louis, 'my publisher in New York having wired me that he had to catch the Christmas trade.'[5] 'These poems were extremely well received by the Press,' Louis added, inaccurately.[6] Reviews were lukewarm at best.

> These verses are smooth and pleasantly-written and some of them are very nearly good.[7]

> 'If we only knew' we would not pay £5 apiece to go hear Cheiro talk for 15 minutes. Suppose we did know, what would become of poor Cheiro?[8]

Louis claimed over a thousand copies a week sold in Boston during the first few months. He did his best to boost sales, reciting If We Only Knew whenever he had chance, often accompanied by music—'Lights were lowered and a soft obligato played on the organ'—and in this twilight atmosphere, Louis solemnly read:[9]

If We Only Knew

IF we only knew, if we only knew
But a little part of the things we see,
Methinks the false would be oft more true
Than what is truth—or what seems to be:
If we only knew—if we only knew!

If we only knew the pain we cause
By the slighting look or the word of shame.
By the seeking out of those old, old flaws
That one scarce could help in the race for fame;
If we only knew that the deeds we scorn
Might some day fall to ourselves to do,
Or if not us, to our babes unborn:
If we only knew—if we only knew!

If we only knew how the man we spurn
Had fought temptation—ay, day and night;
If we only knew, would we so turn
And cast him off as a loathsome sight?
Ah me! instead of the sinner's brand.
We'd gladly help him the right to do;
We'd lift him up with each honest hand,
If we only knew—if we only knew!

If we only knew how the woman fell,
Would we shun her as now, whene'er we meet?

Would we leave her then to that bitter hell
Of self and sin and the homeless street?
Would we shrug our shoulders and toss our head
For trusting too much, or being too true,
Or sinning, perhaps, as some do, for bread?
If we only knew—if we only knew!

If we only knew of that girl last night
Who stood for a moment just at our door,
Ere she turned away from the cheerful light
And sought the silence of Death's still shore,
Would we deem her mad, or turn aside
From half-starved lips so cold and blue,
If they could tell us just why she died?
If we only knew—if we only knew!

...

If we only knew that the hearts we miss
Would have stayed so short in this vale of woe,
How much more sweet would have been each kiss!
But we did not know—we did not know.
Regrets are useless, and tears but blind,
And empty words can no past undo;
It's no good sighing—I'd been more kind
If I only knew—if I only knew!

If We Only Knew was: 'Quoted far and wide through the world but in almost all religious papers it was printed without my name to it; when I protested at such injustice, I was told that "they could not advertise in their columns the name of a man associated with such an illegal profession," yet these same people did not see the inconsistency of making use of the work of my brains'.[10] Maybe they weren't convinced Louis was the poem's author, considering its close similarity to others with the same title. For example, Lottie B Sampson's poem had appeared in 1872:

If we only, only knew,
What the future was to bring,
If our lives should pass away,
As on golden, sunny wings;
Or, if grief must be our lot,
And grim Care or path way strew

Thick with thorns instead of roses,
If we only, only knew...[11]

And there was the uncredited 1876 poem that appeared in several newspapers:

If we only knew
Half the bitter tears we may have to shed,
Half the thorny paths our feet must tread,
Half the gloomy days we will wish to be dead,
If we only knew
How dreary a thing were life?... [12]

Or Bertha Packard Englet's popular poem of 1891.

If we only knew in the early morn,
What we know each close of day.
If we only knew of the battles fierce
That we must wage, by the way.
If we only knew.
Ah I only knew I think we'd pray, ere day begun, That many victories might be won...[13]

Whatever, Louis was proud of it and had the poem printed on the back of his cabinet card.

Not everyone Louis met was part of high society; he claimed to have had five doctors in his classes, including J (Joseph) Heber Smith who taught at Boston University School of Medicine. Apparently, he had a thoroughly marvellous hand because of the multiplicity of lines. 'I consider that one of the best subjects Cheiro has found in this country,' Jehangier said. 'It is a beautifully marked hand and indicates a powerful character, marvellous temperament and strength of mind, as well as delicacy of feeling.'[14]

Heber Smith also used astrology as part of his medical practice, calculating a chart for each of his patients and prescribing treatment based on his interpretations. He also taught astrology to Evangeline Adams who had studied under Vivekananda and attended Louis's palmistry classes in 1896. Later, she discarded palmistry and become America's foremost astrologer. She wasn't as impressed by Louis as most women around him.

Poor Cheiro! His life, as I soon found out by a consultation of his horoscope, was destined to be a stormy one. His palm, too, indicated the same thing. But he was... one of those dashing, daring, handsome fellows for whom the journey through life is just one high adventure after another. Women were 'crazy about him'. And in many ways he was a spoiled child. But he could read palms.[15]

In late December Louis was booked to speak in Syracuse, New York. Pond said he'd got a wonderful deal and had booked the biggest hall in the town for a low fee on condition he took it for three nights running. 'I have advertised you extensively and I expect you will have crowded houses for your three nights' stay,' he said.[16]

But when Louis looked through the curtain before pontificating on 'The Hands of Celebrities I have Met', he was horrified to see the hall was nearly empty. Deciding to give a class instead, he spoke for four hours, only stopping at midnight because his stereopticon was running out of the hydrogen it needed for light.

It transpired that Pond's deal was because the Grand Opera Company of New York was in Syracuse and the proprietor didn't believe anyone could compete with that. But word got around and the next night Louis had a sell-out audience.

Louis and Jehangier next went to Buffalo and stayed at the Iriquois. After the recent near-disaster, Pond decided not to book a hall but instead arranged to use the hotel ballroom. 'People came in such crowds that every inch of available room was in demand, so much so that I had barely space on the platform to stand on,' said Louis.[17] He wasn't exaggerating.

Those parlors of the Iroquois… were entirely inadequate for the many who came to hear the palmist. For two hours he held the closest attention of his audience… The history of palmistry was briefly reviewed, arguments against the science met, and then the stereopticon was brought into use.[18]

With rising popularity came gossip. A local man had said that not only had Louis stolen his books when he'd taught Louis palmistry, he'd also married a young girl for money and left her behind, starving in London. But he failed to recognise Cheiro at a dinner party and:

Looking the man straight in the eyes, I took my cigarette from my lips and said slowly and deliberately: 'Sir, you are either an escaped lunatic or an infernal liar… the man who stands before you is the "Cheiro" that you say you could recognize. I demand a full explanation of your words, or else it will be this very "Cheiro" that will take you to the nearest police station, if he has not in the meantime strangled you.'[19]

The man collapsed in shock and retracted his story, so no-one strangled anyone. Which was fortunate, as Louis and Jehangier needed invitations to private homes to attract clients with real money. And they continued to receive them:

> The reception given by Miss Grace Carew Sheldon on Tuesday evening for Cheiro, the celebrated palmist, was attended by an intellectual and fashionable audience, which listened with delight to the charming talk on the secrets of the hands given by Cheiro... those who were prepared to meet a gentleman of austere and mysterious miein straight from the realm of the occult were made comfortable and happy by the boyish, frank, manly bearing of the speaker...[20]

Some people made more of an effort than others. Mrs Robert Wilson took Louis and Jehangier for a sleigh ride and introduced them to the idea of 'open fires, corn popping and story telling before offering them dinner with 'tiny palms lying next to the plates'.[21]

Apart from a brief trip to Detroit, Louis and Jehangier remained at the Iroquois, performing consultations during the day and then hastily dressing for the evenings events. At one engagement Louis read 44 palms for four minutes each and told a journalist, 'I never before had so many men to consult me during my career.' [22] Then in early February Louis and Jehangier returned to Boston before visiting Chicago:

> Chicago is one of the most abused of all the American cities; its streets are criticized, its buildings held up to ridicule, its men and women stuck into every melodrama that requires money or a villain, and its climate held up to scorn as the worst in the States.
>
> In Chicago, men and women don't think that 'it is a crime to work'; on the contrary, they think it is a crime to be too lazy to toil. These people make a sport of life's hardships. They laugh at her blows, they gamble with her coin, if they lose, or if they win, they laugh all the same—or at least they are too plucky to show their tears.[23]

The city was very lucrative for Louis. Staying at the Auditorium (a building designed to be multi-use and containing offices and a theatre as well as a hotel) it in a suite overlooking Lake Michigan, he worked solidly.

Every second evening he hosted classes and also did the occasional lecture at Steinway Hall. Money kept rolling in. He was so in demand that people paid handsomely to avoid waiting for an appointment.

> One evening, at five o'clock, just as I had finished with my last client, a lady and gentleman, strangers to one another, arrived in my outer reception room at the same moment, and the lady tried to persuade my secretary to arrange an appointment with me at once, when the gentleman said: 'You are taking an unfair advantage both of "Cheiro" and of your sex, madam. We have arrived here at the same moment, if anything I was in advance.' 'Very well,' the lady replied, 'if you think so, let the secretary auction off this extra appointment, and let it go to the highest bidder.' No sooner said than done. They began to bid against one another, the lady only stopping when the figure reached one thousand dollars (£200).[24]

After three weeks, Louis calculated he'd read a thousand palms.[25] And he was paid between $1,000 and $2,000 per lecture.

He may have been getting too cocky. It was in Chicago that Louis fell victim to a scam when a man convinced him that he could create gold from earth, stones and clay. He put money into the scheme after seeing 'proof' but it isn't clear how much he lost. Also in Chicago, a journalist was sent to interview him and catch him out as a scammer. He soon revealed her fate and she sobbed for forgiveness. And he nearly got into trouble on a short trip to Salem to deliver a lecture. On arrival, Louis was informed by a police officer that making money from palmistry was illegal, so he gave people their money back and went on with the lecture, regardless.

That winter was one of the coldest Chicago had seen for years—and Chicago was no stranger to bitter winters. The snow was so deep that Louis and Jehangier were stuck inside the hotel for two weeks. No wonder Louis was delighted to be invited to speak at the Florida Chautauqua. Plus, it was a nineteenth-century palmist's equivalent to being invited to play at Glastonbury.

The Chautauqua (a Seneca word meaning meeting or gathering) movement had begun in 1874 at Lake Chautauqua to provide religious enlightenment and education to Protestant laymen. Its wider appeal was soon obvious and a second Chautauqua was arranged in spring 1885. The movement was supported by famous activists such as Julia Ward Howe.

DeFuniak Springs, Florida was an ideal location. There was easy access by train and being in an uncongested rural area near the coast made it a prime winter resort. Buildings sprang up including the Tabernacle which held 2,500 people. Four new hotels opened, as well as a bank, a general store and a sanitarium. However, ticket sales dropped in 1894, so to pull in a bigger audience, many of the religious classes were dropped and replaced with more entertaining subjects that covered subjects such as politeness, music, gymnastics and politics. Some visitors never went home again. In 1896 the Chautauqua was scheduled from 20 February to 18 March and between four and five thousand people were expected, the largest audience in its history. And on 5 March, 'The crowning event of the day will be the appearance of Cheiro, the world renowned palmist.'[26]

Louis fell in love with the Bay of Penescola.

> I never in all my life experienced the same sensation of rest and peace as we changed trains, and for some hours I wandered through the quaint streets of this old town with its memories of the Spanish Main, or gazed across the tranquil vista of its semi-inland sea...[27]

He was travelling with Jehangier, Pond, an unnamed servant and English actress Elsie Irving who'd arrived in America as part of impresario Oscar Barrett's company and had recently been touring with comedian Joe Cawthorne's company. Elsie's presence caused questions and she was explained away as Jehangier's wife, although his name was oddly given as 'Waite'.[28] In *Confessions* she's described as Pond's wife. She wasn't married to anyone at the time, although, 'The dudes will be pained to hear that she is betrothed to a wealthy young man in Detroit'.[29]

> Her mother was Spanish, and Miss Irving has the jet black hair and flashing black eyes characteristic of the race, while her features very nearly approach the classic. Her eyes are full of witchery, she is very graceful and shapely, and, strange to say, utterly devoid in the arts of the coquette.[30]

Louis may have met Elsie in London as she was a popular and hard working actress, mainly in melodramas, musicals and pantomime. We can safely assume she was with Louis. When they arrived at midnight, they were told there was a problem—that afternoon's entertainer had been delayed. Louis immediately offered Elsie's services as a singer. She was a roaring success: 'If Miss Irving had done nothing but pose for ten minutes before the audience, it would have been worth alone 50 cents. She is ideally beautiful as well as being a trained singer.'[31]

Louis then took to the stage to recite *The Devil in Search of a Wife* followed by one of his—lengthy—poems. People liked it, or at least, they said they did, and it helped him pull ensure a large audience for his two palmistry lectures. Louis and his friends remained in for Florida three weeks, managing to squeeze in a lecture in Tampa Bay:

> Without knowing either the names or the positions in life of any of the people and without asking a question or beating about the bush, Cheiro read from impressions of hands on paper, the life and characteristics of each person with the most wonderful accuracy... Cheiro was pronounced by all last night the greatest living genius on the continent today...[32]

They couldn't stay in Florida forever, and Louis's next stop was in Washington in April.

> It was a glorious day when for the first time I saw Washington, the official capital of the United States. As I drove from the station to my hotel I thought I had never seen a more handsome city or one so beautifully laid out. The capital, set like the centre of a star with wide avenues of white asphalt planted with splendid trees, seemed indeed a worthy setting for the seat of Government of such a prosperous nation.[33]

He rented rooms at No. 1435 K Street and announced his classes. By now Louis had completely adopted the identity of 'Cheiro' and 'Louis Warner' was little more than a memory: '[This] young man keen and cultured will not divulge his identity but has a mission to perform.'[34] Perform he did, and his success was guaranteed when politicians lined up to have their hands read.

> The Vice President [John G. Carlisle], who goes everywhere and does everything in the way of social diversion, was one of the first to call on Cheiro and his example has been followed by most of the dignitaries of the Senate, the Cabinet and Diplomatic Corps... The Secretary was assured of future greatness and power, but Cheiro declined to specify if that meant the Presidential chair...[35]

The high point was when Frances Folsom Cleveland, the young wife of the then President Grover Cleveland, invited Louis to the White House.

She received me with the utmost graciousness and simplicity. 'I have read all your books,' she said... Tea was served—English tea... and also English toast, just as if we had been sitting in any London drawing-room. The President strolled in for a few moments, chatted with me about my tour through the States, and, with a hearty handshake, returned to his duties.[36]

Louis predicted that November would be auspicious for the Clevelands—it wasn't. Cleveland declined nomination, the Democrats lost the 1896 election and their promised son wasn't born. But the story appeared in newspapers throughout the US—the *New York World* even included a nice drawing of the scene.[37]

People paid Louis whatever it took for his sage advice and they came to him in droves. According to his memoirs, amongst his clients on 30 May 1896 was William Q Judge, then President of the Theosophical Society. 'I was... struck by his magnetic dominant personality,' said Louis, 'and pleased him by stating that at that period of his life he had reached the climax of whatever his ambition was; but I added whatever the honour might be it would be of short duration, as "you have already reached the last chapter of your life".'[38]

Judge fell into a swoon so Louis, with a remarkable lack of concern, examined the hand of the woman next to him—Katherine Tingley. Except that Judge had died in March and the Theosophical Society had fragmented since the astrologer Sepharial (Walter Old) had released documents to the *Westminster Gazette* two years previously about Judge's false claim to have received precipitated letters.[39] Theosophists still argue about this today, and it's beyond belief that Louis wouldn't know at least the basics about the affair. A more accurate account might be that Katherine Tingley popped in to see him and while she was there, Jehangier took an impression of her hand.

These are only details. Louis was the most renowned palmist in the world—to many, the only palmist. He was rich and becoming richer every day. He was unstoppable. And then Louis received a cable telling him his father was dying. He hastily packed his bags. 'I had not seen him for upwards of fifteen years,'pointed out Louis. 'Within a few hours of the receipt of the cable, I was on a train making my way as rapidly as possible to catch the next boat sailing from New York. At each stopping-place I cabled my father that I was coming.'[40]

The Cunard liner *Etruria* left New York every Saturday. On 13 June, Louis (travelling under the name of 'Cheiro') and Elsie joined the other passengers. The press announced that Louis had 'sailed to spend the season in London, making a brief trip to Paris and will return to America in the autumn', which was sort of true.[41]

Even while rushing to his father's deathbed, Louis had time for another recitation. On 17 June, Claude Trevelyan, the writer of musical comedies and theatre impresario, gathered people for an impromptu fund-raising concert in aid of the Sailors' Orphanage of New York and Liverpool, om which £60 was raised: 'It was a great artistic and financial success. The singing of Mr Shirley Gandell, Miss Elsie Irving; the recitations of the celebrated Cheiro; the playing of Mrs Binney, Senoritas Anna and Rosa Martinez (pianoforte), and Mr Joseph Weber (violin), being greatly admired.'[42]

The *Etruria* reached Queenstown, Belfast on the early evening of 19 June. Louis had just enough time to get to Maryborough Lunatic Asylum where his father was now diagnosed with 'senile debility'.

Finally, I reached his bedside at 2 o'clock one morning to find him still living. The doctor said that my cables had kept him alive. After the first greetings were over, speaking very faintly, my father said: 'My son, I have used all my will-power to keep living in order to be able to tell you certain things about your family which I should have told you many years ago. God grant that I may have the strength to make up for it now'....

'There are papers valuable to you,' he gasped, 'in the hands of a firm of solicitors in London. You must get these deeds as quickly as possible. The name and address of where they are has failed me for the moment. Lift my head a little higher; open the window, let me get more air; perhaps my memory will come back. My dear boy, forgive me. Like many others, I have left things until it is too late. No, I can't recollect, I cannot remember.'

The effort was too great. Paralysis had already seized the upper part of his body—the poor tongue tried to speak, but no sound came. For four hours the eyes still lived and were fixed on mine, but at dawn the end came and he passed away with his secret.[43]

William Warner died 21 June 1896.

Cheiro and his thought machine, 1897

CHAPTER

EIGHT

It is beyond question or doubt that Cheiro possessed some strange power,
some vital ray, which he was able to project from his body.[1]

*L*OUIS' NEW FRIEND EDITH HAD BEEN AN ODD CHILD. Convinced her stepmother wanted her dead, she began to sleepwalk and have strange dreams when she was nine. As she slept, Edith visited cities filled with wonders and answered her father's questions about what she was seeing. The doctor Edith's father consulted firmly told him to leave her alone and let her get on with her strange dreams. Edith's stepmother was exasperated, accusing Edith of making it up, but Edith continued to travel astrally in her sleep and tell everyone she was doing so.

It made sense when Edith realised, like Blavatsky had, that Louis was the reincarnation of Cagliostro, According to Edith, Cagliostro was the reincarnation of Demetrius Phalerus of Phalerum who'd founded the great library in Alexandria, the location in her dreams.[i]

When Edith's stepmother died, her new stepmother tried valiantly to make friends with her, but Edith was having none of that. So she decided to become an actress. Edith Halford Thompson was eighteen when she moved to London from Exeter to take classes with Ben Greet (Philip Barling Greet), the Shakespearean actor, director, impresario and actor-manager.[ii] Greet was part of a theatrical family—his brother

---

i Edith's account of Louis in her biography *Out of the Silence* is less than reliable. She accepted Cheiro's tall tales as truth and contradicted herself, for example, accusing Louis of both having a violent temper and never expressing his anger.

ii Edith said she'd met Louis in 1895 when she was seventeen, but she couldn't have done

William managed several theatres and his sister Harriet acted as his business manager. He'd formed the Ben Greet Players in 1883 to train up-and-coming actors, and the company frequently toured Britain, often performing Shakespeare in college gardens, parks and on village greens. Greet also ran an Academy of Acting and his students acted in the Players as part of their training.

Louis had gone back into business at 157 New Bond Street, advertising his return in the *Morning Post* from the middle of July 1896. Optimistically, he said that he was only in London for a few weeks before returning to the US.

One morning, Edith left her class and as she walked down Bond Street, she saw the sign 'Cheiro'. She'd heard of him—of course, she had; Cheiro had been all over the newspapers. Plus she'd heard people gossiping about him only a few days before.

> 'Cheiro! Marvellous, but my dear fellow, don't tell me he does it through palmistry!'
> 'How do you suppose he does it, then?'
> 'Through the Devil, I should think.'[2]

Edith entered and went up a flight of stairs to find a room filled with people—the sort of people who made her feel 'up from the country'.[3] She was wearing a simple black dress with a wide white collar into which was tucked a deep red rose that toned with her cerise chiffon hat, so Edith wasn't completely under dressed.

'Not till next week, I'm afraid,' Louis's secretary said when Edith requested an appointment.[4] She added that a lot of the people in the waiting room were only there in the hope that someone else's appointment would fall through.

Then Cheiro's door opened and as a man and woman left, Edith noticed the figure behind them. 'I felt his eyes looking straight into mine,' said Edith. 'I felt also that I was staring and I knew, of course, that it is rude to stare, but I knew also that I was staring for the simple reason that his eyes were holding mine, as other eyes had held mine.'[5]

Louis said, 'Will you come in?' and although his secretary protested, he led Edith into his room where he was 'very handsome in a peculiarly virile way. He seemed to radiate vitality…'[6] Clearly, Cheiro was still gorgeous, and like many before her, Edith:

---

so until the following year as he was in America at the time. And the Ben Greet Academy didn't open until 1896.

Got lost in his strange and beautiful eyes—those eyes which people spoke of as dark, and which were really blue, they were magnetic eyes which made of your soul an open book, of which he turned the pages and read to you strange tales *which came true.*[7]

Louis read Edith's palm and revealed truths of her past, telling her about an upcoming unhappy marriage with an insane husband and 'years of danger and adventure'. 'Your hand interests me,' he added. 'I should like to see you again... It will be after office hours.'[8] It didn't occur to Edith to refuse.

Meanwhile, Jehangier had returned to Greenacre where he swanned around in white robes being a Parsi. That understates the effect. While most people were attired from head to toe in dark colours, photographs show that Jehangier dressed in dazzling white, good enough for a soap advertisement. That summer he helped establish the Monsalvat School for the Comparative Study of Religion, named after the sacred mountain in Wagner's *Parsifal*, where the Holy Grail was kept. With Swamis Vivekananda, Saradananda (Sarat Chandra Chakravarty) and Abhedananda (Kaliprasad Chandra) selling Vedanta, and other speakers focusing on the Talmud, Christianity, Jainism and Islam, Jehangier was a minority of one extolling the virtues of Zoroastrianism.

During that summer, Edith and Louis met regularly and discussed Edith's childhood dreams at length. Sometimes, Louis coaxed her into automatic writing:

I would sit at his writing table with a large sheet of paper in front of me and a pencil or pen in my hand, and he would stand behind my chair. The next thing that I remembered would be that the paper disappeared and that Cheiro was reading intently from several sheets of paper.[9]

Although happy to put Edith into a trance, Louis knew that hiding away in a room with a young woman after hours could lead to problems. Edith was supposed to be staying with Harriet Greet but had moved into rooms and (unusually for a woman of her age and class) could do whatever she wanted.

'He treated me as a child and never spoke of or suggested sex matters to me,' Edith said, defensively. 'Or allowed my mind to dwell on them, after once having explained to me certain facts which he considered were necessary for me to understand clearly...'[10]

Sex mattered because Edith needed to remain a virgin to keep her clairvoyant abilities alive. As well as making sure she understood how sex worked, Louis gradually demanded more and more control over her life. He prevented her from reading books he didn't approve of and kept a close eye on her friends and acquaintances, demanding that she ended relationships with those he disapproved of. Although Edith protested, she eventually complied.

> When he liked he could be a very fine actor, as many men are who possess and control a strong will, for with the extraordinary charm—which must have accounted for much of his success in his meteor-like career—he also had a very violent temper kept under admirable control by this indomitable will... he merely ignored my wish to be an actress until it interfered with his own work, and then he made me give up my engagements.[11]

Back in London, Louis didn't spend all his time bossing Edith around. Shortly after his return he'd called on d'Odiardi who introduced him to the writer C H Malcolm and told him about his 'electric love machine'.[12] There were two such machines, one of them set up at d'Odiardi's Notting Hill hospital. The machine could 'register the effect upon the brain of drunkenness and gluttony' and check people's mental state.[13] It was a diagnostic tool to check the state of someone's mind, allowing d'Odiardi to offer an electric cure based on its results. After all, 'People who have small brain power hardly influence the needle. Drunken men and idiots scarcely deflect it, because they have so few brain waves.'[14] As soon as he saw it, Louis was fascinated.

> Upon an ordinary pedestal were four brass rests, into which a transparent glass bell fitted, so that the upper surface of the pedestal was removed by a couple of inches from the glass, and the hand could easily be inserted between. On the centre of this pedestal there was placed a small metal disc, marked on its upper surface with the 360 degrees of the circle. This disc was not fixed; it could be taken out and examined. Suspended above it, from the inside of the glass, by a fine silken thread, was a needle shaped like a battle-axe. It is the movements of this needle above the disc which register the exertions of will force.[15]

And it *was* a love machine. People queued up to visit d'Odiardi's laboratory to find out if they were in love:

The man stands at one pole and the woman at the other. Both concentrate their thoughts upon it. The young woman thinks intently of the young man and the young man thinks intently of his sweetheart. This is an anxious moment. Both are awaiting the turn of the needle. The one with joyous anticipations, the other in trepidation. Slowly and slowly the needle begins to move, and with a few vibrating movements it swings itself toward the one whose love is strongest. Hate deflects the needle, and if the woman hates the man the needle swings far, away from her. If, on the other hand, they love equally the needle stands still. Married women visit Prof. D'Odiardi to find if their husbands still love them...[16]

It could be useful to see if you'd ever find love, what your true motives for marriage were, to work out the likelihood of you cheating, and in child custody cases to work out the favoured parent.[17] Such devices had been (and continued to be) tested and dismissed as nonsense.

Several forms of apparatus... have been examined, all of which consist essentially of a light body suspended in a glass bell jar by means of a silk or other fibre in such a manner that a very slight force exerted upon it from one side or other causes it to rotate about the point of suspension... The air currents set up by the warmth or movement of the whole body or the hand were quite sufficient to account for any deflection... The 'inventors' of these 'psychic' apparatus are evidently quite ignorant of the methods of scientific research.[18]

Louis had another use for it entirely. Palmistry had vastly increased in popularity, and numerous palmists and clairvoyants occupied the areas near New Bond Street. For example, Celestina shared her rooms with Miss Sheepshanks, a 'complexionist' who'd begun her career as a 'masseuse of the "altogether"'.[40] iii She claimed to have studied under Cheiro who 'took a fancy to me' and only took women clients who'd been referred to her by Miss Sheepshanks.[20] More successful, and less shady sounding, was Madame Voyer, an American palmist and clairvoyant in England since 1893 who operated at 168 New Bond Street. She often saw

---

iii It's hard to decode the euphemisms here, but it's likely it's as rude as it sounds. 'Altogether' as slang for naked had entered the language after the publication of George du Maurier's novel *Trilby* ('I sit for the altogether') in 1894.

eleven hundred people a month and used a crystal ball.[22] There were many, many others.

Working in Bond Street and its environs protected you from the law. Those who practised palmistry or clairvoyance away from the West End were far more at risk of a 'policeman's wife or sister, or some other woman hired for the occasion... employed as agent provocateur, who sets out with a companion to the person marked down for prosecution, and tempts her to commit an illegal act...'[22] Plus, there was much more money to be made in Mayfair than Shoreditch. But it was still risky. Some palmists only saw clients if they'd been introduced. This had the bonus of making clients feel like they belonged to an exclusive club. Or they might only accept money for talking about the past or present and throw in snippets about the future for free. Or they could adopt the American practice: 'Where the sale of drink is positively forbidden. The rum-seller keeps a spotted dog, or some other rarity, for a sight of which he charges the price of a glass of liquor. The customer comes in "to see the spotted dog", and before he goes is presented with a dram.'[23]

Louis didn't have a spotted dog, but he could buy a thought machine, which fitted into a 'good sized hat box.'[24] In September he moved to 47 New Bond Street and was soon advertising that 'The latest great scientific invention for "Thought Photography and Register of Cerebral Force" (lately reported on before the Academy of Science, Paris) is now employed by Cheiro in all his experiments.'[25] And Louis dressed up and had his photo taken, gazing pensively at the machine. He needed to sell its benefits differently to d'Odiardi. 'Cheiro records every motion, directs your efforts in certain directions, and finally explains results, which are invariably in keeping with the lines on the recto of the hand.'[26]

When Louis examined a hand, he verified his analysis by having his client register their thought vibration in the machine which showed vitality, mental and physical strength, nerve force, joy, sadness, confidence or depression. 'The vibrations of mental vitality are given forth by the left hand; those of physical health are good and evenly balanced—the right hand repels the needle and the left attracts'.[27] There were uses d'Odiardi hadn't considered. Louis reported that:

A... gentleman stood in front of the machine, criticising its action, and endeavoring to find some explanation of its power. About the same time several other persons entered the room. In casual conversation one of them mentioned the fact of the sudden drop in the value of South African Chartered Shares. No one knew the person looking at the machine was a large holder of these shares, but instantly the drop in value was mentioned his emotion caused the indicator to swing around and indicate one of the highest numbers that ever has been recorded.[28]

Thirty to forty people a day took advantage of the thought machine in Cheiro's rooms, although not all readings were successful:

A prominent financier fixed his eyes on the dial and concentrated his whole attention on the indicator; in less than twenty seconds the instrument appeared to him to indicate that he was the constant victim of three different kinds of drugs, and finally that he was a pronounced criminal of the most vicious type. He was naturally much distressed until Cheiro informed him that he had been looking at the wrong end of the indicator.[29]

This wasn't the only interesting item in Louis's rooms. Edith didn't like the mummified hand he had 'set in a golden socket, which formed a broad gold bracelet that resembled a fetter... this was fastened by gold chains to the purple velvet cushion on which it lay...'[30] She was particularly bothered when one day fresh blood appeared on it. Fortunately, most of the time Louis put the mummified hand away.

Life wasn't just work for Louis, of course. He was initiated into the Drury Lane masonic lodge (as William John Warner), which Kitchener had also belonged to on 10 November 1896 and had a busy social life. 'Women, the proudest and most beautiful, were his for the asking: he could choose from them as he chose his dancing partners...'[31] Edith pointed out. Women were the source of many of his problems. And Louis told Edith he was once set on by armed assassins but given that he was a ju-jtsu expert and had other fighting talents, he swiftly saw those off. He may have made up the ju-jitsu thing—at least, this is the only time it's mentioned. But Louis didn't like being crossed. On one occasion he was at a house party and a woman challenged him:

'You think because you are a handsome man that you have all the women at your feet. You are an imposter, a charlatan. I suppose you think you could bring me to your feet?...'
'Madam, I don't think anything about it—I *know* it.'[32]

Louis told the woman that at midnight she'd return to the room and kneel at his feet. Everyone gasped and the woman told Louis he was mad and then went to bed. Later that evening, the woman reappeared, sleepwalking, and did indeed prostrate herself at Louis's feet. He kindly took the early train so she didn't have to meet him at breakfast. At least, this is what he told Edith.

Despite repeatedly announcing he'd leave for the US soon in the *Morning Post*, Louis stayed put in London.[33] What prevented Louis from leaving? C H Malcolm thought Louis was having problems with his love life and wrote a poem about it in March 1897.

> STRANGE friend, in thee I sometimes see
> A look that tells of long ago
> A far-off look, that can but be
> Contempt for all thou yet dost know.
> For thou dost hate this mortal earth!
> Thy soul is longing to be free!
> To have perchance its second birth,
> And pass away in happy glee!
> Away! away! I know not where
> And yet I read its life above
> 'Twill pass the bounds of mortal air,
> And fly to seek its only love!
> Its love who lived long, long ago,
> And who for it is weeping still!
> See how yon rays of light do flow,
> And rest on thee by her own will!
> And, noble poet, gentle friend,
> life is watched by spirits
> Angels of peace o'er thee do bend,
> ever whisper, 'She is there!'
> Yes! thou wilt see her soon again
> The queen who gave to thee her heart!
> Oh! there shall be an end to pain,
> For from that hour no more you part.

Malcolm's poems were finally published at the end of 1897.[34] It might have been better if they hadn't been, according to the reviews.

> Had Mr Malcolm never written a line, his girl friends at least might have regarded him as a poetic genius made self-silent through modesty and wisdom. As it is, he has been rash enough not only to write but to publish his rhymes, as presented in his

book. They are so fearfully and wonderfully simple that it is a marvel no friend intervened to postpone their publication.[35]

Whyever Louis was dragging his feet, Jehangier wasn't happy. In October 1896 Vivekananda wrote to a friend, 'I hear your friend Cola is lecturing on Zoroastrian philosophy—surely the stars are not smiling on him'.[36] And in December he commented, 'Poor Cola! is he able now to make a living?'[37]

Maybe Jehangier was short of cash, as he didn't have many opportunities to earn, although he lectured occasionally, for example, speaking at the Boston Home Congress and at the Brooklyn Ethical Association in November.[38] In February 1897 he started fund raising for victims of famine in India with the support of Julia Ward Howe.[39]

Louis announced he'd go back to America in August—probably.[40] He liked to be out and about at society events and attended a reception at the Royal Institute in Piccadilly in May. There was singing and recitations and important society figures were present such as the Duchess of Sutherland, Lady Warwick, and Lady Stamford: 'Cheiro was much observed. His name in private life is Count de Hamong.'[41]

With his father dead, Louis felt entitled to call himself a count, and from spring 1897 had adopted the name of Leigh de Hamong.[iv] As Count Hamong, in July he met the painter Dorothy Tennant, who was married to the explorer Henry Morton Stanley. This led to an introduction and trip to visit William Ewart Gladstone (who'd recently completed his fourth term as Prime Minister) on 3 August at his home at Hawarden castle. '"Your father had the same love of higher mathematics that I have," said Gladstone, "We have corresponded many times on difficult problems"... As he spoke, he unrolled several sheets of paper, covered with calculations and algebraical figures in my father's handwriting.'[42]

Why William Warner would have corresponded with Gladstone about algebra is a complete mystery. But Louis had brought his thought machine and so would presumably know if the story was true or not. The encounter fuelled his lectures for months to come, as well as earning him extensive press coverage.

A few weeks later, Edith told Louis she was going on tour in *The Sign of the Cross*, a popular 1895 historical tragedy by Wilson Barrett. Louis didn't want Edith to go and said, 'You will have an accident tomorrow—

---

iv He changed his name on the records of Drury Lane Masonic Lodge to Leigh de Hamong in September 1898.

oh, nothing that has any lasting effect, just a bang on the head… enough to make you understand that when I tell you not to do a thing, it is best not to do it.' He added ominously, 'You will come when I call you.'[43]

During rehearsals Edith was knocked out after being thrown against a pillar. She left the production, telling the stage manager that her understudy would have to fill in. Returning to London, she went to Louis's rooms and collapsed. 'If he had said to me, "I want you to go to Buckingham Palace and ask the King to lend me his crown," I think I would have answered him, "Shall I start at once or can I finish my tea first?"'[44]

Louis didn't send her to Buckingham Palace but to Eastbourne, to stay with a friend of his. Ben Greet was annoyed about Edith's absence, but as he was being well paid to teach Edith whether she turned up or not, he didn't make too much fuss.

In Eastbourne, Edith spent some time staring into a crystal with Mrs Simmons, the Indian wife of a British soldier. Louis was supposed to turn up on the Saturday night but when it reached midnight and he still hadn't arrived, Edith went to bed. The next morning she woke to find herself wearing a lilac veil over her nightgown as well as a heavy Indian bracelet—and a bowl of roses had appeared in her room. Mrs Simmons turned up with breakfast and told Edith that Louis had arrived the night before with a couple of friends and coaxed Edith into performing temple dances in her sleep. Then he'd carried her to bed, leaving her the roses.

Meanwhile, Jehangier was based in New York though he spoke at the Congress of Religions in Boston before returning to Greenacre in August. It was a boom year for Greenacre—visitors arrived from all over the US and further afield, and lectures drew audiences of up to eight hundred people, many of whom were forced to stand outside the tent where the lecture was being given and strain to hear the proceedings. The Monsalvat School ran for a month, and Jehangier led ceremonies in worship of the setting or rising sun.

It was at Greenacre that Jehangier became friendly with Carl Bjerregaard. An ex-spy for the Danish military, Bjerregaard had run from the army in 1873, heading for New York and a new life. He ended up working at the Astor Library and recreated himself as a philosopher, artist and mystic, becoming a popular lecturer.

And then Louis announced that he intended to leave for the US in September—this time he did. This was a very different trip to his previous one and clearly was primarily to meet Jehangier rather than for work. Indeed, he doesn't appear to have worked at all for the first few weeks.

In October, Jehangier spoke at the Liberal Congress of Religions in Nashville, Tennessee before going on to St Paul's, Minnesota where he spoke at St Paul's church. His and Louis's hats and coats were stolen that night. Louis lost 'a Newmarket of fine blue Melton with a velvet collar and chamois lined pockets' that contained his keys and papers, as well as a silk hat marked with his coat of arms (a crown), plus his white kid gloves.[45] Jehangier was more shabbily dressed in a black frieze coat with a velvet collar and a black cloth cap. They soon moved on to Chicago where Louis began offering palmistry classes at the Auditorium from 8 November.

> Fashionably dressed women and men in box coats, set off with large chrysanthemums, sat nervously in the parlors of the hotel yesterday waiting for their turn to know whether the net work in their palms met weal or woe, obscurity or fame. Most of them seemed to be well pleased when they went away.[46]

Armed with his thought machine, Louis announced that he planned to stay in Chicago for a month. The press were barely interested; there were no invitations to society events and there was a lacklustre attendance at his lectures—despite attempts to liven them up: 'Several days ago Tess, the chimpanzee on exhibition at the Zoo, was obliged to have her left palm examined, much against her will, after which several plaster casts were made for scientific purposes.'[47]

Louis and Jehangier moved on to Milwaukee at the end of December. The plan was to return to Minnesota where Louis had lecture bookings. But Louis had a fall when working out at the Chicago Athletic Club and his arm became so swollen that he summoned a doctor.

> Cheiro, the palmist, was compelled to undergo a surgical operation today, which has necessitated canceling his engagements.... He was told that if he did not immediately submit to an operation that death would ensue. The operation was performed in his room at the Pfister hotel. He will be confined for two weeks, and it will be some time before he can resume work.[48]

Apparently, he'd suffered blood poisoning due to the tight leather straps he wore while exercising. Jehangier went ahead, leaving Louis to recover. The press reported, 'Mr. Cola is... awaiting his friend.'[49] Indeed, he was and Jehangier busily made appointments for Louis in anticipation of his arrival. Rather than cancel, Jehangier performed Louis's lecture on 17 January, accompanied by his stereopticon show.

A week later, Louis arrived in Minnesota and gave a slightly different version of his lecture—this time with the thought machine. He followed this with a talk at the Athenaeum in Milwaukee, and then he and Jehangier moved into the West hotel in Minnesota where he read palms and popped out to give the occasional lecture, for example, at a local music shop on 17 February. Jehangier also offered the odd talk, for example, at the First Unitarian Church on 14 February.

It was mind-numbingly dull. The most exciting event was at a press club reception where Louis gave a lengthy and lurid account of his adventures in India. But things would soon get better. After all, Louis planned to visit every city in America. And then he'd go to Africa, India, Australia and anywhere else that would have him.

Louis and Jehangier returned to Chicago where Louis spoke at the Chicago Esoteric Extension, a group similar to theosophists and part of the New Thought Federation. The society had been established 'for the purpose… of getting together people of all beliefs who are liberal enough to investigate all subjects and try to find out the truth,' which could mean anything, and often did.[50]

Maybe in an attempt to liven things up, Louis predicted in late March saying that the US would go to war on Cuba on 21 March.[51] He was wrong, but not very—the ten-week long Spanish-American War started 21 April 1898.

It's unclear why (there may be clues in what happened later), but Louis abruptly returned to England in early May 1898. He dived into the social whirl, even attending the Chirological Society reception at the end of May, despite them not allowing him to join due to their rules about not using a pseudonym when practising palmistry.

He would have soon heard the bad news about d'Odiardo. To be fair, there'd been rumblings about his abilities for some time: 'Mr. D'Odiardi is an unqualified practitioner, who poses as 'Medical Officer in Charge' of an establishment which he calls a "hospital," but which is not on the footing of a recognised charity.'[52]

D'Odiardi had been diverted by writing with C H Malcolm—their tragedy *Constantine* was performed for copyright in March 1898.[53] He'd regret not paying more attention to his hospital. In April 1898 he attended the inquest of the artist John Slater who'd died while receiving treatment at d'Odiardi's hospital. The lack of qualified staff meant that no-one could issue a death certificate; the doctor on staff never saw patients. Slater had paid £3 for electrical treatment, but—unfortunately for d'Odiardi—had a heart condition as well as kidney and liver disease.

> The jury returned a verdict in accordance with the medical evidence, and added a rider that the professor should not apply electricity except under a doctor's orders and advice, and that only trained nurses should be engaged... advised him for his own sake never to attempt to diagnose internal complaints. The Professor thought this unjust and harsh.[54]

It was a disaster for d'Odiardi. His hospital was already losing money and he went bankrupt in September. Louis quietly stopped using the thought machine.

Back in the US, things weren't going well for Jehangier now he was alone. Hearing that Jehangier was acting oddly—he kept a brazier of coal in his room and spent hours performing rituals before it—Carl Bjerregaard collected him from his home in Thirty-eighth street on Saturday 16 July and took Jehangier to his country home in Montclair to spend the following Sunday with him and his family. He soon regretted his decision. Jehangier was saying strange things and became violent when challenged. It came to a head when he decided that Bjerregard's young daughter was divine. '[She]... was the only one of the household to whom he did not show repugnance. He worshipped her as a deity.'[55]

Bjerregaard swiftly took Jehangier home. His landlady took one look at Jehangier and summoned Dr Bigelow who said Jehangier's mind was imbalanced, and Bigelow and Bjerregard took Jehangier before a magistrate. In court on 18 July, Jehangier—'Between periods enunciating the philosophy of Zoroaster, who came alive out of a burning mountain before Xerxes conquered the known world'—loftily insisted that as a barrister, he'd conduct his own defence.[56] He asked that the British Consul, Sir Dominic Carnegie, then in Boston, and Governor Waleott of Massachusetts be summoned to give evidence as to his sanity and scholarly attainments. This was ignored. The court watched his gestures, which he said were intended to clarify his thoughts, in bafflement and the magistrate summoned a carriage to take him to Bellevue Hospital. The attendants tried to coax Jehangier into the carriage but he'd been in New York for long enough to realise this was a possible death sentence. 'I will never be locked up.' he said. 'I'll hypnotise these men before I will submit to such a thing.'[57]

He submitted.

At Bellevue, the doctors decided that Jehangier was the victim of self-hypnosis because he'd 'centred his whole mentality upon the great mysteries of creation, which no human intellect can comprehend'.[58] They weren't sure what to do with him.

> Clad in the flowing robes of the Parsee, and crooning weird music and uttering strange words, and making mystic passes with his hands, the man spends his time... The wonderful mysteries of the ancient fire of Zoroaster, kindled ages ago, are plain to him, and he is happy. His case is very similar to those hindu fanatics who mesmerize their own limbs, and put them in grotesque positions, and keep them so always... Among the religious fanatics of the East this is not uncommon. But there are few records of such a thing in the Occident... the first case recorded in New York...[59]

Jehangier was diagnosed with 'catatonia', or what we might now call schizophrenia, 'a brain disease of cyclical changing course, with sequential mental symptoms of melancholy, mania, stupor, confusion and finally idiocy'.[60] He was strapped onto an iron bed and 'His face was as red as if he had had apoplexy; his head was constantly moving up and down and his eyes were tightly closed'.[61] When Mrs Theodore Sutro visited Jehangier, the attendant told her that she was wasting her time as he wouldn't recognise her: 'But he knew me the moment I spoke.'[62]

Jehangier died 31 July 1898.[v] He'd survived less than two weeks in Bellevue.

---

v Recorded under the name of 'Ichangier W. Cola'.

ANOTHER RIPPING YARN

One afternoon in the summer of 1896, 'Sir William Standish'—a pseudonym—visited Cheiro. In his mid-thirties, Standish was well-known in London. He'd inherited a fortune and his eccentric father had made it a condition of his inheritance that he gave at least £10,000 to charity each year.

He wanted to consult Cheiro about two odd lines on his hand—a double Line of Head. This rare configuration on his small hands represented a dual personality. Standish said, 'There are times when I confess I feel and want to live as a woman... Then I just as suddenly change, and feel as a person would when waking out of a dream, and trying to remember what the dream was.'

After laughing, Cheiro reminded himself that he, 'had seen in my life so many of those half-feminine types of men,' and said in a joking tone, 'Sometimes, I suppose, you are strongly tempted to darn things, or see how you would look in a woman's hat.'

Standish said he wouldn't do anything like that at home in case the servants saw him. Then he offered Cheiro a cigarette and changed the subject.

The following evening, Cheiro joined Standish, along with his wife and son, for dinner. They had a lovely house, tastefully furnished and containing rare works of art. After chatting over coffee, Standish took Cheiro up to his private rooms. Cheiro remarked 'It certainly does not look as if you did any sewing or darning up here.'

'Yes, but I would like to show you where I do it,' said Standish.

The next evening, Standish took Cheiro to a flat just off Oxford Street. The silk-covered chairs, along with the curtains and lamp, were rose coloured. 'The whole effect was that of a lady's boudoir,' said Cheiro. 'As if to add to the effect, several small pieces of silk were on the table, and near a rocking-chair a large well-filled basket was lying half turned over on the floor. It was just as if a lady had been serving, and had left the room for a moment.'

While they sat and chatted, Standish absent-mindedly picked up a piece of silk from the table along with needle and thread and made a flower from it. He said that sometimes he spent months away from home but had no memory of what he did during that time. Fortunately, his wife thought he had business interests in Paris and Rome and he'd arranged to have his letters sent on to addresses in those cities, and then re-forwarded to the flat. His wife didn't mind his absences as, 'She always hated the ordinary idea of married life' and they'd agreed to be simply companions. She knew he wasn't interested in women in that way so wasn't worried that he had a mistress. Though he'd tried, Standish couldn't fight his urges to live his other life. It was as if he was possessed—every twenty-eight days the urge came upon him.

The following week Cheiro turned up for dinner to be told that Standish had suddenly been called to Rome. Lady Standish said she didn't mind, after all, she had her own independent life. Plus her husband had some rather unfashionable religious tendencies and it was better he indulged them privately in Rome. After dinner, Cheiro read Lady Standish's hands and saw 'the sign of some terrible tragedy... some shock that would paralyse her very senses.' But he couldn't work out what would be behind it.

Months later, Cheiro was in London's Green Park when he bumped into an old friend, Algy—a poet with an odd personality. 'He really did live in the clouds,' he said. Algy had odd views on marriage, saying it should be a mental and not a physical association. 'He would have divided the world into two sects,' said Cheiro, 'the breeders and the thinkers—but for the unfortunate " breeders " he had nothing but contempt.' Although he was odd, 'This man had eyes—wonderful eyes— great violet eyes, with black lashes—eyes that dreamt and thought and held communion with other worlds so that under their spell one forgot the rest of the picture.'

To Cheiro's surprise, Algy told him that he'd met the love of his life. And he'd found a way of surviving on very little food. His system was to sleep all day, get up in the evening and wander throughout the night. By avoiding being jostled by crowds his clothes lasted longer and only eating when hungry meant he needed very little. One night, he was sitting by the river when he became aware that a woman was sharing his bench, staring out onto the water as he was. They began to talk and it was only natural she should follow Algy home.

Although Algy's servant Pat was puzzled by her presence, he managed to pull a simple breakfast together, after which Algy offered the woman his guest room. When he got up for dinner, he was astonished to see that the furniture had been re-arranged, cushions dug out of where they'd been hidden and two vases of roses stood in the room. Pat said the woman was responsible and she was in the garden, tying up the roses over the porch. The woman entered the room and announced she was going to move in as Algy clearly needed someone to look after him. And she agreed with Algy's thoughts on eating. But the woman had forgotten who she was—she didn't even know her own name.

After dinner the woman settled down to do some sewing while Algy admired his own poems. They lived like this for several weeks until one day the woman disappeared.

'I am so sorry for you,' said Cheiro with suspicion. 'How do I know it is not one of your fantastic poems that you are trying on me, to see how it goes?'

That was easily solved—Cheiro could meet the woman. She'd returned a month later. And they'd got married. 'Married!' cried Cheiro. 'Surely you were not mad enough to marry a woman whom you knew nothing about—and with your queer ideas about marriage, how could you do such a thing?'

'She has just as strong views on marriage as I have' said Algy. 'She only believes in the mental side of it, as I do... we live like brother and sister together.'

The woman still disappeared regularly and Algy was expecting her back at any moment. When she returned, he'd invite Cheiro to meet her. A week later Cheiro received a telegram and went out to buy a supper basket and a couple of bottles of wine. 'I was not going to take any chances with people who could go for weeks without food,' he said.

Cheiro arrived to find the lamps already lit and flowers on the table. 'All over the room, one could see the touch of a woman, and a woman of taste at that, ' he said. The woman rose to greet him.

There was nothing very remarkable about her beauty, I thought. Her brown hair, with just a glint of gold, was unmistakably like a wig. Of figure, she did not appear to have much, but in any case it was hidden in a straight up-and-down kind of costume. She wore no rings or jewellery of any kind—a bunch of roses at her waist was the only attempt at ornament. She looked at me in a dreamy kind of way, as if she were not quite awake.

It was fortunate Cheiro had brought food as there wasn't much to eat. While they were chatting, he wondered if the newly-weds planned to have children. That didn't go down well. To retrieve the situation, Cheiro hastily suggested that Algy read them some of his poems. That did the trick.

While Algy was reading, the woman pulled out her sewing equipment and 'in a few minutes she had formed two odd-shaped, but beautiful flowers, which fell at her feet, as if she had hardly noticed she had made them.'

Cheiro picked them up and as he handed them back to the woman, his eyes met hers. They looked somehow familiar: 'No, it could not be possible, I thought ; it could not be possible.' He asked if he could look at thewoman's hands. Then 'My brain turned icy cold—across both left and right was the "double Line of Head" that I had seen on a man's hands and not so very long ago.' Jumping up, Cheiro said it was getting late and promptly left. Once he got home, he fretted and wondered if he'd got it wrong. But there was no mistaking that double Line of Head. What should he do? If he told Lady Standish, it could drive her mad. If he went to the police, there'd be a huge scandal. Finally, he went to the Standish's house. Lady Standish invited him to have a cup of tea with her; her husband was away.

'You are looking ill and tired,' Lady Standish said. 'What is the matter?'

Suddenly, they heard footsteps rushing up the stairs and Algy was there. 'My wife, my wife,' he screamed, 'where is my wife?'

Cheiro jumped up and said, 'For God's sake, calm yourself, man… what is the matter?'

Algy said that after Cheiro had left the previous evening, he'd tried to kiss his new wife. She struggled but he planted a kiss on her lips. His wife screamed and ran out. He managed to trace her to London and saw her enter the house and followed her in. 'My wife is here—I must find her,' he screamed. Cheiro was horrified.

'The man is mad,' Lady Standish said. 'Ring the bell.'

Suddenly, they heard footsteps on the landing and a fumbling at the handle. Lady Standish stood frozen and as white as death as the door slowly opened and a figure stood before them. Algy leaped towards the figure.

The figure stood with a bunch of roses at its waist, looking from one to the other. Then its eyes focused on Lady Standish's white face. As his trembling hands slowly stretched out towards her, Sir William Standish cried out, 'My wife, my wife' and fell dead at her feet.

Cheiro, *Confessions*, Chapter XXXVIII.

CHAPTER

NINE

Cheiro was a great Soul who carried on the torch of spiritual Light handed down the ages by the Masters of Light.[1]

CLAIMING A NOBLE HERITAGE when that claim is sketchy at best is nothing new and continues to this day. Frauds are often uncovered. Indeed, Count Cagliostro was reputedly expelled from St Petersburg by Catherine II for being neither a count nor a Spanish Colonel, despite the uniform he wore.

And in 1898 'Sir Henry Onequi' was sentenced to twelve months' hard labour for stealing luggage at Kings Cross Station. He was really ex-journalist Evans Wheeler, a New York palmist who listed amongst his clients Queen Victoria, as well as Lilly Langtry, the Prince of Wales, the Czar of Russia, Gladstone and others on Cheiro's client list. He also claimed to be a Russian count—'Baron Musgrave'. Wheeler had worked at the Auditorium in Chicago in 1896 and 1897 until accusations of fraud forced him to flee to New York in June 1897. There he gave advice on stocks and shares based on his readings. Oddly, Wheeler made notes of his readings and sent his client a written report the following week, refusing to say anything at the time. He defrauded dozens of clients and in 1899 he advertised for a wife in London. Gladys Fenton agreed to marry him the moment they met. He borrowed money from her and she never saw him again.

Did Louis know Wheeler? There is no evidence he did, but he probably knew about him. And how useful Wheeler found his assumed title. Calling himself 'Leigh de Hamong' was perfectly legal. Under English common law you could (still can) call yourself whatever you fancy so long as you don't commit fraud or shirk your obligations. Later, Louis adopted the French form of the name—'Louis Hamon'—although he used both names interchangeably at the turn of the century.

Maybe Louis genuinely believed he had a right to the title of 'count' now his father was dead. But he had another reason for his new name—he wanted a pen name for his novel. *A Study in Destiny* appeared in October 1897 and attracted little attention.[i] That changed the following year when someone realised who 'Count Leigh de Hamong' was. Reviews pointed out that it was a supernatural thriller that would go down well with those who liked such things.

> I would not advise nervous ladies to read the Count de Hamong's story late at night, but it may be commended to those who like a powerful story with an element of the gruesome.[2]

> Such a book as this suggests to us how very carefully children should select their parents.[3]

Set in Egypt, *Destiny* is 'saturated with moonlit deserts, mysterious and therefore evil foreigners, torchlit passageways, tombs piled high with riches and the mummies of ancient royalty, confounding riddles, black magic and unimaginable terrors.'[4] The plot has everyone charging around the Valley of the Kings looking for a tomb. One of the main characters is Professor Heller, an Egyptologist who wore an ancient mystical ring, which strangely resembled Louis's ring.

> Within a few pages we are treated to all the clichés sacred to this kind of novel. The explorers hear strange noises in the dark; they are attacked by bats; they have to restore their superstitious servants to their senses with some good stirring rational words; they see men doing unspeakable things with snakes and find that they are being watched by a silent onlooker who seems possessed by some fearful and all consuming melancholy. When they fail to find the hidden tomb, the heroes nearly give up.

---

i The novel appeared under the title *The Hand of Fate* by 'Cheiro' in the US in June 1898. It was 'discovered' at regular intervals and reprinted and a version of it featured in horror anthologies as a short story—for example, in *Great Untold Stories of Fantasy and Horror* (New York: Pyramid, 1969). More recently, it was republished in 2006 as *The Curse of the Yogi's Tomb: Cheiro, A Study in Destiny* (Tampa, Florida: University of Tampa Press, 2006). Do read it.

Suddenly the silent figure appears and reveals that he alone knows the whereabouts of the tomb; and, being a sporting Englishman, he is happy to reveal it.[5]

This review also describes *Destiny* as 'the kind of novel that H. Rider Haggard would have written if he'd leaned too heavily on the laudanum' and comments on Louis's philosophical asides with 'In many ways, this is really just gibberish, but the important thing is that it sounds awesome.'[6] It was so awesome that in 1934 Louis re-used *Destiny* in *Real Life Stories*, claiming it was a record of true events.[7]

By early 1898 Louis's mum—as Countess de Hamong—had moved to London and was living in Gledhow Terrace, Kensington. Lest anyone think she stayed in a poky hovel, it's worth mentioning that her rented flat contained 'Four bed-rooms, two reception-rooms, kitchen... electric light, dinner lift' along with a servant.[8] Margaret Warner was unwell, so Louis put his plans to go to the western US and Australia on hold. There'd been some mysterious knocks in the house, which in his family heralded death within twelve months, so he was concerned.

Maybe not concerned for too long. Louis said that he spent Christmas 1898 with Princess Monyglyon (Countess Rose de Mercy Argenteau), the last member of a Belgian royal line and friend of the Prince of Wales.[ii] Rose was a lively character. Her husband, the Marquis d'Avaray, had spent their wedding night with another woman and gambled heavily. Rose left him to marry her childhood sweetheart, but finding him in bed with her maid spoiled that relationship. She spent much of her time travelling in search of her half-brother whose existence she'd discovered when her father was on his deathbed. At one point her travels took her to Bangkok where she developed an opium addiction that she claimed she cured with smelling salts. Chances are, Rose could be relied on for a good party.

Despite the bad weather, Louis set off for the Chateau d'Argenteau. No other guests were fool enough to attempt to cross the Channel that night, but Louis would do a lot to get to a good party. While he sat on the train, snow fell even more heavily, and by the time he reached Liege, the roads were almost impassable. Swift talking acquired Louis a sleigh and horses. He reached the castle and ended up snowbound with Rose and her English companion for nearly a week. Louis told the unlikely

---

ii Rosalie Francoise Adelaide Caroline Eugenie Mercy d'Argenteau. Louis doesn't give a year but says Rose was about thirty-five and it couldn't have been 1897 or 1899, when he was in the US.

story that things livened up when they were joined by King Leopold of Belgium and his daughter Princess Clémentine. They merrily played poker—which the King won—and Louis finally left four days later.

Louis knew the best events to be seen at. He attended the Japan Society's annual *conversazione* at the Institute of Water Colours in February 1899, enjoying the Bijou Orchestra playing 'the "Geisha" and several Japanese airs'.[9] He also became a life member of the Royal Geographic Society.

In March he attended a lecture on telepathy and wireless telegraphy at the London Spiritualist Alliance. Amongst the attendees were sparkling lights of the occult scene including Herbert Burrows, the socialist activist and theosophist who had worked with Annie Besant as one of the organisers of the matchgirls' strike in 1888; Mabel Collins, the novelist who had been linked with Robert Donston Stephenson, an early candidate for Jack the Ripper; George Wyld, Vice President of the National Association of Spiritualists and an early member of the Society for Psychical Research; George Sutcliffe, the astrologer; and Bessie Leo, wife of the astrologer Alan Leo.

By this time, Alan Leo was gaining a reputation as an astrologer. He ran the *Astrologer's Magazine* (later *Modern Astrology*), and had recently become a professional astrologer, having lost his job as an ice-cream salesman when the company he worked for failed. Leo ran classes and set up one astrological society after another. If you wanted to improve your astrological skills, this was the man you consulted. Louis and Leo exchanged letters in March 1899 about the nature of Saturn, and Leo's 'Many thanks for your practical support of our work' suggests that Louis offered his ventures some financial support.[10] Leo added, 'My fate line stops at the heart line dead. I do not know how this measures out but my end is 57 by my map' which was repeated as one of Louis's predictions.[11] (Leo did indeed die at the age of fifty-seven.) Louis continued to correspond with the Leos for many years.

Although Louis wasn't involved in the multitude of astrological societies that appeared, he may have attended meetings. He certainly knew other prominent astrologers—for example, he wrote a testimonial for George Wilde saying how 'wonderfully true' one of his horoscope readings had been.[12]

Louis said that it was around this time he attended his first séance. (In reality, he'd attended séances on and off for years.) While waiting at a station just outside London, he picked up an abandoned copy of the spiritualist paper *Light*: 'I laughed as I opened it—imagine anyone reading such trash I thought—but I was soon looking it over and reading it myself.'[13]

A séance with Cecil Husk was taking place nearby that afternoon and Louis decided to go along. Husk had been a professional singer until his eyesight deteriorated and he became a full-time medium. In 1891 he was exposed as a fraud when caught leaning over a table pretending to be a spirit by covering his face with phosphorescent paint.

Louis arrived just in time. Before they'd even finished the hymn singing, a pale floating light danced around the room. *Easily faked*, thought Louis. Then he felt something soft and cold pass across his face and pat his head. '"More fake," I mentally said, and wondered how they did it.'[14]

Husk announced that a spirit was going to manifest and to Louis's astonishment, he saw a likeness of his father. While the rest of the group burst into song, Louis's father (via Husk) told Louis that he'd left papers with a solicitor on the Strand. The next day Louis found the solicitor's office and collected these papers. Disappointingly, he never disclosed what they contained.

Margaret Warner's health had worsened and in April 1899 she sent to Ireland for her niece. Unfortunately, shortly after she'd arrived, Margaret's niece's husband fell ill and she was torn whether to return or not. Louis knew the end was near.

> I had just made the remark: 'If we could only get some definite idea how many weeks or days mother will live, you could go over and see your husband and perhaps return in time.' The words were hardly out of my lips when one of the chains on the pendant in the centre of the ceiling was slowly but steadily pulled—the room was plunged in darkness for a second; then the other side moved, the lamp lit up again, and this was repeated three times. 'Does that mean,' I said aloud, 'that mother will only last three days?' In exactly three days my mother breathed her last.[15]

On 2 May 1899 Margaret Warner died and was buried the next day.

Louis was now free to travel, but this couldn't be arranged at the drop of a hat, and it would have been in extremely bad taste to leave immediately after his mother's death. Plus, he was in the midst of the London season.

Edith Halford Thompson was often present at receptions where Louis was a guest. 'He usually arrived late having come on from another "crush" probably at the house of some famous Edwardian hostess where he was one of the lions of the evening.'[16] Edith felt uncomfortable meeting him socially, although they were still conducting their occult experiments, and she usually slipped away before he arrived. But she was there often enough to observe that 'to dance with him was an experience that no woman ever forgot. His partner was drawn into a rhythmic vortex, an ecstasy of movement, in whose harmony the dancers floated' and 'to women he was always courteous, even when their rudeness didn't merit his consideration.'[17]

All this attention from society women was probably behind the assertion that Louis joined an anti-marriage society in early 1899. Such societies certainly existed, although they were usually made up of women who wanted to lead an independent life. Louis maintained he'd been initiated into a society in his early twenties.

> The one I joined consisted of five hundred members bound under a common oath never to enter the bonds of wedlock... Each member paid dues of one hundred pounds per year into a kind of pension fund, which money, with compound interest added, came to a considerable amount when one reached the supposed unmarriageable age of sixty years—called in our ritual, 'the age of wisdom'.... we took an oath to help women in every way that was possible...[18]

'He would have broken his vow to marry me,' said Edith later, although Louis never suggested such a thing.[19]

Many occultists advocated celibacy, including numerous theosophists. Blavatsky had maintained that sexual indulgence had caused untold misery throughout the generations while birth control interfered with the law of reincarnation. Other occult groups and orders also advocated celibacy, including the Golden Dawn. Claiming celibacy not only helped Louis keep women at a distance, it added to his occult credentials. So when he met Katie Bilsborough, who made it clear her interest in Louis wasn't simply occult, he had an easy get-out clause.

> There came one day to my rooms in London... a young girl whose small and beautifully formed hands attracted me even more than she did herself. Beautiful hands have always been a weakness of mine... I foretold that this young girl would have a cruel fate before her; she would marry within a year, lose her husband in some mysterious way that would for a long time

prevent her remarrying. She would meet again and again the man she would eventually marry, but be prevented from doing so for many years…

Looking me straight in the eyes, this young girl of sixteen said quite innocently but impulsively: 'You are the only man I would want to marry; if, as you say, I am fated to lose my first husband, can't you try and make the second come off a bit sooner?'

'What do you mean?' I asked.

'Simply that I mean to have you for my second husband, if I cannot have you for my first.'[20]

Katie *would* get what she wanted and marry Louis, but a lot has to happen before we reach that story.

Louis claimed Katie was descended from Prince Edward I. That's unlikely, but she did have an interesting heritage. She was the granddaughter of Martha Brotherton, an early British Mormon who has gone down in (Mormon, at least) history for refusing, at seventeen, to enter a polygamous marriage with Brigham Young, the second president of the Church of Jesus Christ of Latter-day Saints and the founder of Salt Lake City.

Martha's family had joined the LDS Church in 1840 when Brigham Young was seeking converts in Manchester. The Brothertons were amongst two hundred passengers who left Manchester in September 1841 to join the Saints at their headquarters in Nauvoo, Illinois.

They hadn't been there long when Martha was left alone with Young who wanted to secretly ask her some questions. He asked her what her feelings were towards him and if she'd marry him. Martha was horrified; Young was a married man in his forties and she was under age. She tactfully demurred and was told that Joseph Smith had had a revelation that it was fine for men to have two wives—he had six at the time. Martha wouldn't consider such a thing without consulting her parents. Young locked her in the room and called Joseph Smith who tried to persuade her to marry Young. After all, he was a prophet and knew what was right. He added, 'If you do not like it in a month or two, come to me, and I will make you free again; and if he turns you off, I will take you on.'[21]

As soon as Martha's parents discovered what was going on, they packed and moved to St. Louis, Missouri. They'd been in Nauvoo for nine weeks.[iii] Once the story got out, the Saints denied advocating polygamy

---

iii Martha's sister Elizabeth remained in Nauvoo and polygamously married Parley P Pratt

and dragged Martha's name through the mud, accusing her of being a prostitute. Brigham Young ended up with an estimated fifty-five wives.

Martha remained in America and married James Purnell. Amongst their five children was them Felicia Hemens Purnell and Kate (Catherine) Florence Purnell.[iv] Kate moved to England and married Thomas Bilsborough and their daughter Katie Florence (our Katie) was born 26 April 1882. Martha died in 1863 and her three youngest children, including Felicia, travelled to England to be adopted by Martha's brother Edward.

Katie was no innocent. She was three months pregnant when she married Henry Hartland in June 1899, shortly after Louis met her.

June was a particularly busy month for Louis. He continued to work and perform lectures, for example at the Homolegical Association, an organisation that focused on reading character by external signs—such as physiognomy, palmistry and graphology. His tales were 'amusing and pathetic, and narrated so humorously that all were interested and amused.'[22]

After hours, when not dancing and fending off attractive young girls, he met Edith. Often, he put her into a trance where she recalled glimpses of them being together in past lives. But the real world sometimes intervened. Edith was acting in Ben Greet's company when one of the leading actors who played Macbeth approached her one evening to say, 'I have never seen such eyes in my life... Where are you staying? I will come and see you.'[23]

A few days later he arrived at her boarding house and asked her if she fancied accompanying him to on the midnight train to Edinburgh the next day. Somehow, Louis discovered what was going on and told Edith that unless she wrote to turn him down, he'd write to her father. 'That man is a blackguard,' he said, adding, 'Has he ever kissed you?'[24]

Edith denied anything improper had taken place, 'hiding my face in my hands, murmuring, "I hate you."'[25]

Despite her tears, Louis was adamant and said that one day she'd thank him.

> His eyes... flamed into my own. I gave a sharp cry, for a stab of agonising pain had shot through my right eye and... into my brain... the strange feeling came to me that I was being overpowered, overshadowed by some intense force that, though

---

who went on to have twelve wives, though he was later killed by one of their husbands.
iv Presumably named after the then-famous poet Felicia Hemens.

it came from him was not part of his personality. Instinctively, I felt it was useless to resist any longer...[26]

Now word had got around, Edith's reputation would be forever soiled if she went ahead with the trip. Greet turned up at her lodgings the next morning, scolded her for considering such a thing and said he was taking her to Exeter—Edith's home town. When Edith petulantly asked, 'Who told you?' Greet said, 'Your friend Cheiro. I believe he is in love with you.'[27]

'Anything more unloverlike than Cheiro's friendship with me it would have been hard to imagine,' Edith said sulkily, but she did as she'd been told.[28]

And then Louis had to turn his attention in a different direction, entirely. In the mid-1890s, there was a singer/actor in London. He liked reciting poetry and took up palmistry for a while. He also went through a multitude of names, at one point claiming descent from a French count. His own story is a ripping yarn, but more to the point Cheiro testified in court that he'd known him and his wife in 1890.

Louis had been subpoenaed as a witness for palmist Edith Valentia Keighley, who worked under the name of 'Satanella' at a waxworks in Cardiff and was suing the magazine *Society* for libel. Going to court wasn't going to be comfortable for Louis. There'd recently been rumblings about the legality of palmistry and further arrests of palmists. On one hand, in June 1898 Sir Matthew White Ridley had said in the House of Commons that palmistry was perfectly legal so long as there was no attempt at fraud. On the other, in April 1899 Georgina Jones had been fined for practising palmistry in Manchester. Some palmists called themselves 'palmist entertainers' to indicate they weren't trying to con anyone, only offer them a good time.

That Louis seemed to be above the law often drew comments: 'Is it because he is a man of good birth, breeding, and education, and would know how to defend himself, and the art in which he honestly believes; or is it because he has been consulted by hundreds of the élite of London?'[29]

Louis couldn't fly completely under the radar and turned up to court prepared to defend his profession. The story went like this:

In 1896 Edith Keighley worked for a few weeks as a palmist under the name of 'Satanella' in Bond Street, which was when Louis had met her. She was married to Frederick Keighley (the man whose life sounded like Cheiro's) and their marriage was a disaster.[v] Not only did Edith's husband give her gonnorhea in 1894, he also punched and kicked her. Edith left the

---

v Born Frederick Timothy and also known as Donald Cornwallis.

country with their two children and returned in 1897. Again, she endured her husband's violence and irrational behaviour—in May 1897 he forced her to go skating by making her drink potassium bromide (a common sedative). She began divorce proceedings and moved to Wales. Later she discovered Frederick had started living with 'May' Brown in 1897.

When Edith Keighley read the article in *Society* she was horrified:

> Callan was the co-respondent in a divorce suit, while the respondent was the notorious Satanella... who practised the mystery of psychometrist and clairvoyant. Callan assisted this person in her nefarious work, who, it must be admitted, was a most attractive woman, and whose fascinating personality was largely influential in bringing grist to the joint mill... Satanella for the time is lost to sight, if not to memory dear. Were she to get her deserts, she should be made to join the scoundrel Callan in that retirement where the wicked cease from troubling.[30]

Owen McDonnell Callan (sometimes Willie Terris) was the worst person anyone could be associated with, although he 'used to live in Hyde Park Mansions, was always faultlessly dressed, and was well known in Fleet Street and the Strand and in theatrical circles.'[31] In 1893 he'd been convicted of fraud after he and Mabel Nesbitt conspired to extort money from James Westwood Meakin by charging him with being the father of Nesbitt's baby, although no child existed. In 1897 he appeared in a divorce case after being accused of adultery with Minnie Brown. Minnie was living with a Mr Russell when she married and took up with a Mr Hancock before she started seeing Callan and was divorced. This was the 'May' Brown who lived with Frederick Keighley.

In May 1898, Callan was arrested for attempted murder. He'd taken out life insurance worth £50,000 on Hubert Birkin while working as his secretary, and the two had travelled to Tangier. Late one night, Callan asked Birkin to look out of the hotel window to see whether the street lights were out. When Birkin obliged, Callan tried to throw him out of the window. Birkin ran downstairs calling for help, so Callan chased him, grabbed Birkin by the throat and fired his pistol at him. Then Callan began to beat him about the head with a life preserver. The two were taken to the British Consulate where Callan said Birkin had attempted suicide and he'd acted in self-defence. It was down to the cocaine Birkin had taken, he said. Given that Birkin had 'contracted tastes which have led to misunderstandings now and then' and was one of the three people who'd offered Oscar Wilde £1,000 towards a fresh start when he was released from prison, Callan's suggestion that Birkin was insane was seriously considered.[32] However, Callan was arrested and convicted of murder.

Edith Keighley insisted that readers would understand her to be 'Satanella' and sent a solicitor to see the owners of Society. He called at the publishing office and said if they didn't tell him who was responsible, he would take further steps and was told, 'You can take any steps you like as long you don't take the office furniture.'[33]

It may have been an understandable error given that Frederick Keighley and 'Mrs Cornwallis' advertised their services under the names of 'Saturn and Satanella' in 1898, but Edith Keighley insisted her reputation was damaged and Londoners would no longer give her business. (It didn't help that she'd been charged with fortune telling in Swansea, although charges were dismissed.)

Those in court regularly broke into laughter at the long exchanges about palmistry and clairvoyance. There was also much discussion about how beautiful Mrs Cornwallis was, and everyone decided that nice as Edith was, she couldn't be described as beautiful—she happily agreed. Louis identified Edith Keighley as Frederick Keighley's true wife and said how respectable she was—not like Mrs Cornwallis.

I felt extremely nervous when from my seat at the back of the court, I heard the name 'Cheiro' called, and I found the plaintiff's solicitor ushering me into the witness-box.

'You will have the redoubtable Marshall Hall to cross-examine you,' he whispered, 'for God's sake keep your head.'...

I only wonder I did not drop dead with fright... Q.C. Marshall Hall was already standing up, looking at me with a curious, sarcastic, ironical expression on his face that pulled me together as nothing else could... to my mind... he seemed a kind of intellectual god calling me before the judgment seat of Truth.[34]

Edward Marshall Hall was already famous, although his major cases, when he'd successfully defend numerous people accused of murder, were yet to come. He'd featured heavily in the press in 1890 when his wife Ethel had fallen pregnant by her lover and died of a botched abortion. Her lover, the abortionist, and several others were indicted for Ethel's murder, and the abortionist, Dr Albert Laermann, was convicted. Marshall Hall became renowned for defending women maltreated by men.

The first questions posed to Louis came from Mr. Macaskie, acting on behalf of Society's printers. He asked what palmistry was. Louis said:

'If we went into discussion upon that I am afraid would take up a great deal of your time and too much of mine. (Laughter.)...'
'You know better than we do?'
'I should rather hope so. (Laughter.) It would take much too long explain it to you.' (Laughter.)[35]

By the time Marshall Hall questioned Louis, he was playing to his audience. Oddly, Marshall Hall felt the same and they engaged in banter that delighted their audience.

'Do you suggest you can foretell the future?'
'So far as the tendencies of the person are concerned I can do that.'
'Perhaps you have told the Plaintiff what the result of this action will be?' (Laughter.)
'I have not read her hand.'[36]
Ah, but you have not seen my hand, you know. I don't know whether you can read it that distance?
'No, your character is too deep to read that distance. It... would make [an] interesting study, I'm sure. (Laughter.)
'I'm afraid it would. It is rather blistered. (Renewed laughter.)[37]

Finally, Justice Wills said, 'it was such a libel that it was not easy, even for a judge, to look on it without indignation.'[38] He awarded Edith Keighley £1,000.[vi]

That evening Louis was dining at the Carlton and bumped into Marshall Hall. After a jolly exchange where Marshall Hall said how impressed he'd been with Louis's prowess as a witness, they arranged to meet so Louis could read his palm. Marshall Hall had been interested in the occult since 1894 when he'd observed an experiment in automatic writing.

---

vi Frederick and Edith Keighley were finally divorced in 1900. He worked as a palmist under the name of 'Kismet' and married Minnie in 1901—she filed for divorce in 1906 on the grounds of cruelty. Although a decree nisi was granted, it was withdrawn the following year as she was found guilty of adultery. They never divorced. Keighley moved to Australia and turned to film, directing *The Newsboy's Debt* in 1914 and producing *The Veil of Kismet* in 1915, in which he recited his poems. By now, he called himself Count de Cassinette. He remarried in Australia in 1923 (despite never having divorced Minnie) and was convicted of fraud in 1926. The 1911 census shows that Edith Keighley ended up in the Convent Home Of The Good Shepherd in Finchley, working as a laundress with her daughter, Dorothy.

He'd handed the medium, Mrs Labouchere, a letter and asked her who'd sent it. Labouchere had said that the letter's author had died the day before which turned out to be true—or rather, he'd died two days earlier which wasn't too much of a discrepancy. That Louis's reading took place is attested to by a letter Marshall Hall wrote in 1924 referring to a reading he'd had in August 1899.

But Louis's planned American trip didn't happen, even though he'd engaged Major Pond to arrange a lecture tour. In August he was summonsed as co-respondent in a divorce case. He rushed to Marshall Hall for advice. Marshall Hall responded with, "'I am very sorry,'" and then under his breath, he added, "Guilty, of course.... Well, don't be frightened, better men than you have been in the same position, but let us hope the woman was at least pretty'".[39]

Louis told Marshall Hall a long involved story about a client who'd visited him every fortnight for the last six months—she'd also sent him piles of letters, unfortunately now stolen. In June Louis had attended a ball where he'd danced with a veiled lady. At the end of the evening he'd approached a woman believing it to be her, and as he did so her husband punched him. After a scuffle, it transpired this was another woman entirely, so Louis offered to escort her back to the Savoy. Then he exited via the back door and the watching detectives reported he'd spent the night with this woman. Louis then decided to take a holiday and while at the French seaside, he saved a woman from drowning. Serendipitously, she was the woman he'd been dancing with. Everything was sorted out and Louis was able to go to the US.

It didn't happen like that. Louis was accused of having sex with a client in his consulting rooms.

On 28 August 1899 stockbroker Shaftesbury Edward Henry Walmisley filed for divorce stating that ten days earlier his wife Mary had committed adultery with 'Leigh de Hamong'. Walmisley sought divorce and £5,000 in damages from Louis, as well as custody of his son. Although I haven't tracked down any press reports of the case, word would soon have got around. Louis simply denied it. The case dragged on and after oral affidavits (unrecorded) were submitted, it was finally dismissed in July 1900 due to a lack of evidence.

One evening, Louis told Edith Halford Thompson he was leaving and she'd soon meet her future husband, although she'd be a widow after not too long. And she'd have a child who'd die in an accident. All Edith heard was 'I am going to America.'[40]

'No, I cannot take you with me,' Louis said, although Edith hadn't asked. 'This marriage is inevitable... but it is only a phase, you will come back to me. I shall probably be in America three years. Three years is not a very long time... What is the matter? So you don't hate me any more?'[41]

'I don't think I ever hated you,' said Edith. 'I—I love you.'[42]

'Child—my dear—little child,' said Louis.[43]

Edith, maybe prudently, didn't say what happened next.

Louis had had a narrow escape. Maybe more than one. On 14 December 1899, Edith Halford Thompson married the actor William Ashcroft.[vii]

---

vii Real name William Nelson.

CHAPTER

TEN

*Search, student then, within my hand, and see
The warp and web of things that yet may be.*[1]

FTER A SHORT VISIT TO PARIS in October 1899, Louis—as Count Hamong—finally arrived in New York on 24 November. This wasn't the glorious return of Cheiro. The cancelled contract with Major Pond remained cancelled.

In December Louis visited Boston to lecture on behalf of Lady Jennie Spencer-Churchill, the American-born British wife of Lord Randolph Churchill, and mother of the later Prime Minister Winston Churchill. One of hundreds of American heiresses who'd married into the British aristocracy, she was known as 'the panther' and had a snake tattooed on her wrist. Throughout her marriage Jennie had taken hundreds of lovers, including the Prince of Wales. Randolph Churchill had died in 1895 and Jennie had moved to Paris. At this point, she was raising money for the Boer War effort.

Louis's talk gained scant attention, though he was determined to convince Americans of what good fighters the English were: 'In all my life I never knew the English people to be so united and full of the war feeling. They would fight in this mood any nation of Europe without another thought.'[2] It wasn't the most tactful comment given the unsteady relationship between Britain and France at the time and the fear of war breaking out.

Louis moved on to Washington before returning to Boston and then onto New York. At least his identity couldn't be under doubt as he displayed the portrait painted of him by Jean Paul Selinger. 'Cheiro's name has been appropriated by a man in Buffalo,' pointed out one newspaper, 'and another in Boston, Christy, rightly called, on whom an injunction had been served lately restraining him from appearing under that title, and should he persist in the deception, imposing a penalty of $700 if detected.'[3]

Another 'Cheiro', Oliver Brownwell, had recently featured in news reports after he was shot in Baltimore by a Dr Whiting after an argument about a screen he'd left in Whiting's house after being evicted.

To be fair, Cheiro's name wasn't original with him and numerous Madam Cheiros had appeared in the 1890s, such as Miss Alexander who worked under that name at a church bazaar in Grantham, Lincolnshire in 1894.[4] There was also Madame Cheiro who appeared in Dublin alongside a 'Specially engaged flying lady... graphologists. The greatest novelty of the age, the cyclophoron. Chinese shooting jungle with birds flitting through the foliage' in 1895.[5]

Once Cheiro had achieved fame, Cheiros popped up all over the US. For example, in 1900 there was Cheiro Junior of St Louis; Mrs Cheiro the famous scientific palmist of San Francisco and Prof Cheiro of Oklahoma.[6] Some tried to suggest a more direct connection to Louis such as Madam Hamong of Massachusetts in 1902.[7]

Most of them used the name 'Cheiro' simply as a description of their work. A few hinted at a connection with Louis, but didn't try to suggest they were Louis. Except for one.

Carl Roth was an occult wonder. At least, that's what he said.[8] It's unclear who Roth was or where he was from (a report of his wife's death suggests he came from Connecticut) but he thought he was the 'world's famous and greatest medium and astrologist'.[9] Roth was so certain of his abilities that he had a notary public take his sworn statement that as a clairvoyant, he'd refuse a fee unless the client was satisfied.[10]

Ambitious Roth pulled in plenty of clients in San Francisco. By March 1899 he claimed to have another office in New York and had taken up palmistry. He happily displayed photos and plaster casts of hands of his eminent clients, including those of many of Cheiro's clients.

But he shared more than a few clients with Louis. By March 1899 he was to travelling the country as 'Karl von Roth', a German (or perhaps Swiss) phenomenon. Apparently, he'd graduated from law school in Hedielberg and then travelled to India with Countess Constance

Wachtmeister, a close friend of Helena Blavatsky's. That month, Roth also revealed he was *really* Cheiro.

He worked under that name in Utah, somewhere Louis had never been, or expressed any interest in visiting. In summer 1899 Roth also visited Boise, Idaho and Santa Fe, New Mexico as 'Cheiro'. By September he was Karl von Roth Hamong and claimed to have written Cheiro's Language of the Hand, as well as Blanca de Ovies' *Psycho Palmistry Key*, a series of lessons on palmistry.[i]

Roth settled in El Paso, Texas, saying he was the brother of Émile de Hamong and the two of them combined were the real Cheiro. Or they were both instructors at a national school of palmists in New York and Karl had written the books.

The names of Cheiro's famous clients were public knowledge, but Roth's careful efforts to ensure he conducted business in places Cheiro never visited or indicated he might visit is worthy of note. When he ended up somewhere Louis might be known, he claimed to be his brother.[ii]

It helped that Roth was attractive. 'He is a slim man of medium height, good looking, has a beautiful complexion and is a tasty but not loud dresser'.[11] Unfortunately, he was less of an occult wonder than he said and rumours soon circulated that Roth was less than honest. Finally, the authorities began to catch up with him. In May 1900 he had to hurriedly leave Hartford, Connecticut to escape creditors; in May 1901 he narrowly escaped conviction because his victims refused to testify; in January 1903 he was convicted of grand larceny in Utah; and in 1906 he was convicted for practising medicine without a licence. Most of Roth's victims were women and the majority refused to take legal action due to embarrassment.

> [Roth] a man who, attired in a high silk hat and a long Prince Albert coat, was wont to disport himself in front of the Kenyon hotel and in prominent places, for the benefit of the fair sex. With an American Beauty rose in the lapel of his coat, and a Turkish cigarette held tightly in his glove clad fingers, Mr. Roth would attempt conquests of the fair sex by stepping in front of women who were passing in the street and attempting to intrude

---

i Countess de Ovies—originally Minnie Blanche MacDonald—described herself as a 'society entertainer' and her husband was both a Chilean ambassador and an exiled Spanish count.

ii As he did in Chicago in September 1899.

his personality on them. Repulsed as he often was, he was not ruffled... many threats made against him.[12]

Without professional help (he could have done with Major Pond) there was little Louis could do to retrieve his reputation in the US. People prepared to con society women of thousands of dollars (Roth wasn't the only palmist to do this) were hardly likely to worry about who had the right to use the name 'Cheiro', especially as it was long established as a name for palmists. The damage had been done and Louis needed to go elsewhere. Which is exactly what he did.

Most of Louis's world—the society world—was heading to Paris for the Exposition, scheduled from 15 April to 12 November. Louis was among the many who sailed from New York to Paris on 10 April.

The first international exposition had been held in London in 1851— the Great Exhibition of the Works of Industry of All Nations at the Crystal Palace. Numerous world fairs followed, several hosted by France. (Famously, the Eiffel Tower was built for the 1889 Exposition.) The 1900 Exposition had been planned since 1892 when the French heard the Germans were planning a 1900 exposition. Determined to be the country that hosted the exposition at the threshold of the new century, France announced their intention.

The site covered 216 hectares and would be visited by nearly 50 million people—60,000 visitors an hour passed through the gates. The temporary buildings sat on iron frames covered with plaster and staff (cheap artificial stone), many still under construction when the Exposition opened.

The main entrance, the Porte Monumental de Paris on the Place de la Concorde, was crowned by a huge statue, La Parisienne, dressed in modern Paris fashion. At night the gateway was illuminated by 3,200 light bulbs and forty arc lamps. Forty thousand visitors an hour could pass beneath the arch to approach the twenty-six ticket booths.

Once inside, you could choose from thousands of sights and activities. Perhaps you'd visit the Palace of Electricity and the adjoining Water Castle. The enormous Palace (420 metres long and 60 metres wide) was in the form of a giant peacock spreading its tail and its central tower was crowned by an illuminated star and a chariot carrying a statue of the Spirit of Electricity. Thousands upon thousands of electric lights graced the site, and you could even visit the steam-powered generators that provided the electricity. The Water Castle was formed of two domes between which was a gigantic fountain that which was illuminated at night by continually changing coloured lights.

The Gallery of Machines showed advances in industrial technology and featured a huge cinema. However, the best display of motion pictures was at the Phono-Ciné Theatre where the screen image was synchronised to the sound from phonographs. Or you could enjoy the Cinéorama which simulated a voyage in a balloon with a film projected on a circular screen below the spectators.

You could visit the Palace of Optics with the Great Paris Exposition Telescope, the world's largest refracting telescope, which enlarged the image of the moon ten thousand times. The image was projected on a screen in a hall which seated two thousand visitors. And a giant kaleidoscope, attracted three million visitors, plus you could see demonstrations of X-rays and dancers performing in phosphorescent costumes, or visit the Palace of Illusions which created a show from mirrors and electric lighting.

There was also the largest aquarium in the world; the Grande Roue de Paris Ferris wheel; moving sidewalks (with handles to hold onto if you got worried); escalators; the telegraphone (the first magnetic audio recorder); the *Mareorama*, which simulated a voyage by ship (viewers stood on the railing of a ship simulator, watching painted images pass by while the ship rocked the 'ship' and fans blew gusts of wind); the Globe Céleste, an immense planetarium; the Rue des Nations with pavilions representing the participating countries, each containing their own wonders; the Palace of Furniture and Decoration; and the Agriculture pavilion, which included the hugely popular Champagne Palace.

Less worthy options included Vieux Paris, a recreation of the streets of old Paris; recreations of bazaars, souks and street markets of Algiers and Tunis and Laos; the Swiss Village; theatres (Sarah Bernhardt had her own) and music halls. The Rue de Paris was lined with music venues, a comedy theatre, marionettes, American jazz, a Grand Guignol theatre, and the Backwards House, which had its furniture on the ceiling, its chandeliers on the floor, and windows which gave reverse images.

And there was much, much more, including thousands of vendors—one of whom was Louis. [iii]

Many of the illustrious clients Louis wrote about were people he met at the Exposition, including King Humbert of Italy whose assassination

---

iii At his rooms at 4 Rue de clement Marot.

he claimed to have predicted. And after making a speech at a lunch hosted by American Commissioner Senator Thomas Walsh, Louis met King Leopold II of Belgium.

Today, Leopold is viewed as one of the worst representatives of colonialism, a corrupt leader who laid claim to the Congo and was responsible for numerous atrocities, including torture and murder. The hands of men, women, and children were amputated when the quota of rubber was not met and ten million Congolese were murdered. The scandal was yet to break when Louis met him, and Leopold didn't relinquish control of the colony until 1908.

A few days later, Louis encountered the King at a reception also hosted by Walsh which led to Leopold attending Louis's rooms for a consultation. After smelling Louis's lunch, the King decided he wanted an Irish stew, so Louis commanded his cook to make one. Apparently, this led to an invitation to Laeken Palace in Brussels and Louis hastily made a trip there to read the King's palm. Leopold cooked an Irish stew shortly after Louis's arrival and then they got down to palm reading. This story may be taking the idea of the unreliable narrator to the extreme, considering that Louis states in the same telling that the encounter took place both while he was at the Paris Exposition and in 1907. He never explains why the King was such a fan of Irish stew.

Louis didn't need to meet royalty to make predictions about them. Shortly after his arrival he told a journalist from the *American Register* that Queen Victoria would die in 1901. The *Register* had better manners than to print the prediction at the time, so it didn't appear until after the Queen's death. That didn't matter. Business was booming and Cheiro was soon 'the great palmist, whose success here is phenomenal'.[13]

On 10 July he was amongst the largely American audience who watched Loie Fuller perform her famous Serpentine Dance, in which her silk costumes were illuminated by multi-coloured lighting of her own design. Her performance was widely reproduced in photographs, paintings and drawings, although no film remains of her.[iv] Fuller, who was later credited with defining modern dance, was then at the height of her powers.

It was her dancing, her graceful and original swirling of draperies, and her marvellous manipulation of coloured lights that suggested certain effects to the young artist's sculpture,

---

iv Marie Louise Fuller was from Chicago. The film that pops up on YouTube claiming to be of Fuller is actually of 'Papinta', Caroline Holpin from Minnesota.

jewellery, and house decoration, whose is the admiration of all visitors to the Exhibition... Around the stage are great dark curtains ready to open upon the dance. Outside the whole of the lower part of the facade formed of a figure of the dancer with tier skirts swirling and stretching away on either side, the whole being coloured plaster... After the lights went out the band played soft music, and Loie began to dance. It was indeed a feast for the eye to watch those graceful movements, those ever-changing, but always perfect, combinations of colour...[14]

Another of Louis's royal encounters was with Muzaffer-ed-Din, the Shah of Persia, then the guest of the French Government and a source of endless fascination.

The Shah... preferred to employ his fingers in dealing with meats and salads. Another story told of him is that he caused his Persian servants to be flogged almost daily for the least offence, and once even ordered one who had upset a candle-stick on the table, burning the Shah's hand slightly, to be decapitated. French advisers had great trouble in making the Eastern ruler understand that he must refrain from such practices...

The thing that bewildered the Shah more than all the other wonders he saw was the affection of the European husband for his one wife; even long after age had rendered her unattractive.... 'In my harem all the women are young.' The papers say that he engaged two young and pretty women acrobats whom he noticed at the Hippodrome Circus to perform later at his palace, and that five French girls, four of whom were dancers and one an expert photographer, were sent to Teheran to await his return....

The... cost of the Shah's purchases while he was in Paris was more than 1,600.000 dollars. When the Shah and his Persian colony vacated the sumptuous mansion provided by the French Government for visiting Royalty it was found necessary to thoroughly clean the entire establishment. Many priceless tapestries, carpets, and pieces of furniture were ruined.[15]

On 31 July Louis predicted that the Shah would be victim of an assassination attempt, based on similarities with his relationship to numbers (or astrological factors) as King Humbert had. On the morning of 4 August:

A man dressed in the ordinary clothing of a Paris workman darted forward from between two automobiles where he was hidden and rushed toward the imperial carriage, overthrowing a bicycle policeman, who rolled under the feet of the horses. In an instant he was on the carriage step. Holding the door with his left hand, with his right he pushed a revolver toward the breast of the shah. He seemed to hesitate for a moment, as though undecided where to aim. This hesitation saved the Persian monarch's life, for, before the would-be assassin could pull the trigger, a strong hand grasped his wrist and wrenched it so that the weapon dropped harmlessly to the bottom of the landau. 'I'd like to have a photograph of that man,' nonchalantly exclaimed the shah.[16]

Louis was summoned to the Palais des Souverains. 'I will confess that I felt a little trepidation at having to face such an ordeal. However, I determined to keep myself well in hand and to endeavour to treat him exactly as though he were an ordinary consultant.'[17] He was challenged to ascertain psychically what was going on in Tehran at that moment. Of course, Louis got it right.

He genuinely did go to the Palais. And he received a medal for making his prediction: 'The Grand Vizier of the Shah... introduced 'Cheiro' to the Shah at the Palais des Souverains, when the Shah conferred upon him the decoration of the Lion and the Sun of Persia, which decoration (the green ribbon of Persia) 'Cheiro ' has now the pleasure of wearing.'[18] However, it wasn't the private audience he made out: 'During his visit the shah decorated 240 people, including Cheiro.'[19]

Louis also met the astronomer Camille Flammarion:

I received an invitation to go and dine with him and Madame Flammarion *en famille* in their apartment close to the celebrated Observatory in Juvisy close to Paris... One magnificent night in June, a night I shall never forget, high up in the Observatory, we watched the stars for hours, until the dawn came... Our conversation had turned from the wonders of Nature to the probabilities of life after death, and my host listened with rapt attention to some of my experiences in research work in spiritism...[20]

And later he bumped into Oscar Wilde. Back in early 1895, the Marquess of Queensberry, father of Wilde's lover, Lord Alfred Douglas, had left his calling card at Wilde's club, inscribed, 'For Oscar Wilde, posing somdomite' [sic]. Wilde prosecuted Queensberry for libel but the trial unearthed evidence that caused Wilde to drop his charges and led to his arrest and trial for gross indecency with men. Wilde refused to leave England and he was eventually sentenced to two years' hard labour and jailed from 1895 to 1897. Once released, he left immediately for France and never returned to Britain. When Louis claimed to have encoutered him, Wilde was poverty stricken, drinking heavily and depressed by embarrassing chance encounters with people he'd known in better days.

> I had been dining… with friends, and as we sat on the terrace of one of the principal restaurants, a strange, gaunt, broken figure passed and took a seat far away from the crowd. I should not have recognized him if some of our party had not exclaimed, 'Why, that's Oscar Wilde!' Instinctively I rose. 'I must go and speak to him,' I said. 'If you do,' my host replied, 'you need not return.' I accepted the challenge and went to Wilde and held out my hand. In his terrible loneliness he held it for a moment and then burst into tears. 'My dear friend,' he said, 'how good of you! Everyone cuts me now. How good of you to come to me!'[21]

Whether Wilde then rushed to the riverside and contemplated ending his life is more debatable.

> As he stood on the parapet the moon shone out and outlined every curve of the massive, broken figure that seemed about to plunge into the quiet river at his feet. I reached his side, and clutched his arm, but he as suddenly turned, and with the most satirical laugh I have ever heard, said: 'No, my boy, they shall not say that Oscar took his own life. How the dogs would yelp and the Press would ring with their graphic descriptions!'[22]

Wilde would die from meningitis in November 1900, only a few months after Louis last saw him.

Once the summer had ended, Louis was worn out. He was friendly with Prince Marco Colonna of Rome who'd suggested Louis should call on him if he was ever nearby. *I need a holiday*, thought Louis. And he never turned down an invitation, even if it was made from no more than politeness.

> A doctor friend called to see me… 'You are seriously overworking; your nervous system cannot stand the strain without some rest, if you do not take even a few weeks off, there will be a collapse.' Just then I received a letter from an old friend who was living

in Rome, asking me if I could come over and be his guest for a few weeks... On arriving in Rome, I sent a message to Prince Colonna, mentioning that I had arrived.[23]

Prince Colonna might have sighed, but he also took Louis to the Vatican and arranged for him to meet Pope Leo XIII. Louis and the Pope had a nice chat about occult number symbolism, and the Pope introduced Louis to Cardinal Guiseppe Sarto. According to Louis, Sarto was interested in astrology and they had many other meetings, during one of which Louis predicted he'd be elected Pope from his horoscope (he'd become Pope Pius X in 1903). But more excitingly, he offered Louis a tour of the Vatican library. It was here that Louis discovered manuscripts that revealed 'chemical discoveries... of the greatest importance...' [24] The story of these manuscripts will be told later.

In November that year, Louis met Mata Hari, the Dutch exotic dancer who was convicted of being a spy for Germany during World War I. Born Margaretha Zelle, Hari had married Dutch Captain Rudolf MacLeod after he'd advertised in the newspapers, and moved to Java, Indonesia to live with him. Their marriage was a disaster as MacLeod was an alcoholic and regularly beat Margaretha as well as keeping a concubine. In 1896, Margaretha joined a dance company and adopted the name of Mata Hari (in Malay, 'sun'—literally, 'eye of the day') but she returned to her husband.

> I was walking home one night from a meeting organized by an English woman for the aid of the badly treated cats and dogs of Paris, when I noticed a few paces ahead an extremely graceful figure of a woman that I could not help but admire. It was a bitterly cold night, the woman before me had no coat: vanity, I thought—women will do anything for vanity, just because she has such a graceful figure she will risk pneumonia to show it off.
>
> I turned and went back towards the brazier; she was still standing there with her hands stretched towards the fire. I suppose I said the wrong thing. Men always do when they try to be kind.[25]

Louis said he took her home and she spent the night on a rug in front of the fire. That he did meet Mata Hari is confirmed by her handprint in Confessions, dated 1900. But his predictions are based on a horoscope calculated for a completely wrong birthday.

'He did not love Mata Hari,' pointed out Edith.[26] But Louis did keep a large photo of her displayed in his Bond Street rooms and was certainly taken with her: 'Mata Hari was... handsome as a queen, fascinating, intelligent, beautiful.'[27]

Things were going well for Louis, but he was growing too confident, too inflated with self-importance. In late December 1900:

> Cheiro... was ignominiously ejected from an Embassy reception in Paris, by order of the Ambassador, General Porter. The palmist had been invited to the reception by General Porter's wife and daughter, who were among Cheiro's most devoted adherents... the United States Ambassador did not like the way the Oriental conducted himself at the function, and accelerated his departure therefrom in a manner more practical than poetic.[28] v

After this, Louis went quiet. Indeed, he disappears from newspapers for several months. He'd ceased working as a palmist and in summer 1901, newspapers announced his retirement.

> Cheiro wishes to notify that since January last he has ceased his Professional Career as CHEIRO, and warns his numerous clientele and the public against persons fraudulently imitating or using his name in both London and the provinces.[29]

> Count Hamong... has retired from the business a millionaire... The only known man to make a million telling fortunes has bought a chateau in the champagne country, where he has gone to cultivating vines.[30]

Although he spent most of the year in Paris, Louis took a brief holiday at the Hotel Metropole in Brighton in September. He was certainly in Paris in late April 1902 as he attended a reception for Helen and Josephine Bowen at the home of Charles Holman Black and Frank Holman. Nothing more is recorded in the press or in his own writing. But he obviously got up to *something*—that something was Katie Hartland, the girl with the beautiful hands.

Katie and her husband Henry, along with their five-month-old son Jack, had arrived in Boston in May 1901. Unfortunately, Henry was unable to find a job in Boston and so went to seek work in New York—he

---

v Although Louis didn't look 'oriental', the fact he performed palmistry was enough to land him with this description. It was, after all, primarily an 'oriental' activity.

soon found a job as a purchasing agent for the Mallory Steamship Line in Manhattan.

Henry left Katie and their baby in Boston, occasionally visiting them at weekends. Katie was furious. 'I told him it was terrible to leave me, a nineteen-year-old girl and our child here in a foreign country, and he said he'd send for me as soon as he got a job.' she said later[31] But he didn't, although he sent Katie $7 out of the $11 he earned each week. When they did see each other, there was 'constant bickering on money matters.'[32] 'I was giving her all I had,' Henry explained.[33]

Katie wanted to go on the stage but Henry firmly opposed that idea, although she threatened to do so, anyway. Even worse, 'She was running around with someone else and I was jealous,' Henry said.[34] 'She was sick and tired of me and paying attention to somebody else.'[35] He told Katie, 'If you are to continue as you are doing I shall go away.'[36]

The someone else was Louis.

It isn't clear how Katie made contact with him again, or precisely when Louis was in the US, but she did and they didn't even make a half-hearted effort to be discreet. Louis said Katie was a widow, so that didn't matter:

> She was in widow's weeds, but as her husband's body had not been found, they being both of English nationality, she would have to wait seven years, she told me, before the courts would allow his death to be presumed.[37]

Except Henry wasn't dead when they met. He was very much alive and at the end of his tether. Henry threatened to leave Katie, but she was unperturbed. In desperation he wrote to her, 'I will try to live happily if you will; if not we can but go on as we are until something happens.'[38]

On 23 June 1902, Katie visited Henry in New York. They attended a show and spent the night at a hotel. The next day Katie returned to Boston and sent Henry a letter saying, 'I send this in fond remembrance of our last night spent together… Goodbye. Sincerely, your wife.'[39] She enclosed a photo of their son Jack and this was the last time he saw her for forty years.

Then without further ado, Katie became a chorus girl. Maybe Louis used his contacts to help her get started—it's anyone's guess. For the next two years she toured the US as part of the cast for *The Prince of Pilsen* and *Babes in Toyland*.

Back in England, Louis needed something to occupy his time. It was all very well retiring as a palmist, and he had more than enough money, but he was bored. So in December 1902 he decided to buy a newspaper and move to Paris.

Cheiro [is] better at palmistry than wine making and lost a lot of money in champagne… [He] has now bought the American Register.[40]

Cheiro, 1898

OCCULT NUMBERS

Cheiro won't tell you he uses 'numerology', because that meant 'arithmetic' until after the 1910s. But he can tell you how to make the occult significance of numbers work for you.

First you need to know that there are really only nine numbers. Anything over 10 is reduced to its root number. For example, 11 is 1 + 1 = 2.[i]

The number of your zodiac sign has a special meaning to you, even more so if the date you're born on is the matching number.

Aries: 9 positive	Taurus: 6 positive
Gemini: 5 positive	Cancer: 2-7 (negative 2, positive 7)
Leo: 1-4 (negative 4, positive 1)	Virgo: 6 negative
Libra: 6 negative	Scorpio: 9 negative
Sagittarius: 3 positive	Capricorn: 8 postive
Aquarius: 8 negative	Pisces: 3 negative

Positive numbers are more physical while negative numbers are more mental. The best time for success is during a month that matches your number. Your number is more strongly emphasised on a date that corresponds with your number. For example, if your number is a 3, the 3rd, 12th, 21st or 30th of the month are most positive for you.

You're also likely to be attracted to people with whom you share a number. However, the Sun and Moon numbers (Leo and Cancer) are always attracted to each other.

People often ask Cheiro how they can change from an unlucky

---

i This used to be called 'theosophical reduction' because theosophists were fond of the method, but it's much older than that.

number to a luckier one, especially those born under a 3 or 4. If this is you and you are also born on a 4 day of the month, avoid doing important things on dates making an 8. It's best to rely on your month number rather than date number in these cases.

However, if you are born on a 3 or 4 day in an 8 month, don't select the number of the month, because that will make the power of the 4 and 8 even stronger. Instead, choose the opposite month number (count 6 signs forward).

CHAPTER
ELEVEN

Cheiro has been the rage in Paris for some time past and has been particularly petted by the feminines of the 'American' colony, who admired his peculiar beauty even more than his palm divination.[1]

*W*HAT WAS PARIS LIKE WHEN LOUIS ARRIVED? BUSY. His was the world of Right Bank Paris. Not the Paris of artists and writers of the Left Bank but one of money—serious amounts of money. Amongst heiresses and self-made millionaires were also lawyers and entrepreneurs. Paris was a relatively cheap place for Americans to live and many travelled between different addresses, so it's difficult to work out how many Americans were in Paris at any given time, but there were a lot.

From summer until late autumn, much of Paris was more American than French. Wealthy Americans socialised in London during the season, and as soon as summer approached they moved to Paris. They stuck together, forming groups for everything from drinking coffee to attending lectures. Groups often formed around their state or city of origin or among people of comparable wealth and similar family backgrounds. Slightly more American women than men lived in Paris, and although many lived with family members, a large number lived in a way that was impossible back in the US.

This was the American Colony, the home for those who regarded themselves as residents rather than tourists. Everyone knew each other's business—at least, they tried their best to know each other's business.

Despite arriving to experience European culture, they wanted an American version of it. Therefore, American shops and businesses blazed with electric lights. You could find an American dentist, jewellers, shoe shop, bookstore or café. Trams, cars and buses were at least half-American. Several of the better hotels were advertised as 'American' meaning they had up-to-date plumbing and heating systems. In these you could run a bath instead of buying hot water from a man on the street. When it came to meals, you had the option of American food or drink—including ice-cream soda.

Offices appeared in American-style with fashionable furniture and electric elevators—with no need for an operator. All you needed to do was enter and sit down. The doors closed and the electric power turned on so you could press a button for your floor. And the idea of women typists had also been imported from the US. Although American employers expected hard work, they also introduced the idea of Saturday afternoons off. There were limits, though—no self-respecting French person could tolerate people drinking water instead of wine with their lunch.

Anyone who was anyone featured in the French versions of American newspapers or in the regularly issued directories. As a Brit, Louis didn't appear in such lists and he needed to advertise his presence if he was to infiltrate the Colony. There may be simpler ways of getting good press coverage, but buying a newspaper would work.

The *American Register* (which Louis retitled *The American Register and Anglo-American and Colonial News*) was the oldest English language paper in Paris, established in 1868. After its owner Thomas Evans died in 1899, it was sold to James Buckworth Dixon, whose father was a partner of Lloyds and financed his initiative. Dixon found the paper more trouble than it was worth after he had to take the manager of the London office, Albert Miles, to court in February 1902 for embezzlement. Miles was found not guilty, but the *Register* wasn't making much (if any) profit—its circulation was only 800 copies a week. Dixon was probably relieved when Louis agreed to buy the paper in early 1902.

For a few months the *Register* disappeared, before re-emerging at the end of December. Cheiro might have 'retired', but there was plenty of life left in him. Advertisements for his books appeared in the *Register* in December, as well as a jaunty note reporting that *Language of the Hand* had now sold 60,000 copies and *Guide to the Hand* 100,000. And the *Register* now carried a column called 'Occult Notes', penned by Cheiro, the first instalment of which described a new thought machine invented by a Professor Gates of Washington.

The primary purpose of the *Register* was to chronicle the activities of smart American society in Paris—arrivals and departures, at-homes, supper parties and fund raisers, what Countess XX wore and Marquise YY had to say, where you could buy one thing and sell another. It helped ensure not only did you mix with the right people in the right places, everyone would know you'd done so. It was only fair that it also regularly carried advertisements for Louis's champagne—Royal Imperial, an 1892 vintage from Reims, and it chronicled Count Hamong's involvement in the social whirl.

Louis sensibly retained some of the original staff of the *Register*, including Rowland Strong, who'd long been a writer before becoming the paper's editor. Strong worked as a correspondent for several British papers, including the *Observer, Morning Post* and *Pall Mall Gazette*, as well as the *New York Times*. He was best known for his role in the Dreyfus affair: his article, based on conversations with former French military man Ferdinand Esterhazy, revealed Esterhazy's confession that he'd written the paper that resulted in Dreyfus's indictment.[i] Strong had also published the widely popular *Where and How to Dine in Paris* (1900) and was a member of Oscar Wilde's Parisian social circle in Paris.

Another regular contributor to the *Register* was the Countess de Montaigu. Born Annie Kershaw, she'd married Count Frederick Oliver Raimond de Montaigu in 1862 and he'd died a year later. Annie took up journalism and worked for newspapers in St Louis and Washington as well as contributing to a variety of women's magazines under the name of 'Countess Annie de Montaigu'. The sort of hard-hitting journalism the Countess wrote included advice such as on how to make full use of your hairpin: 'Naturally, the legitimate use of the steel or tortoise-shell pin is to keep the hair in place. Women, however, utilize it for many purposes.'[2]

You might need your hairpin to button your shoes or gloves; pin on your veil; clean your nails; open your letters; cut the pages of your

---

i Captain Alfred Dreyfus was convicted of treason in December 1894 and sentenced to life imprisonment for allegedly communicating French military secrets to the German Embassy in Paris. He was imprisoned in Devil's Island in French Guiana, where he spent nearly five years. In 1896, evidence came to light which identified the real culprit as Major Ferdinand Walsin Esterhazy. When military officials suppressed the evidence, Esterhazy was acquitted and the army laid additional charges against Dreyfus, based on forged documents. Émile Zola's open letter *J'Accuse* prompted support for Dreyfus and put pressure on the government to reopen the case. In 1899, Dreyfus returned to France for another trial. The scandal divided French society between Dreyfus's supporters (including Sarah Bernhardt) and those who condemned him (including Oscar Wilde). A new trial resulted in another conviction and a ten-year sentence, but Dreyfus was pardoned and released. In 1906, he was exonerated.

magazine; pin back your net curtain; clean your gas burner; blacken it in a gas flame to use as an eyebrow pencil and clean the waste pipe in the sink, said the Countess, desperately listing as many things as possible that could be achieved with a piece of wire while remaining ladylike.

By the time Louis bought the *Register*, Countess de Montaigu had been living in Paris and London for years. She beavered away supplying society news designed to appeal to Americans in Paris for the *Register*, plus church and religious news.

When out and about, Louis kept his eyes open for other potential contributors. One was W Herbert Thomas, who would become editor of the Cornishman for fifty years from 1902.

> An American lady... introduced me to an attractive, suave good-looking man who was the Editor of her newspaper, 'The American Register',... She said he was Count Hamon, and his personality was pleasing and impressive. She told me that they were severing their journalistic connection, and she wanted me to... become Count Hamon's successor. It seemed a rather precarious enterprise, and I politely declined the offer.[3]

Although Louis was a hands-on owner, he wasn't the paper's editor and neither was he looking to dispose of it. On the contrary, he sought to expand it. Relations between England and France were difficult and there were fears of war breaking out. In 1898 France and Britain had clashed near Fashoda (Sudan), leading to the French withdrawing their claims. This led to bitterness in France and the view that the British were usurpers and bullies. Louis asked the *Register*'s readers what sort of reception they thought King Edward VII would receive if he visited France. 'The feeling in Paris at the time of which I am writing was so bitter against anyone who even happened to "look English" that I often saw Americans when walking through the boulevards hold some American paper prominently in their hands.'[4]

The mixed responses were forwarded to Sir Edmund Monson, the British Ambassador to France. A few weeks later Louis was called to the Embassy, the letters were returned to him and Monson said the King was due to visit in the near future. In April 1903, Louis launched *L'Entente Cordiale*—an 'illustrated International Review of politics, diplomacy, industry commerce, art, science, literature etc.'[5]

Due to problems with the French printers, Louis decided to launch the new paper in London and rushed back to London overnight from

Paris, hoping to find the paper ready to print. In the Piccadilly office, the 'principal editor', a French editor and an Irish editor were working on the paper.

> The Irishman... was the 'powder magazine' of the ship... his Irish sense of humour was... a somewhat serious drawback... he thought 'International Peace' such a huge joke that he nearly split his sides with laughter the first time he saw our ambitious sub-title.

Louis could hear fighting as he got out of his cab.

> 'What's the matter?' I said to the porter. With a significant grin he replied: 'It's the first night of the Peace journal upstairs, sir; that's all.' There was a crash of glass, and the Frenchman came tearing down the stairs like a madman. In the editorial room it looked as if a Cydonia had paid a surprise visit—proof sheets were flying in every conceivable direction, my venerable editor had a nose so damaged that it spouted blood like a water-cart, while my ex-war correspondent [the Irishman] looked as if 'he had just returned from the front.' I never knew exactly what happened—for I never asked.[6]

The King visited Paris in May 1903: 'It was anything, in fact, but a warm, or even a lukewarm, reception,'said Louis. 'It is true that the Avenue du Bois de Boulogne and the Champs-Elysées were crowded with people, but they were for the most part a very silent crowd; very few even raised their hats.'[7]

In the end, the French decided they needed a good relationship with Britain in case war broke out between France and Germany, and this led to the Entente Cordiale of 1904. Despite preening himself and believing he'd made a contribution to world peace, Louis was forced to admit this wasn't the best business decision he'd ever made. *L'Entente Cordiale* lost money with every issue and closed down after a year.

This wasn't the only dabbling in politics Louis attempted. He wrote several articles about promoting Irish industry and welcoming the possibility of home rule. As far as he was concerned, 'Ireland should become wealthy and the most prosperous country in the world'.[8]

During this period Louis suggested Edith Halford (now) Nelson wrote for the *Register*. Since last seeing Louis, Edith had acted alongside her husband, William Ashcroft.[ii] Although living in Battersea, she hadn't seen

---

ii For example, in *Coriolanus* at the Lyceum in April 1901.

Louis for three years. One reason for this was that early in her marriage Edith had a son who'd died at the age of ten weeks. She'd also spent time in the US with her husband who was touring in a play.

Shortly after they returned to London, Ashcroft bumped into Louis in London and told Edith, 'I have met an old friend of yours—Count Louis Hamon; used to be Cheiro the famous palmist, but seems to have given up all that bosh because he is now a very successful business man.'[9] He went on to tell Edith that Louis had suggested she should write an article about one of Nellie Melba's protégés and she should go to see him.

> 'I would rather not meet Count Hamon again.'
>
> 'You are surely not afraid of that man, now that you belong to me!'
>
> 'You don't understand what I mean and you don't realize what Count Hamon is.'
>
> 'What he is!...You talk about him as if he were the Devil incarnate. I don't understand why you were ever afraid of him, he doesn't seem at all alarming to me. Delightful fellow, no nonsense about him, but a great deal of personal charm... Very clever fellow and he knows everybody. He offered to give me introductions to anyone I want to know.'[10]

Never good at saying 'no', Edith acquiesced and went to see Louis at Devonshire Lodge on Marylebone Road to see, 'He was no longer the athletic, clean-limbed, handsome man I had known. His shoulders stooped slightly, his still handsome face was beginning to look heavy, even the expression of his splendid eyes had changed. There was something of the snake in them now.'[11]

Louis made it clear that writing articles wasn't what he had in mind for Edith, saying, 'Your husband is a fool. He has sent you back to me... you are very unhappy... it is not long now. Less than a year and you will come back to me.'[12]

Presumably, Edith did some swooning or similar at this point. In any event she doesn't appear to have written anything for the *Register*, although she did continue to see Louis from time to time.

Trying a different tack completely, at the end of October 1903 Louis launched a sports supplement to the *Register* and gathered a number of sports journalists for a celebratory dinner. A very small number—despite the offer of a spiffing meal at the Excelsior 81 restaurant, many invitees refused as the dinner clashed with a meeting of La Presse Sportive. The supplement sank without trace.

Let's not pretend Louis had given up the life of a mystic seer in favour of journalism. Or that he wasn't still as gorgeous as ever, despite what Edith thought. As mentioned above, 'Occult Notes' was a regular column in the *Register*, and as well as rehashing old stories such as that of his encounter with Gladstone, Louis advertised his courses of '12 or 24 lessons which will enable any one [*sic*] of average intelligence to become successful in the art of reading hands.'[13]

And he was gradually developing a greater interest in spiritualism and in psychic phenomena. In May 1903 he introduced Charton de Boyon's first London performance, a French musical medium whose gift Sarah Bernhardt, amongst others, raved about. He used his own unique fingering and couldn't play the same piece twice—or remember it once he'd played it. To most of the audience, he played badly, rather than mystically.

> Upon piano, organ, and clavecin M. Boyon attempted to extemporise in the manner of the great masters, and his methods were curious enough. Apart from many eccentricities of fingering, he, apparently dissatisfied with the volume of sound to be obtained by the mere finger-tips, frequently made use of his wrist and knuckles in an endeavour to obtain all the noise possible from his instrument. It was a little difficult to know whether it all was intended seriously.[14]

Not everyone claiming to display psychic phenomena was as honest as they might have been. However, Louis thought some investigators were full of themselves and ought to realise that:

> Trickery and deception are practised daily in every walk of life apart from that of the medium... It may be true that mediums resort to tricks at times, especially when the power they rely upon fails to make its appearance, and as the selfish public must have some thing [*sic*] for its money, it is hardly to be wondered at that there are mediums who yield to the temptation of using a brass wire or a piece of clockwork.[15]

After all, Louis had seen phenomena:

> During a recent visit to Naples, I myself witnessed a strange phenomenon, at the house of a friend of mine, living in that city. In order to amuse his guests, this gentleman had asked a medium to... entertain them with a séance... Our host was sitting in the library with half-a-dozen of his friends, when the young girl... entered the

room. Seeing her slight girlish figure our host asked in amazement: 'Is it possible that during these séances you are able to move heavy tables and chairs about the room!' To which she quickly replied: 'It is not my strength that does it. It is some unseen power that carries out these phenomena, when I am present?' She had hardly ceased speaking... when... the heavy oak library table rose from the floor fully three inches, and moved towards her. Our host got up from his chair to look for the supposed steel wire, which he was certain must exist, but to his amazement, the table turned and followed him into the corner of the room, from which he could not move without using all his strength to push away the heavy piece of furniture.[16]

Such views are why he attended and spoke at a meeting of occultists and spiritualists to protest against negative newspaper articles in 1904.[17]

On balance, however, Louis devoted more energy to his social life in Paris than anything. He'd set up his rooms with the curiosities he surrounded himself with—statues of gods, mystical veils, draperies of sumptuous colours and other treasures, plus his mummy's hand which he kept in his bedroom. And he was a frequent guest at receptions to welcome American visitors to Paris, often at the home of Charles Holman Black and Frank Holman where he read palms.

'Count' Hamon has been a dashing figure in Paris since his arrival here... He lived in costly apartments in the Bois de Boulogne.[18] [iii]While there was considerable mystery about his title of 'Count', he was so clever and such a pleasant entertainer that people soon forgot about that. He succeeded in working his way into the drawing rooms of prominent residents by his agreeable, suave manner.[19] Cheiro entertained guests by reading palms and telling the future from a crystal. His interesting discourses on their futures charmed his patrons.[20]

Louis's introduction into the social aspects of the American Colony was largely due to a friend he made early in his stay—a priest known as the Abbé de la Fresnaye.[iv] Well-educated and erudite, as a priest, the Abbé

iii Frank Ellis's *Directory of Occult Practitioners* (Blackpool: Ellis family, 1906) lists three addresses for Louis: 5 rue clement marot, Paris; 107 New Bond Street, London and 275 Fifth Avenue off Holland House, New York.

iv Born about 1857 in Montreal, Canada, the Abbé seems to have been born Gustave Leclere. At different times in his life he went by the names of Louis Henri Le Clere de la Fresnaye, Louis Gustave Leclere de la Fresnaye, Henri Gustave de la Fresnaye and other

could easily wangle invitations to events, and a bilingual respectable ally was more than useful for new arrivals to the Colony. Living on the rue de Lille, the Abbé inserted himself into events, performing marriages and selling raffle tickets for fundraisers from his home. It was said that he was responsible for introducing Comte Boni de Castellane to American heiress Annie Gould who he married in 1895.[v] He was also involved in selling fake works of art. The Abbé happily introduced Louis to everyone he knew.

Although it seems Louis would happily attend the opening of an envelope, it's only fair to point out that he also hosted 'Frequent receptions, at which he dispensed champagne in a most liberal manner'.[21] These often involved singing and recitations: 'Count Hamong gave a delightful musicale in his house in rue du bois de Boulogne last Thursday... handsome Gaveau piano made expressly for him.'[22] And he was still popular with the ladies— sometimes, too popular:

> A story is told here [Paris] of an American woman who carried on a flirtation with Cheiro. She at first found him amusing, but in the end was obliged to appeal to her friends to have the palm reader cease his attentions to her. Eventually she left here to escape the gossip caused by the episode.[23]

On 23 January 1904 there was fighting in the Place de la Concorde and talk about the possible downfall of the French cabinet. A military guard surrounded the chamber of deputies while they were discussing the case of Father Delsor, an Alsatian priest accused of plotting against the government. Sixty people were arrested during the pro-Alsatian demonstration and the German embassy was placed under a strong guard. Paris was again filled with the animosity that had arisen in the Franco-Prussian War. It wasn't the most fun place to be and this atmosphere may have contributed towards Louis's decision to take a break in Russia in February.

St Petersburg, the 'window to Europe', was an extremely popular place to visit from Paris during the years of the Franco-Russian alliance. And with heavy Russian investment in the French press during the early twentieth century, there may have been a business angle to Louis's visit. Plus, St Petersburg was renowned as a sympathetic environment for the occult. The

---

combinations of these names.

v Anna obtained a civil divorce in 1906, after the Count had spent about $10 million of the money given to her as a wedding present. Anna remarried and Castellane sought an annulment from the Vatican, which was the source of gossip for years. The annulment was finally denied in 1924.

royal family were interested in all things mystical, and the famous Parisian occultist Papus (Gerard Encausse) visited them on numerous occasions.[vi] It was exactly the type of location to appeal to Louis, despite the journey there being arduous.

> The journey from the frontier station of Wicrzbolow to the Russian capital is wearisome and uninteresting, and the distance of five hundred and sixty miles over bare, monotonous, characterless plains is usually traversed by night... for there is nothing in the landscape to rest or please the eye of the traveler. Night closes in upon a weird scene of jagged pines rising from a desolate heath against a lurid crimson sky. Low fir-woods and open corn-fields greet the eye at dawn, and we watch for the joyful moment of excitement when two vast domes appear beyond the hitherto feature-less waste, one purple and the other with a brilliant gleam of gold upon its surface,—the dome of the Church of St. Alexander Nevsky and of St. Isaac's Cathedral...[24]

St Petersburg was extremely cosmopolitan. Foreign enough to be interesting but not so Russian as to be alien. The hotels weren't as smart as in Paris, although they weren't dreadful. There were plenty of impressive buildings to see and historical sites to visit. And everyone who mattered would be in town at this time of year—they retreated to the country in summer. Louis said little about his visit beyond that:

> The Minister of Foreign Affairs, Alexander Isvolsky, arranged for me to dine with the Czar and himself at the Summer Palace at Peterhof.... On this occasion the Czar showed the Minister and myself calculations I had made for him when he had visited me in London. These calculations foretold that the most fatal war Russia had ever been engaged in would break out during the summer of 1914, ending in revolution and the fall of the Romanoff dynasty...[25]

> The Minister... laughed heartily over my predictions. 'You may be correct Cheiro in your description of my character and disposition, but your sinister forebodings at to the future are absolutely absurd.'[26]

---

vi Encausse had his finger on every occult pulse. He'd been a Bishop of the French Gnostic Church, studied theosophy under Madame Blavatsky and joined the Golden Dawn in Paris. In 1888 he'd joined the Kabbalistic Order of the Rosicrucians. Encausse had also studied medicine and served Tsar Nicholas II and his family as both doctor and occultist.

It wasn't long before Louis was back in the Paris/London social whirl. For example, in April he was at a dinner hosted by the Baron Oppenheim in Paris, and around this time he claimed to have read the palm of Baron von Bissing. And on 7 May, he was one of the three or four thousand guests present to celebrate the re-opening of the Savoy after its expansion and enjoy the three orchestras in attendance along with the steady supply of champagne.

The *Register*'s move to new offices in Piccadilly Circus provided an opportunity for more champagne on 27 May. That afternoon, an Austrian band played and the 400 hundred attendees enjoyed Arthur Wellesley's recitations, Maud Percival Allen's singing and a Mr Hoering playing the Steinway piano Louis had bought.

Back in Paris, it was around this time that Louis met Mata Hari again. She'd separated from her husband in 1902 and had moved to Paris in 1903, where she performed as a circus horse rider under the name of Lady MacLeod. By 1904, she was gaining renown as an exotic dancer, and she became an overnight success after her debut at the Musée Guimet in March 1905. However, Louis's accounts contain multiple errors about her life so it's unlikely they were as friendly as he implied.

Louis had also met up with Rose, the Princess Monyglyon. On 31 July they went to the theatre together.

Bonavita, the famous American lion-tamer, was to appear for the first time. We had front seats in the orchestra stalls. The great crimson curtains rolled open. The entire stage was replaced by a steel cage; enormous African lions paced up and down before us, glared and growled at the audience, snapped and snarled at one another... Bonavita was a man of splendid physique; dressed in a kind of semi-military uniform, he made an imposing appearance. The audience gave him a magnificent ovation... Suddenly the great beast gave a roar of defiance that echoed through the theatre. The moment had come. With another roar he sprang on the defenceless man, knocked him to the floor, and commenced mauling his left shoulder and arm. Then the unexpected happened. With everyone paralysed by fear, the Princess sprang from her seat; in a second she had reached the cage, jabbing and striking the lion's face with the handle of the parasol she carried. Pushing the man one side, the Princess entered. Kneeling down, she lifted the injured man's head to her lap, then with the attendant's help carried him through the lions and out of the gate into safety.[27]

Despite sounding like one of Louis's wilder stories, this actually happened. Bonavita (John Friedrich Gentner) had started his career as an acrobat before discovering his true vocation. He'd been performing at Dreamland, an amusement park set up by Frank Bostock that had opened at Coney Island in Brooklyn, New York in May. The Captain was one of several animal trainers there and one of the main major attractions, appearing with as many as twenty-seven lions at a time.

That night, his lion Baltimore left claw marks that extended from Bonavita's right shoulder to below his elbow, and several of his fingers were damaged. However, the lion wasn't repelled by Rose's parasol—Bonavita grabbed an iron bar to force him back and finally got the lion to retreat by firing blank cartridges at him. His arm became infected and was amputated in February 1905. Rose stayed at his side and cared for him while he was recovering. In fact, Rose became obsessed with Bonavita, following him from show to show across the US before they secretly married in Paris in April 1905. Their marriage only lasted two years, but Bonavita continued to work with wild animals that took offence to him until he was killed by an angry polar bear in 1917.[vii]

Louis was back into the public eye when a piece of Paris gossip about the bad effects of his predictions hit the press.

> An American woman well known in San Francisco society consulted 'Cheiro' in Paris in the spring of 1900, and among other matters was informed that the two months most prejudicial to her welfare were those of July and August. Strangely enough, her lover and sister died on the following July 4 and August 13, respectively. Since then she has been a changed woman. Upon one who had previously been exceptionally strong-minded, the apparent fulfillment of the palmist's 'prophecy' produced a pitiable effect. Acute hysteria and neurasthenia were the immediate result, followed later by the most grotesque eccentricities. Imagining that almost every ordinary occurrence had some bearing on the occult, she would immediately seek out 'Cheiro', on one occasion even crossing to New York for that purpose. Of ample means, she had in turn sought the advice of the most eminent medical practitioners of London and Paris. But she invariably ceases to persevere with

---

vii Bonavita went into films from 1913 to 1917 as a stuntman, actor and director. He appeared in *The Wizard of the Jungle* and *The Woman, the Lion and the Man* in 1915. He also continued to work with Bostock's Circus, training animals at Frank Bostock's farm in Los Angeles.

their prescriptions in the middle of the treatment, with the result that she is now mentally and physically a wreck.[28]

And Louis hit the headlines again in October when Charles and Martha Stephenson, known as the 'Keiros', were in court after being charged under the Vagrancy Act. 'I suppose it is the *Daily Mail*,' Martha said with resignation when told of the charges.[29] The similarity of name meant that many believed Louis to have been arrested and for years to come the story was repeated in the press to illustrate his criminality. To be fair, Charles Stephenson tried his best to allay the confusion:

Mr. Gill: When did you adopt the name of 'Keiro'?
—In 1879.
Did you happen to adopt that the time another Cheiro disappeared from Bondstreet?
—Cheiro must have been a boy at school then. He adopted my name, if anything.[30]

Prudently, Louis refrained from comment. However, he did treat himself to a new pianola in January 1905, which he showed off at a party. (That's two new pianos and a pianola, in case you're keeping count.)

Shortly afterwards, in February, Louis visited St Petersburg for the second time. By now, unrest had spread throughout the Russian Empire, leading to strikes and military mutinies.

When the first snow of winter made the streets almost impassable, I met a procession of some fifty men with a few women handcuffed together being driven to a station to be entrained for Siberia. They had been arrested at their work, some were in shirt-sleeves, some in their overalls, but just as they were, they were being marched through the streets...[31]

The newly emancipated peasants suffered from poverty and weren't allowed to sell or mortgage their land; ethnic minorities were suffering from discrimination, being unable to vote or serve in the Imperial Guard or navy; strikes and unions were banned causing resentment amongst workers; students were taking on board new radical ideas; and soldiers returning from the recently ended war with Japan organised protests against the inadequate factory pay and shortages they found on their return.

The shift from unrest to revolt occurred on the Bloody Sunday of 22 January 1905 when soldiers fired on a group of people attempting to present a petition to Czar Nicolas II in St Petersburg calling for reforms. Hundreds were killed or wounded. The event led to the 1905 revolution and finally the Russian Constitution of 1906. When Louis went to St Petersburg for his second visit, strikes and violence were commonplace.

But business is business. Despite the potential danger, deals were being struck, funds being sought and entrepreneurs frequently travelled between St Petersburg and Paris. Society continued as it always had, albeit with one eye peering over its shoulder in case of attack.

Also staying in St Petersburg was Mata Hari, who had taken an expensive suite of rooms at the Hotel l'Europe.

> She entertained largely, but I noticed the guests were chiefly important heads of the Government or Staff officers in the Russian Army. The name she lived under was Baroness von Mingen; she was considered extremely rich with a weakness for doing charitable and eccentric things.[32]

One evening, Mata Hari interrupted Louis's writing because she fancied a chat. *How could any man refuse?* thought Louis.[33] Extraordinarily, Mata Hari launched into an account of how when she was in Berlin, the German Secret Service had convinced her to train as a spy. She was posing as a German baroness and was throughly enjoying life. "'Espionage" is the greatest game of all,' she said.[34] Louis pleaded with her to give it up but to no avail. After all, this was a career women could excel in. She left the next morning so Louis turned his attention elsewhere. Famously, Rasputin had arrived in the city the previous month, and Louis claimed he met him during this trip.

> Habited as a kind of peasant monk, corresponding to the old-time wandering friars in England, he walked with long strides across the carpeted floor, halted in front of me, and speaking a few words in very bad French, then rapidly in Russian... [he] said something to the effect that he did not believe in hand-reading—but he believed in Fate.

> His features were large and coarse, his eyes brilliant, his mouth mobile and the lips full and red. He wore an overgrown light brown beard, partly reddish, and his head was covered with a tangled mass of unkempt hair. On his forehead was a dark patch-like scar of an old wound. His voice was deep, authoritative, and sonorous.[35]

When I first met Rasputin, I could not help but realize… that I was in the presence of one of those extraordinary men who are born into the world as instruments of Fate…[36]

Whether Louis met Rasputin at all, let alone predicted from a reading of his hand that he'd suffer a violent death within a palace, by poison, knife and bullet and the icy waters of the river Niva flowing over his dead body, is open to debate.

There were other wild adventures. Louis was taking a walk one night when it began to rain so he jumped into a *droshky* (open carriage). A man appeared and asked if he could share the droshky and before they reached the hotel, the driver went off-route and the man said, 'You will not see your hotel tonight' before offering a glimpse of his revolver.[37] 'You must come quietly,' he added. 'Otherwise you will never see your hotel again—either tonight or any other night!'[38]

Louis was taken to a house where he saw men making bombs. A woman there asked for his help. She said her son had been taken after Bloody Sunday and was awaiting his death sentence.

'She would give herself up if that would save his life,' the man interrupted at this juncture, 'but the only result would be that two lives would be lost instead of one.'

'But what can I do in all this tragedy?' I asked. 'I, a stranger here—what good can I do?'[39]

What indeed? The man told Louis that the Princess he'd had dinner with earlier that evening could wield her influence over the Czarina so the boy could be spared. There was only two days before his execution, so Louis had to move fast. When he returned to the city, he told the Princess what had happened, talking her out of going to the police. Finally, she agreed to see the Czarina the following morning. The next day the Princess sent for Louis. "'I have not been successful,' she said, "but I have at least obtained one slight concession. The boy is to be shot at 6 o'clock to-morrow morning, but I have been promised that his body will be placed in a coffin and given over to his relatives… you… will be allowed to witness the execution, and can take the coffin away with you at once'."[40]

At the execution, Louis watched as the boy's body fell forward to the ground. The warders put the body in a coffin and moved the coffin into a hearse. Louis and the man who had accosted him in the droshky followed the hearse back to the boy's mother's house. As his mother sobbed over the corpse, Louis turned to leave and:

As I did so, I heard a scream that seemed to freeze the blood in my veins. I rushed forward. The mother was clasping her boy in her arms, as if waking out of a dream, his eyes opened and were looking straight into hers. 'Maya, Maya,' he said in Russian. 'Don't be frightened! I am not dead.'... The Princess had kept her word. She had influenced the officer in charge of the firing-party to have the soldiers served with blank cartridges. He had, in his turn, told the boy to fall forward, as though dead, when the shots rang out, and the lad himself had involuntarily added realism to the deception by fainting at the fateful moment.[41]

Louis had saved a revolutionary's life, and no-one had got into any serious trouble. More believable is that Louis spent much of his time partying. As he said, 'There were balls, dances, dinner parties, and assemblies; there was hardly an evening but I was whisked off to some lordly mansion to meet beautiful Russian women, highly placed soldiers and naval officers, diplomatic figures, and those who then emphatically made up the ruling class.'[42]

That was the class Louis wanted to be part of. So when the *Register* published *Who's Who in Paris* in April 1905, he ensured he was included in it with the suitable pastimes of rowing and travelling listed against his name.

Social gatherings in the *Register*'s London office had become regular occasions—and highly popular. In April 1905 about seven hundred guests enjoyed the afternoon's entertainment, which included recitations from Louis and from Loie Fuller with Hamilton Harty accompanying several songs. Edith may have been there—she attended some of these receptions. At one, she turned up alone as her husband was out of town. It was coming to an end when Louis took her into a back room, saying he wanted her to meet the American ambassador's wife. As he turned away to get the ambassador's wife, Louis told Edith to wait 'with a peculiar note in his voice... which made his words sound like a command.'[43]

Feeling strange, Edith decided to leave. But she found herself crossing the main reception room and walking towards Louis. He was standing with the ambassador's wife who said, 'But Count Hamon, what have you done—what you are doing is very cruel. That poor girl is suffering, I am sure she is going to faint.'[44]

Louis took Edith's hand and she immediately came to her senses. She hadn't the foggiest what had happened but assumed Louis had used a psychic power on her.

In May Louis took a break at a hotel in Bexhill-on-Sea and followed up with a night out at the Shakespeare Ball at the Royal Palace Hotel for the Actors' Benevolent Fund. He whizzed back to Paris in June and went to a stag party which was 'attended by many of the well-known musical stags of the gay capital... and some of the songs rendered in harmony astonished the neighbours in the vicinity of the Champs Elysees.'[45] This was followed by another seaside break in Folkestone in September.

Back in Paris, Louis had lunch with W T (William Thomas) Stead, the newspaper editor and journalist who's credited with inventing the new journalism that paved the way for modern tabloids. He was also responsible for *Borderland*, the spritualist quarterly which ran from 1893 to-1897. Stead had just returned from Russia where he'd spoken at public meetings in Moscow and St Petersburg in an attempt to reconcile progressive Russian society with the Russian government. Also present was Maud Gonne, the Irish republican revolutionary, suffragette and actress, and a past member of the Golden Dawn. Louis understandably felt that he had to wear his medal from the Shah of Persia while in such illustrious company.

Louis had settled into a socialite routine, filled with pianos and champagne, with a friendly priest to hand if he needed helping out. Things might have carried on in this way if he hadn't met Hugo Loewy.

Undated, around turn of century

CHAPTER

TWELVE

*Society greeted him rapturously for he had money to burn and right
swiftly, and without a thought of the morrow, did he incinerate the lucre.
All the waiters knew him and so did all society that basks in the sunlight
of American dollars.*[1]

Y OU MAY BE WONDERING WHAT KATIE DID.
Louis said her voice had been damaged by diphtheria
and that's why she gave up the stage. She may have been
worried about the tax problems some of the chorus girls
of *Babes in Toyland* experienced in the summer of 1903. The
Chicago Board of Review's request for accounts had been splashed all over
the press, with jabs at the morals of the chorus girls. The actresses played to
their audience—for example, the actress Helen Hilton said her only notes
were her beautiful contralto ones. Most of the cases were dismissed due to
the actresses claiming to be New Yorkers and not subject to Chicago taxes.

Babes in Toyland had opened in Chicago in June 1903 and played in
Washington in October 1903. In summer 1904, two tours began of the
production—one with most of the original cast and a smaller tour—that
ran until May 1906. Newspaper reports mention Katie being on the stage
for two years, so she could have returned to the UK at any time between
1904 and 1906.

She'd stayed in touch with Louis, and they bumped into each other
in 'China, Cairo, Monte Carlo, and Paris, but as by my oath I could not
marry, we remained good friends and nothing more. In the end, perhaps

to forget, she went to Egypt and lived for over four years in her own caravan, travelling on the confines of the Sahara.'[2]

While in Mexico, Katie was apparently kidnapped by bandits. Fortunately, 'the head of the troop of brigands chanced to be an English Peer who had sacrificed his name and fortune in order to shield a woman he was in love with'.[3] Katie told people she'd also spent time in a harem.

> Decorations the Countess [Katie] wore came from the Khedive of Egypt following her kidnapping by Prince Yusef. 'They were given me,' the Countess smiled, 'for keeping my mouth shut!'... when she was a very young and very beautiful woman, she had been kidnapped by the Prince while she was travelling on a private yacht on the Nile, with the intention of presenting her to the Prince's uncle, Sultan of Turkey, for his harem. Her bodyguard was killed, she said, but she was rescued by a member of the Prince's staff who took pity on her—not, however, before she lived in a Turkish harem at Abdin Palace in Egypt for two years. She did not report the matter to the English Government when she finally got free, and the Khedive presented her with the medals in token of her prudence.[4][i]

Katie doesn't appear in public records for many years and was presumably using a different name (not one connected with her family) or actually was overseas. But she was there, a shadowy figure in the background of Louis's life.

In 1905, Louis ceased to be 'Count Hamong' in favour of 'Count Hamon'. His occult interests were now just that—interests. Although he still wrote 'Occult Notes' for the *Register*, and could be called on for a quick reading at parties, Louis was recreating himself as a businessman— with some help from his friends.

Abbé Lefrasnay acted as Louis's agent in several ventures, including his champagne business. Together, Louis and the Abbé used their social connections to 'arrange' marriages between rich American women and financially challenged European nobles. This doesn't mean they were running an early twentieth-century version of Match.com; it was more subtle.

In the late nineteenth century, British (and to an extent, European)

---

i This story reputedly later formed the basis of Katie's novel, *Outlawed*.

aristocracy was struggling. Some families disappeared completely, others survived through American money—by marrying 'dollar princesses'.

This period was an era of rapid economic growth for America and had created a newly moneyed class. However, the nouveau riche soon discovered money couldn't buy social status. Despite America theoretically opposing markers of privilege such as titles, in reality those who came from old money refused to accept the new millionaires. Money alone couldn't break down entry barriers but a title helped to whittle away at them. If that failed, you could enjoy your privileged position in Europe. Mothers and daughters from newly wealthy families arrived in London every year for the social season (often also spending time in Paris) in search of suitable beaus, offering huge dowries to suitable candidates for their daughters' hands. And American heiresses became ladies, countesses, marchionesses and duchesses.

It didn't always turn out to be as grand as they'd hoped. Many dollar princesses ended up in run-down and dreary houses that lacked the most basic of amenities, ostracised by 'true' aristocrats (especially by English women who'd lost out to them) for their lack of social skills and horrified by their husbands taking mistresses as they had done for centuries. Others pragmatically saw it as a business arrangement both sides could benefit from and enthusiastically entered their new world. New money gained a shortcut to social acceptance via a title and blue blood could afford to survive.

To marry the right candidate, you had to meet them first—and that was easily achieved. Musicales, soirées and other events enabled women to meet members of the aristocracy. Although it might be gauche to pay for an introduction, many had no problem in paying for services rendered and a lot of money could be made. Plus, who would blink at paying a priest to conduct or facilitate a marriage? These weddings were meticulously listed in the Register. Paris gossip said that Louis arranged marriages (especially for American women who were no longer young) and was rewarded handsomely for his service. He was specifically credited with having arranged a marriage between an unnamed wealthy but elderly American woman and an Englishman thirty years her junior.

The practice faded after George V was crowned in 1911 and expressed his disapproval of such unions, but by then millions of pounds had been brought into the economy—about a quarter of the British aristocracy married American money between 1890 and 1910. But Louis sought bigger money. And what better way to get your hands on it than open a bank?

In the early 1900s (it isn't clear precisely when but they were both at a dinner party in June 1904), Louis met Count Reginald Henshaw Ward, an American millionaire born in Massachusetts in 1862. Ward had started his professional life as a clerk in a Boston bank at seventeen and later opened his own banks in Boston and New York. From the start, Ward knew he was destined for greater things; he dressed well and took French lessons as soon as he could afford to do so. (It helped that he married the millionairess Edith Newcomb Ward.) Ward arrived in England in 1897 to represent his company, Clark, Ward & Co. For a number of years he dealt in mining ventures—hence being known as the 'copper king'. After converting to Catholicism, he donated enough to the Church to be made a count by the Pope—the alternative easy route to entering the aristocracy: 'Time was, and not so long ago, when anybody with the necessary assurance and a little money could go to Portugal or Italy or one of the Balkan principalities and come away within a week a full-fledged Count, at least.'[5]

As if to be on the safe side, Ward also acquired decorations from almost all the crowned heads of Europe. Part of his reinvention involved leaving his wife behind in the US and they later divorced. In April 1902 Ward leased Fulwell Park in Twickenham, becoming famous for his weekend parties. During the week, he travelled to the city every morning in one of his five cars. (One was fitted as a small room with dressing tables and a couch for use on long journeys.) By July 1903, he was Consular-General for Romania.

As well as hosting the sort of parties Louis would give his right arm plus any other requested limbs to attend, Ward knew everyone worth knowing in the banking world. Louis was ill-qualified to become a financier on his own, so Ward introduced him to Hugo Loewy (Löwy), a German-Jewish banker.

Loewy had a chequered past—in 1891 he'd been convicted of falsifying accounts and sentenced to two-and-a-half years in prison in Berlin. And while still in prison, in December 1893 he'd stood trial for fraudulent bankruptcy, receiving a sentence of nearly five years. Loewy often dealt with the sale of mining stock, and this presumably is how he knew Reginald Ward. His dodgy past was no secret, having made the English speaking newspapers, but it seemed an occupational hazard for a late nineteenth-century financier. It probably wasn't much to worry about; after all, it was years ago. However, those acquainted with Loewy more intimately, or who were involved in the financial scene on the continent (people like Ward), knew this story barely scratched the surface of Loewy's shenanigans.

Leaving Berlin in 1877, Loewy had founded his first bank in Vienna. Shortly after, he went to Paris and then on to Odessa. After doing something to upset the Russian police enough to make them want to keep an eye on him, Loewy sharply returned to Paris. He declared bankruptcy for the first time shortly after his arrival in December 1881 after losing money through a mechanical sawmill industry. Two year later, he became bankrupt for the second time. Unfazed, Loewy set up the Banque Populaire de l'Epargne. That went wrong and he declared bankruptcy again in April 1885. Following yet another bankruptcy in April 1886, Loewy served six months in prison for fraud.

Once he was released in August 1887, he went to the Ardennes and set up a company for the manufacture of parquet floors and wooden chairs. Apparently, an office boy found a list of shareholders of the Panama Company in an office cupboard which Loewy took full advantage of in order to become a banker. 'Loewy et cie', with its headquarters in Paris, was successful for a while—but like everything financial Loewy was involved with, the company collapsed and after the police chased him across the rooftops, he was once again made bankrupt.

Once freed, Loewy borrowed a hundred francs from a friend and became a money lender. Somehow, he made four hundred thousand francs with which he left for Berlin—where he opened a bank and called himself 'Herr Breuer'. Along the way, Loewy had learned the power of advertising, and he wasted no time in promoting his new establishment. From his offices in Friedrichstrasse, Loewy surveyed his new empire. There were four branches of his bank in Berlin alone and he lived like a prince.

Things went wrong when a woman tired of waiting for her papers for shares she'd invested in consulted a lawyer. And this brings us back to the early 1890s. We'll ignore the stories of orgies Loewy organised, and suicides he caused, that he'd been convicted of indecent exposure in Bordeaux, and he had a criminal record for arson, because this tale is long enough already.

At the time of his arrest, Loewy had been living with Helene Goldstein, who had played a major role in his fraudulent activities. She was also arrested but somehow Loewy managed to marry her while they were still in prison in the hope of making it impossible for her to give evidence against him as his wife. It didn't work. But Loewy clearly had friends. He wasn't in England after serving his term simply for a new start. He'd escaped from prison in October 1894 and settled down in Kensington, buying himself a French poodle.

Why Ward thought that this man with a 'grubby moustache' was who Louis needed to help him enter the financial world is unclear.[5] Perhaps he didn't know Loewy's full story, but it beggars belief that he didn't at least know about more recent events. Ward was a skilled linguist—he travelled extensively in Europe and wasn't restricted to English-language newspapers and discussions by any stretch of the imagination. It's as if he wanted to offer Louis the worst possible option.

Maybe that was the case. Maybe Ward disliked Louis. Maybe he hoped to profit from the arrangement himself. Both Ward and Loewy were at the Register's monthly 'at home' in March 1905 so whatever talks took place probably started about then.

Loewy certainly needed a new venture. When Louis met him, Loewy was a director of the Financial and Commercial Bank in Lombard Street, which had been set up to carry on the business of the Berlin Financial and Commercial News. The bank decided to close down on 24 May but continued to accept deposits for the next three days. A petition to wind it up was presented in June 1905 as the bank then had debts of £600,000. The company went into liquidation and it became clear the trustees had no financial experience but had taken directorships on Loewy's advice. News of what had happened soon reached Berlin and a warrant was issued for Loewy's arrest. It was time for him to leave town.

As 1905 drew to a close, Louis and Loewy went into partnership and rented 8 Place de L'Opera, a former tailor's apartment above the offices of the *Echo de Paris*, paying 30,000 francs in rent. The Avenue de l'Opera was filled with American businesses, including the American consulate and an English language bookshop, making it an ideal location. Louis provided £2,000 in capital to start the bank with three other partners (one of them Loewy) adding a total of £14,000. Louis's contribution was lower because he was liable for all debts.

The bank's offices were sumptuously furnished with uniformed servants, an army of typists, a huge dispatch room and a reception room where visitors could browse through copies of the *Register* and admire the antique furniture. Louis and Loewy had the main office and behind it were two newsrooms and the office of the *Register*'s editor. (Apparently, for a period this was the Abbé.) The name of the *Register* was emblazoned on the front of the building in electric lights and Louis and Loewy sent out thousands of flyers announcing the bank's services.

And then they opened for business. Through the pages of the Register and elsewhere, the Banque Hamon-Americaine (or Hamon & Co.) advertised cheque and current accounts, orders on stock exchanges, advances made, telegraphic transfer money, bills negotiated or forwarded for collection and currency exchange—all the services you'd expect from a bank. Loewy focused on recommending shares in the Eastern Japanese Corporation and the Korean Water Works of which he was the representative.

By March 1906 the London office had opened in Gracechurch Street with Loewy as its manager. On Loewy's advice, Louis kept books referring to the bank's French business in London and those referring to its English clients in Paris.

As if a champagne business, a newspaper and a bank weren't enough, Louis established the Anglo-French Herald Motor Company. Louis loved cars—evidenced by long discussions about them in the *Register*. It was some years before mass production would make them available to a wider market, so there was a sense of exclusivity—as well as uncertainty—about driving: 'Switzerland is a horrible country for automobolists. The rural population does all it can to make the motor car impossible, throwing heavy stones at the sight of a car.'[7] Louis sold cars or, if you were more financially challenged, could rent you a vehicle for three months at a time.

The Anglo-French Herald Motor Company wasted no time in expanding. It bought out La Société Anonyme des Moteurs et Automobiles

Herald, a company established in 1901 that dealt with the manufacture and sale of anything to do with cars, lorries and cabs. To cover costs, shares were sold from mid-May. The company also bought twenty taxis in London, with a view to expanding a large taxi service. But things were starting to look shaky and people were suspicious: 'If the public glance at the difference between the price which Messrs. Hamon and Co. are paying for the property, which includes not a halfpenny in cash, and the price to be paid by the public, they will see that Messrs. Hamon and their friends are making an uncommonly good profit out of it.'[8]

Louis hadn't seen Edith for months. She didn't mind much, because she was convinced he was a spy.

> Cheiro frequently disappeared, sometimes for long periods at a time. These disappearances have since been explained by the fact that Louis Hamon was often engaged in dangerous businesses in foreign lands. In his memoirs he speaks of 'business engagements' but the business was so secret that no one ever knew where he was unless it were some Minister or financier whose delicate scheme he was working out in some foreign country. He sometimes worked for the Secret Service, which fact was told to me by my brother, Major Halford Thompson, a well-known police officer.[9]

It's true that Ralph Halford-Thompson was a 'well-known police officer'—he later became Deputy Chief Constable of Devon. But Devon policeman aren't usually authorities on secret agents, although maybe Halford-Thompson did tell Edith this to shut her up. Although Louis probably wasn't responsible for 'the economic future of a whole country' as Edith thought, he did want to expand the bank's business and the Abbé suggested opening a hotel in St Petersburg might be a good idea.[10] Louis was there in August 1906.

> Returning one day to my hotel, I found that some of my most important papers had been stolen. I went at once to my friend, Monsieur Isvolsky, at the Foreign Office and protested. He listened, smiled his enigmatical smile, and said: 'Take my card to the Chief of Police and explain the loss of your papers to him.'... Within twenty minutes I was shown into the presence of the Chief. By the time I returned to my hotel, the police were already at each entrance to

prevent anyone leaving. Within an hour my papers were restored; a secret agent of Rasputin joined a Siberian chain-gang that night, and never again was I subjected to any molestation.[10]

In reality, Louis probably spent much of his time looking at hotels and saying, 'That's nice.'

While in St Petersburg, Louis had entrusted his business concerns to Loewy. One of the deals Loewy made was with Julia Newell and Josephine Pomeroy. Newell had married her second husband, New York lawyer George Baldwin Newell after he'd successfully defended her interests in a suit over a large estate left by her brother, George Pomeroy, ex-American Consul-General in Egypt. The Newells had settled in Paris in 1904 with Julia's sister, Josephine who'd been due to marry Josef Klimke, the Transvaal State mining engineer, in summer 1901 but the wedding never took place. As soon as they arrived, they were at the centre of the American colony and entertained lavishly.

One of Loewy's letters advertising the bank's services reached them and appeared to offer a good deal. Another account says they were introduced to Louis and Loewy by the Abbé. Some of the sisters' assets were still under litigation in the US, and they were short of funds, so they decided to use their railway stocks as security for a loan. The stocks were worth about £16,000 (although again, there are varying accounts). The sisters cabled their New York broker to transfer the stock and bonds to Hamon and Co. It was later reported that they received a $150,000 loan raised through London banks for stocks that had a market value of $500,000.

At the time, it was just another transaction and Loewy turned his attention to appointing new staff to the Register. One of these was Ernest Bryham Parsons who had a reputation to compete with Loewy's own. Given that Bryham Parsons had such a gloomy view of his prospects, it's surprising he decided to live in Paris. 'The Man in the Newspaper Shop which I frequented in Bloomsbury told me before ever I started that people who went to Paris rarely came back,' he said. 'They were not all murdered, said he, but a good many were. They got run over, and killed in the Underground Railways, and assassinated in broad daylight.'[12]

Parsons had lost his job and was short of money, so he decided to take a holiday. 'I do wish they would hurry up and make the Channel Tunnel,' he complained during a stormy crossing.[13] The train from

Boulogne was no better, considering he could only afford to travel third class. He wasn't a natural traveller: 'I once went to Venice in London, and spent half an hour in its market-place and on the bridges, listening to the Venetian boatmen swearing at each other, and Paris reminds me of that…. hundreds of thousands of foreign faces…—the real foreign type—not the sort you meet in Bloomsbury, London.'[14]

On his second visit to Paris, Bryham Parsons gained employment at the *Daily Mail* offices as a shorthand writer taking down night calls. The calls were hard to hear and the pay bad. Fortunately, he discovered: 'The French are a gay, jaunty race. They trust to each other's good sense in the open streets and are seldom run over… they radiate with a sort of Continental sunshine, as though each one of them possess a sense enabling them to place the highest possible value on life.'[15] To keep things in perspective, he also commented, 'I travelled once or twice on the Metropolitan railway—not without a sense of impending danger.'[16] Bryham Parsons wasn't simply beset with misfortune—he went out looking for disaster.

He'd met actress Mary Fitzpatrick (who acted under the name of May Travers) in 1897 when they were boarding at the same lodging house and was instantly enamoured with her. When he refused to take no for an answer and wrote to the manager of the theatre where she was appearing asking for a permanent pass to see her act, Fitzpatrick moved house. Bryham Parsons showered her with unwanted attention between 1897 and 1902, sending her books, flowers, fruit and pornographic drawings. One day when she was out for a walk, he grabbed her arms—finally, she could charge him with assault.

> The prison doctor had certified that the defendant, although not insane, was a person of weak mind and excitable, and there could be no doubt that his excessive affection for Miss Fitzpatrick had led him to do regrettable things. As to his having ordered a band to play outside Miss Fitzpatrick's window, that was intended purely as a compliment.[17]

The request for this band was read to the court:

> Dear Sir,—I want a flute, harp. and violin to play… at nine o'clock on the morning… the repertoire to commence with The Amorous

Goldfish, to played at sufficient length, but not to a point that would weary, and to continue, say, for an hour, with other tunes, preferably 'Good bye, Dolly' and 'Stars and Stripes.'[18]

Bryham Parsons also advertised in the *Telegraph*, announcing his wedding to Fitzpatrick at Downpatrick Castle in Ireland, from which they rode away on a tandem on 1 May 2000 (not a typo). Because he hadn't been physically violent, Bryham Parsons got off lightly and had to pay two sureties of £50 each to keep the peace for twelve months. Unable to find the money, he spent two months in prison.

The day Bryham Parsons was released, he went to Fitzpatrick's home, rushed past the servant who opened the door and ran upstairs to Fitzpatrick's room. Finding it locked, he yelled that he'd break the door down if she didn't open it. Fortunately, the servant had called a policeman. Back in court, Fitzpatrick denied having let Bryham Parsons kiss her and that she'd met him in the pub and he'd told her he'd written a novel about her. Cross-examining Fitzpatrick himself, Bryham Parsons tried to sully her character by asking if she had a drink problem and if it was true she used to 'lap up champagne.' He ended up spending another six months in prison, and after this he needed work a lot more than he let on. This is how Bryham Parsons ended up on the *Register* staff.

Although seemingly oblivious to the quality of his staff, Louis may have heard that Edith's husband had died in October, a week after Louis had left London to return to Paris. Fortunately, Edith received a vision from Louis via an Indian lady who told her everything would work out well. To ensure it did, she contested her father's will, won the case and spent the next year travelling. She visited France and Italy before ending up in Tunisia where she became the wife of an Arab sheikh who she believed she'd known in a previous incarnation.[ii] While in Tunisia, Edith had a daughter, Saluhah, but her husband's family took her from Edith for the first year of her life and again when she was three years old. Edith remained in Tunisia for the next eight years.

While Louis spent his time out and about, imbibing large amounts of champagne (for example, in December he was at the Savoy mingling with names such as Baden Powell, T P O'Connor, Lloyd George, and Rider

---

ii Edith later wrote a book about her experiences: *Desert Sanctuary* (London : Skeffington and Son, 1946).

Haggard), Bryham Parsons was causing havoc in the office due to having fallen in love again.

> Baby Peyter is so bright, but I can write no poetry about her...
> Baby Peyter will sit still while I sketch her—still as a mouse.
> Afterwards, with a heavenly smile, she will ask for the sketch and
> pout if it is refused. Baby Peyter drank my tea yesterday and was
> to have given me a kiss for it— but she owes me that still... finding
> Miss Peyter was engaged in a long conversation with Clement,
> I took offence, and tore in half the water-colour portrait of her
> that I had begun. It tore across the neck, just under the chin, in
> a slanting line. The drawing lay in two parts for her to see as she
> went out, and, like a born phraseur, I framed the words of my
> excuse: 'I have torn it because you have torn my heart.'[20]

There is much, much more of this, but you probably get the idea. While Bryham Parsons wallowed in angst, he heard a man say to Miss Peyter, 'Beware of that man. I know him.'[21] Miss Peyter politely made excuses to Bryham Parsons and kept out of his way.

Fortunately, Bryham Parsons managed to fit in some work. He wrote a column headed 'News of the Week in Paris' and in December 1906 he produced an article about Henri Rochefort who ran the *Intransigeant*, a popular right-wing French newspaper.

> This man, who has travelled all over the world, seems to make his
> soul the harbouring place for every bitterness and animosity that
> politics can excuse or indigestion cause. Yet occasionally, strange
> to say, he turns his envenomed pen from some human target,
> and sits down to talk sense.... In his article... with regard to the
> Channel Tunnel, he says that he is convinced that this project will
> never become a reality...[22]

Bryham Parsons harboured a hearty disapproval of anyone who opposed the Channel Tunnel, but his comments didn't go down well.

> Rochefort... threatened to send his seconds up to Count Hamon,
> the then proprietor of the 'American Register.' Count Hamon
> reported the matter to me, saying that I must take care what I
> wrote, as he might have had to fight a duel over this matter. I

replied: 'Thank you, sir. If you will allow me to defend my own article, I shall be very pleased to do so. A duel with Henri Rochefort would certainly be a new experience, and I am quite prepared to meet this man, who wishes to fight with everybody!'

'Oh!' replied Count Hamon, with a laugh in his voice, 'M. Rochefort would not fight with you! He would challenge me, because I am the proprietor of the journal.'[23]

Bryham Parsons remained with the *Register* for at least the next year and never fought any duels.[iii]

Business was going well and the bank had made a profit of about £6,000 in its first year of trading. Louis seemed oblivious to the fact that Loewy was making deals with other companies he had a financial interest in, such as the Japanese and Eastern Corporation, or maybe he wasn't worried.

In February 1907 Louis made another visit to St. Petersburg where he met Isvolsky again and received an invitation to visit the Czar at his summer palace in Peterhof.

His Excellency [Isvolsky] drove me through the wonderful gardens surrounding the palace. Below us lay the private yacht, with steam up and ready at a moment's notice to convey the Czar to a place of safety should events necessitate a flight. 'What a terrible way for the Czar to live,' I exclaimed...

'Yes,' replied his Excellency, 'but this is Russia. You may not have observed, perhaps, but this car in which we are motoring has not an atom of wood In its structure; it is fashioned of steel, and is bomb-proof.'

Just then we passed the famous waterfall of the golden steps, sheets of crystal water flowing over wide steps of beaten gold. What a land of contrasts, I thought.[24]

---

iii Bryham Parsons married a French girl, Leone Lacombe, in 1913 and was locked up after they separated and he refused to pay alimony, believing his ex-wife should pay him; in 1914 he was found guilty of selling tickets for an Irish sweepstake (illegal in France) and received a suspended sentence of eight days' imprisonment; in 1930 his seventeen-act play was published (but not performed) in Nice; and in 1924 he wrote a fictionalised version of his life describing how he'd been blackmailed by one man and attacked on a train from Liverpool by a madman who was King of the Cannibals.

Isvolsky told him they were going to have dinner with the Czar and warned Louis to steer the conversation away from any predictions promising doom for Russia.

> 'But, your Excellency,' I protested, 'how can I possibly dine with the Royal family like this— In a blue serge suit? It is impossible!'[25]

Instead of questioning Louis's priorities, Isvolsky pointed out he was also wearing a serge suit and the dinner wasn't formal—indeed, there was a fair chance that the Czar was also wearing a serge suit. Isvolsky was right, although the Czarina wore 'a kind of semi-evening dress'. Apparently, they ate sturgeon.

Louis then spent some time travelling. He visited Jitomir and Baku, where he saw the oil wells and huge refineries, crossed the Caspian Sea to visit Turkestan, and went onto Mount Ararat where he saw a supposed piece of Noah's Ark, Finally, he reached Kiev—this was the point of his trip.

> I presented a letter of introduction from His Excellency Monsieur Isvolsky in Petrograd to Count Vorontzoff-Daskoff, the Viceroy, who received me in a most courteous and charming manner. I carried with me from the Minister of Ways and Communications, a signed Government concession... This concession had been represented to me to be worth a fortune.[27]

The Anglo-French Herald Motor Company was seeking a concession from the Russian government to run buses from Tbilisi, the capital of Georgia, to Vladkiaffcasse, the capital of the Republic of North Ossetia-Alania, located at the foothills of the Caucasus Mountains on the Terek River. This would shorten the journey by two days. Louis decided to take a look around to see precisely what he was dealing with:

> I went by automobile by the once great national road to Jitomir [Zhytomyr]. This wide, magnificent route was made for military purposes and is almost a straight line across the country for a distance of about forty-five miles between the two towns. As this part of the country is very badly served by the railway, the traffic is carried on by the most old-fashioned diligences that one could possibly imagine. To see these odd-shaped vehicles drawn by six or seven horses lumbering along would make one believe one was

suddenly transported back to the heart of the Middle Ages.[28]

He had little to do while waiting for his tender to be considered, and so decided to explore the area: 'The Grand Patriarch was a marvellous-looking old man in his robes of black and gold, and a beard white as snow that almost reached his feet... He gave me a monk as a guide to show me the wonders of the place.'[29]

Louis viewed catacombs and the mummified heads of the ancient monks who had built the cathedral and carved out their own tombs. His guide drew his attention to a small painting suspended on gold chains and framed with gold and diamonds. '"That picture," he said, "was painted by a monk about the year A.D. 400; it is made on human skin taken from the breasts of those monks who started the foundations of the cathedral".' [30]

We'll skip past Louis's belief in the multiple uses for human skin. The guide continued to say that the painting was only lowered to be kissed by special people—the most recent being the German Kaiser. But Louis was so important it was to be lowered for him. Which was nice.

To be thorough, Louis decided to travel the whole route he was offering to arrange transport for. 'The Viceroy, whose guest I was... laughed and said, "If I gave you an escort of my best Cossacks, I doubt if you would ever get half-way".'[31]

That area of the country was wild and infested with bandits. Fortunately, Louis had made friends with a Georgian prince who said that for a small consideration he'd accompany Louis. The next morning, they left at sunrise in a carriage stuffed with provisions and furs. Prudently, Louis had packed a revolver. It wasn't long before they ran into trouble:

> Our horses were dead beat and they had to rest, our men too were hungry and they had to eat. We opened our provisions, we spread them on the upturned face of a massive granite rock. We filled our glasses—we had brought with us a bottle of French champagne, it sparkled in the sun, but, like ourselves, it looked out of place in such surroundings. For hours we had not seen a human being, not a single bandit—as if such worms could live in such a scene! We clinked our glasses, we had raised them to our lips, when from behind our shoulders two huge hands appeared, took them out of our fingers and with a laugh emptied them into two big fierce-looking mouths. They first ate our provisions,

drank our champagne, and with charming consideration gave us two chunks of dry bread for ourselves.[32]

Horrified by the audacity of bandits who stole champagne, Louis and his party were marched for an hour until they reached the bandits' fortress. Apparently, they planned to hold Louis to ransom.

Outside the hut there was no one to be seen, we could wander where we walked. We climbed the edge of the rocks; on two sides there was a precipice with a wall of unbroken rock that looked straight down as far as our eyes could see, and on the other side there was a wide plain of unbroken ice and snow.[33]

The bandits returned to Tbilisi leaving Louis and his party to await their fate. They returned a day or two later in a good mood as they'd met a Muscovian merchant en route and lightened his load by taking from him several thousand pieces of gold, a watch and one of Fabergé's jewelled cigarette cases. To celebrate, they made a venison stew and offered Louis and his party some vodka to wash it down. Then to Louis's astonishment he heard someone say, 'My God, to imagine we should meet like this.'[34]

It was the man whose life Louis had saved from a rifle squad three years previously. He'd become an outlaw and was fighting for the revolutionaries in the north. 'All men are bandits,' he said bitterly, 'until they become successful: if they have luck enough to rob countries, they become kings.'[35]

The bandits took Louis and his party back to Tbilisi where he fully expected to sign the deal. However, he'd been too optimistic. A German company had been negotiating for the same service and had tendered a much lower price—too low for Louis to consider competing against. (Apparently, the German motors turned out to be too light and the service was dropped in the long term, although that version of the story might have been sour grapes on Louis's part.) The deal had come to nothing. Never mind, there'd be other deals and Louis's businesses were doing well; Loewy was taking good care of things so he'd no reason to worry.

Or so he thought.

CHAPTER

THIRTEEN

The count is a very clever talker and has a fund of interesting stories.[1]

ONFIDENT THAT THE ABBÉ AND LOEWY could deal with the boring ins and outs of running his businesses, Louis decided that after the recent excitement, he deserved a holiday. He crossed the Black Sea, stopped off in Constantinople, and then headed to Genoa. After relaxing in Italy, he arrived in Monte Carlo at the end of February 1907. The plan was to test if applying numerology and astrology to the gaming tables would help him turn a profit. It did: 'After considerable practice I was able to gain on an average about 5,000 francs (£200) during the hour that I had selected to play.'[2]

The problem was that making the relevant calculations, and maintaining his nerve, left Louis worn out, so he didn't hang around for long. After failing to make a deal with the Russians, Louis had decided to give up complicated activities and focus on having a good time. 'Money to him meant so little that he flung it to the winds like rain.'[3]

He was back in Paris in March and then nipped over to London where he met up with Hamilton Harty and attended a private concert given by the singer Marthe Gavarett at the Carlton hotel. In May he attended a fundraiser for the animal charity Our Dumb Friends League at the Wharncliffe Rooms at the Grand Central hotel, and in June he was a weekend guest at Guilsborough Hall, home of American novelist Irene Osgood.[i] Osgood said she barely knew Louis and he came to the

---

i Our Dumb Friends League became the Blue Cross in 1950, as this is what it was

Hall on business. This is probably accurate, as an interview with Osgood appeared in the *Register* in September that year.

From time to time, Louis imparted financial insight. 'Tell Count Hamon your troubles... He is a business man who knows all about stocks. Besides, he is very wise and can give you the best advice,' the Abbé apparently told Julia Newell and Josephine Pomeroy.[4]

Two things happened in 1907 to make Newell and Pomeroy question this wisdom. First, Julia's husband died unexpectedly in Paris on 15 May, leaving them feeling insecure. Second, the US was heading for potentially the biggest financial crisis in its history.

In 1906 the US economy had been booming, but a series of events had unsettled the market. The banking system in the US was different to that of Europe. There was no centralised bank and most investors used trust companies which had appeared in the early 1890s to hold investments and gradually taken on other activities until they'd effectively become banks. But trusts weren't as regulated as banks and didn't need to hold as many of their assets as cash.

There was a drop in the stock market after the Standard Oil Company faced financial difficulties in February. Then a shipping conglomerate failed in the summer. Tight credit markets in Europe and the Bank of England raising its bank rate from December 1906 added to a sense of insecurity. The seriousness of the situation was yet to become apparent, but by summer 1907 things were uncertain enough for Americans in Paris to be seriously worried. Stories of embezzlement were rife, and fear of war with Japan in June added to the general sense of panic.

In the US, copper kings Augustus Heinze and Charles Morse had borrowed huge amounts to invest in United Copper, a copper mining company. When the economy slowed down and depressed the prices of raw materials, the value of United Copper's shares fell. To prop up the market, they tapped funds from the banks they ran—and made huge losses. This led to the closure of the Westinghouse Electric Company and the Knickerbocker Trust Company (plus the suicide of Knickerbocker's president) in October, accompanied by a mass panic.

Worried that banks and trusts were short of cash, people rushed to withdraw their money. The New York Stock Exchange promptly fell almost 50% from its peak the previous year. Some states declared emergency holidays while others limited withdrawals. The US was

popularly being called by then due to it being the name of one of its fundraising campaigns.

suddenly in the midst of a recession—unemployment increased and production plummeted.[ii] Americans all over the world suddenly lost money as their stocks and shares dropped in value.

By the end of 1907, Louis's bank was broke. And he'd lost another £14,000 on a failed financial paper—*La Gazette Financiere*. Desperate for money, Louis sold the *American Register* in January 1908 for £20,000 in shares and a director's salary of £500 a year.

Everyone in the Colony was suffering financially, but from the outside Louis didn't appear to have problems. He held *musicales* at his apartments during January 1908, one of his guests being Count Rudolphe Festetics de Tolna. The following month Louis attended Count Festetics's wedding.

Count Festetics was a well-known adventurer, one of those characters who if he appeared in a novel, you'd describe as too unrealistic. This was his second marriage. When he'd married millionaire's daughter Ella Haggin, her parents had given the happy couple a yacht for their wedding present. In 1893, the Count and Countess set off on a cruise that was to last eight years. They sailed to Sydney and the Solomon islands, up to Japan and back down to Singapore, before going west to the Indian Ocean.

The Festetics encountered cannibals, collected souvenirs, visited Robert Louis Stevenson and tried to enter Manila at the beginning of the Spanish-American war. After leaving Ella behind in Singapore in 1897, Count Festetics continued his cruise until his yacht was wrecked in the Indian ocean and he lost many of his treasures. Two months later, he and his crew were picked up by a British ship. But Ella had had enough of this adventuring. Complaining that her husband had tried to feed her to cannibals and he was guilty of cruelty and neglect, she filed for divorce in 1901.[iii]

Festetics was marrying sculptor Alice Wetherbee—it was also her second marriage, but that didn't stop the couple hosting a grand reception at their home and inviting anyone who was anyone in the Colony.

Gossip about the state of Hamon and Co wasn't enough to stop Louis

---

ii The situation was resolved when J P Morgan with other leading financiers raised enough funds to support financial institutions. However, the American economy didn't begin to grow again until 1909.

iii The Count wrote a book about his experiences *Chez les Cannibales: Huit Ans de Croisiere Dans L'ocean Pacifique A Bord du Yacht le Tolna* (Among the cannibals: Eight years of cruising the Pacific Ocean on the yacht Tolna) , which became a bestseller in 1903 and was followed by a second volume in 1904.

from partying. In March 1908 he hosted further receptions and was one of 600 guests at a St Patrick's Day ball in London. Possibly in a bid to take life more seriously, in April and May he organised and hosted anti-vivisection meetings and attended fundraisers for Our Dumb Friends League in London.

Newell and Pomeroy had been asking for months what had happened to their railway bonds and wrote to Louis asking for them back—or enough cash to cover their value. Louis said he didn't know what they were on about as he'd never made a deal with them. The sisters insisted that although it might not be him *personally* they'd dealt with, the Hamon bank had their shares so it came to the same thing. They mentioned money they'd put into the bank in 1906 and Louis pointed out he'd been in St Petersburg so they couldn't possibly have dealt with him.

Oddly, instead of putting their energy into extricating themselves from Hamon and Co, Newell and Pomeroy dug themselves in more deeply and asked Louis to extricate them from a stock market deal in New York where they'd handed over their American Coal Company shares to a broker. In November the Hamon bank asked Newell and Pomeroy to redeem their accounts. When they didn't respond, their shares were sold.

In early December, Loewy abruptly left Paris. Although Louis at first thought he'd gone to Germany, that's unlikely considering there was a warrant for his arrest waiting in Berlin, plus he soon turned up in London.

Newell and Pomeroy were becoming insistent. Louis checked the records of sales made by Loewy and said the shares had been sold in London. He insisted that Loewy had stolen them and he'd had nothing to do with it. He asked Newell and Pomeroy not to make a formal complaint because that would send Loewy into hiding, saying, 'If we keep this thing quiet a few days longer, we will be able to trap the fellow.'[5]

What about the American Coal Company shares? Louis had put them as collateral in the name of Baroness Epstein, who'd pledged 130,000 francs (about $30,000) in the bank. Several attempts had been made to sell these shares, one by an unnamed woman who said she'd bought them from Louis.

Louis appointed a Greek lawyer, N D Antoniadis, to look at the bank's finances. Antoniadis told Baroness Epstein it was Loewy's fault and things could be worked out. Somehow, he persuaded her that the best way of doing this was to give him a cheque for three thousand francs, saying a cash injection was needed to save Louis from embarrassment. The Baroness agreed and gave Antoniadis a cheque. He pocketed it, promptly disappeared, and the Baroness realised she'd been duped.

She lodged a complaint with the magistrate and he referred the matter to M Valette, the commissaire aux délégations judiciaires. Antoniadis was found and offered multiple excuses as to why he didn't return the cheque—he'd given it to a friend, left it at home by mistake, and left it with a lawyer. Frustrated, Valette threatened Antoniadis with prison; he handed the cheque back and threatened to call his embassy. In a startling display of hubris, Antoniadis then lodged a complaint against Valette for abusing his powers—which was immediately rejected. Throughout the arguments, Antoniadis continued to hold onto the bank's books and papers, which only added to the confusion. The case wasn't resolved until July 1909 when the Court Corectionalle sentenced Antoniadis to six months in prison.

Newell and Pomeroy went to the American Ambassador for advice and were told to lodge a formal complaint with the Public Prosecutor. They promptly did so. Word got around and several of the bank's creditors seized the furniture at the offices to cover their debts. Gossip said that when they turned up, Louis put on his doorkeeper's coat and hat and told them the 'count' had left for London.

On Christmas Day, Newell and Pomeroy obtained an injunction against the sale of their American Coal stock in New York or London. The magistrate told Louis to return their stocks and bonds or reimburse their money in full. Louis refused and said he preferred to leave. The case was adjourned for three days. True to his word, Louis left Paris for London that evening.

His absence wasn't noticed until police arrived at his offices to serve papers on him—possibly with a warrant for his arrest, although accounts are unclear. Despite claims he'd completely vanished and police were desperately searching for him, the search seemed only to comprise visiting his London offices and not finding him in. Indeed, Louis turned up the next day. He told reporters in exasperation that he was in London on business and hadn't been hiding at all. The business he had in mind, according to some accounts, was to find Loewy.

Louis's secretary told journalists in Paris that it was a misunderstanding and Louis had recently lost $60,000 and so was struggling to pay his creditors. One of his typists, Madame Laharpe, agreed, saying she hadn't been paid for the last year (she was a wealthy widow) but Louis was the 'grandest man in the world.'[6] Another employee said Newell and Pomeroy had ordered certain purchases and when they made a loss, they wanted to put the blame elsewhere. Shortly after the story of Newell and Pomerory's case hit the English-speaking press, news of Baroness Epstein's complaint appeared.

Not everyone wanted Louis to return to Paris. It was the last thing many women wanted. When the police made a thorough search of Louis's offices and his apartment, there was no money in the safe but they uncovered lists of banking clients and similar documents. And they were astonished when they broke open his desk and found four hundred love letters (yes, four hundred; they were carefully counted) addressed to Louis.

> Never before was there such a collection of love letters to one man. Some of them were comparatively innocent, the gushing outpourings of girls, the sentimental rhapsodies of their older sisters. But these were in a minority. Many of the others were absolutely shameless in their self-revelation, in the utter abandon of their tone.[7]

The letters were from women from all walks of society, single and married. Most were written in English although some were in French. They were filled with endearments and reproaches for not having written to them. A man who read the letters told the press:

> It is absolutely incredible that women of such position could have dared write such letters. The letters should be destroyed. I have not tried to discover the identity of any of the writers, but some of the names were well known to me. Apparently, the women who wrote to Cheiro were so infatuated with him that their hearts ran away with their heads and they threw caution to the winds. Nearly all of the letters were written by women of high position, as could be seen from the nature of their correspondence. I hope that the letters will be burned, whether Cheiro is ever brought back here or not.[8]

One letter was different—it showed Louis's infatuation for 'a woman well known amongst the boulevards.'[9] Who she was is unknown.

Women all over Paris held their breath. If Louis was brought back to stand trial, the letters would form part of the evidence against him. They could be read in open court and reported in the papers. Gossip would spread like wildfire and bring in its trail one divorce after another, accompanied by shame, embarrassment, financial difficulty, and feeling generally silly. The simple existence of the letters had already led to whispers on the boulevards. And the police would have a real headache. There'd be chaos in court. Louis may have been guilty, but much of Paris wanted him to go away and be guilty somewhere else.

Louis was safe in London. Britain didn't allow extradition of her citizens (hence lengthy discussions regarding Louis's Irishness), and the transactions had been made in England so might not have fallen under French law. Indeed, Louis suggested that the transaction on which the charge of fraud was based was legitimate and wouldn't have caused any bother in London or New York. Due to heavy losses caused by the state of the market, he now only owed Josephine and Julia $7,000, although he'd pay up if the courts found more was due.

Once it was obvious that Louis and Loewy weren't coming back, although convinced Louis had been duped by Loewy, the French press struggled to find anything interesting else to say. An interview with the hotel manager of the Hotel Continental revealed that Louis had stayed there fifteen days before the complaint had been made and had looked worried. On being pressed, the manager added that Louis and Loewy stayed there often, although not necessarily at the same time, and Loewy brought his wife. And they had no trouble in getting him to pay his bill. He tried, but there wasn't a story to be had.

The story hit the American press when the police search took place— and a different story was told. Louis was presented as a mastermind criminal and Loewy barely warranted a mention. Some newspapers dug into their files and repeated Louis's stories about India. A few came up with facts, but more put two and two together and made five. Learning he'd been an actor, they assumed he must have been an actor in the US: 'Cheiro came to this country as a member of Wilson Barrett's theatrical company when that great star made his first trip to America... He had too strong a personality to suit Wilson Barrett and was dropped. In casting about for something to do, Warner decided on palmistry.'[10][iv]

Some accounts were simply bizarre. Refusing to believe Louis was Irish, they described him as being born in New Orleans, and said 'his father was a German, his mother Creole French.'[11] Louis couldn't be Irish because he wasn't Catholic, and he was so nasty that his landlord had thrown him out, being a good Irish Catholic himself. Or he was Irish, but

---

iv Barrett had indeed formed his own touring company and had managed the Princess's Theatre where Louis had acted between 1881-1886. By the time Louis became part of the company, Barrett was no longer its manager, although he was still associated with the theatre in most people's minds.

not proper Irish—he was of 'Irish Hebrew origin.'[12] Like many reports, this one pointed out that Louis had been forced to leave London after being investigated by Scotland Yard.[v]

Sometimes, the press sidestepped the issue of Cheiro's origins and said he was really someone else. One newspaper reported he was the German Charles Pscherhofer (Count von Pscherhofer) who'd served time for financial fraud and had picked up palmistry in prison.[13] Pscherhofer had disappeared years ago…

What about his title? He'd probably 'inherited it from his father, who received it from the pope.'[14] Or it had been conferred on him by a ne'er-do-well adventurer.

> In Paris Warner met a man who called himself King of Sedange and Hamon, two small islands near the Malay peninsular. This king was really Count Meyrena, an Italian adventurer and explorer. The king was seated with an American and 'Cheiro' at a table in a cafe one day when he asked the American if he did not want to be made Count Haman [sic]. 'No,' the American said, 'I will take a cigarette instead'. The honor was offered next to Warner and he was forthwith ennobled.[15] [vi]

When it came to how Louis become a palmist, the consensus was he'd been taught by Oscar Wilde (or at least discovered by him), who'd come up with the name 'Cheiro'. Louis wasn't even a real palmist. He had a 'distinct hatred for the superstition of his patrons' and burned incense that smelled like rotten onions.[16] It was all about conning money out of people, primarily women.

> He was quite willing to gossip about the fools who came to him, laughing at their credulity. Over and over he asserted that there was nothing in the so-called 'science' of palmistry—that it was all a fake, but a profitable one….
>
> Some of the information he extracted from woman clients seemed so valuable to him that he attempted to force their husbands to pay money. Complaints were made to the police and though

---

v Other reports make it clear that this misconception derived from him being confused with Charles Stephenson (Keiro) who stood trial in 1904.

vi King Sedange was French adventurer Charles-Marie David Mayréna, who had established his own country in the Kingdom of Annam of French Indo-China (south Vietnam) in 1888 after helping locals deal with an epidemic. During his two-year reign, King Marie sought support from the British and Belgian governments and declared war on France. He ran up enormous debts in Paris at the end of the 1880s and died in exile in 1890 of a cobra bite—or he was poisoned or committed suicide, no-one knows.

Cheiro was not arrested he was driven out of town.

He knew his clients down to the bottom of their silly and sordid little hearts. What was more to the point, he knew their histories... Small wonder, then, that his predictions so often came true... If he predicted an affaire du coeur of the tenderest nature, he was in a position to secure the fulfilment of his prophecy... It was the frequency with which he was consulted upon finance that led to his downfall.[19]

One place where Louis didn't feature was the *American Register*. No one said anything about Count Hamon's troubles, but he vanished from its pages. 'Cheiro' re-appeared in January 1910 with his 'Occult Notes' column and continued to write for the *Register* but 'Count Hamon' had ceased to exist.

Back in the real world, a 'for rent' sign went up at 8 Place de l'Opéra... The bank... fell under a shadow, and its collapse is a matter of public notoriety. The geraniums and azaleas disappeared from the window-boxes... all of us were swept away.[20]

Louis came to a settlement with Newell and Pomeroy—it's unclear how much money they got back, but they lost a lot. He was also sentenced to thirteen months' imprisonment in his absence (which he never served). But it wasn't over yet. In May Count Festetics claimed he'd been swindled out of nearly a million francs ($200,000) and brought his own complaint. Other complaints were rumoured to be forthcoming, although they didn't. Louis had to pay 500 francs in restitution to Count Festetics. The Count now leaves our story but you may be pleased to learn that he and Alice spent much of the next years sailing his yacht.

Josephine Pomeroy left Paris to live in London while Julia Newell continued to make bad decisions. In February 1911, at the age of fifty-two, she married thirty-year-old George Draper. She thought he was American, although he was English, despite trying to convince everyone he was Romanian. Believing Draper to be the protector she needed to stop her from getting into further financial scrapes, Julia announced a reception and invited her friends to meet him. Unfortunately, she fell ill and a friend had to take her place. Even more unfortunately, Draper was a gambler and used Julia's money to support his hobby. And he was verbally abusive. Draper soon disappeared and Julia had to pay agents to pursue him around France to serve divorce papers on him.

And Louis? 'This adventurer, palmist, journalist and financier has come to the lowest ebb of his fortune.'[21] He declared bankruptcy in

September 1910 with debts of £43,000, though Louis said most of them had already been settled by someone else.[vii] All he had left was ten shares in an unnamed company worth four shillings.

So he decided to bring aviation races to England.

---

vii A later report suggested the debts amounted to about £72,000 but they were mostly paid off.

INTERLUDE

PLAYING THE TABLES

Before you risk any money on the tables, it's wise to examine your hand. Should your third finger—the finger of the Sun—be longer than your first finger, success is more likely. This is especially so if the Line of the Sun is distinct on your palm. Take care if it's especially long, as this suggests you can get carried away. If this finger is also crooked, handling money sensibly is beyond you, and it would be better if you took up a safer pastime

Cheiro will tell you of the time he met Princess Lavalia, and how when she took his advice and based her bets on the number 6, which was personally lucky for her—she won back her earlier losses. You could do the same by using numbers that are a multiple of your personal number.

But there are times when some numbers are more powerful than others. If you use astrology to calculate these times, your chances of success will be greater—especially if you combine this with your personal number.[i]

---

i Although Cheiro didn't detail his methodology, his comments suggest he was using the system described in John Roye's *Astrology The Key to Roulette* (London: Nichols and Co., 1908) so some astrological details are derived from this text. I've been unable to identify Roye (it appears to have been a pseudonym) who claimed to have based his theory on spending a month at the tables in Monte Carlo in 1905. It's possible that Louis is Roye. and it's notable that the only lengthy review I've traced (one of very few reviews) appears in the *American Register*, 11 April, 1908. The same system is used throughout the astrologer Sepharial's work—for example, in *Cosmic Symbolism* (London: Rider, 1912)—and forms the basis of his horse racing prediction techniques. Like many of Sepharial's techniques, it appears to be based on the astrology he learned in India.

Astrology will help you succeed at roulette because the wheel represents the zodiac itself. The 36 numbers and zero combine to give 360—the number of degrees in the zodiac. The four-pointed cross by which the wheel is turned corresponds to the four cardinal points of the zodiac, and the four seasons. And when you add the numbers that lie on the green cloth together (the colour of which represents the element of earth), they total 9, the number of the planets in the solar system.

The colours of the numbers given in roulette as red and black symbolise qualities of the planets and each of the classical planets rules a day of the week:

Moon	2, 11, 20, 29	black (feminine)	Monday
Mars	9, 18, 27, 36	red (masculine)	Tuesday
Venus	6, 15, 24, 33	black	Friday
Jupiter	3, 12, 21, 30	red	Thursday
Uranus	4, 13, 22, 31	black	
Mercury	5, 14, 25, 32	red	Wednesday
Saturn	8, 17, 26, 35	black	Saturday
Neptune	7, 16, 25, 34	red	
Sun	1, 19, 28	red	Sunday
	10	Number 10 of the Sun and zero is black.	

The first calculation you need to make is that of the *planetary hour*. For this, you need to know the local time of sunrise and sunset for the date you plan to place your bets. Then take the time of sunset and divide the time span by twelve. The first hour is governed by the planet that rules that day, and the following hours are then ruled by the planets in the following sequence: Saturn, Jupiter, Mars, Sun, Venus, Mercury, Moon and then back to Saturn and continue the sequence until you run out of hours.

If you are playing the tables at night, divide the time between sunset on the day you begin and sunrise of the following day.

Don't forget that because you're using the time of *apparent* sunset in your initial calculations, your times won't match with clock time. Just adjust your watch so it matches the times you're using.

Once you've noted these planetary hours (which will not be the same length as clock hours and will be longer during the daytime in summer), you will need to make a further calculation to divide them into their *planetary periods*.

These periods are the time occupied by the Sun in passing through one degree of its apparent daily rotation about the Earth. In one solar day (the time between sunrise and sunset), the Sun passes through 180 degrees. This takes about sixteen hours in midsummer but only about nine hours in midwinter. A single period is therefore between three and five minutes in length.

Next you note the planetary hour you plan to gamble in and divide it by 15—the number of degrees or planetary periods in an hour. The first period of your planetary hour is ruled by the planet that rules that hour.

For example, your planetary hour is ruled by Venus and lasts from 21:46 to 22:34. That makes it 48 minutes long.

Dividing it by 15 gives 3 minutes and 12 seconds.

Use the planet that rules the period to decide which numbers to play.

The first period is from 21:46 to 21:49:12 and is ruled by Venus. At this time you should play the numbers associated with Venus.

The second period is from 21:49:12 to 21:52:24 and is ruled by Mercury (using the sequence above) so you should play Mercury's numbers.

The next period will be the Moon's and it's usually best to avoid the Sun and Moon periods because they take two numbers each and you'd need to play higher stakes or risk choosing the wrong number. (Also, remember while playing roulette that the ball must register before the period ends.)

When this planetary hour ends at 22:34, the next one will be ruled by Mercury. However, you don't need to make any new calculations but can simply keep adding your period number (in this case 3 minutes and 12 seconds) as Mercury will be the ruler of the first period of the Mercury hour.

You also need to examine the relationship of the planet to other planets at the time of play. If it's applying to a square or opposition of another planet, this will weaken it. (If you don't know what that means, a friendly astrologer can help you.) Rather than take a risk, it would be better to sit back and have a drink at these times.

If all this sounds like too much work, stick to your personal number. That will still give you an advantage.

Cheiro in 1916

CHAPTER
FOURTEEN

The count is a very clever talker and has a fund of interesting stories.[1]

ON SUNDAY 25 JULY 1909 French aviator Louis Blériot took off from France and landed in England thirty-six minutes and thirty seconds later.

The *Daily Mail* had offered a £500 prize in October 1908 to anyone who made the flight successfully. When no-one won it, the prize was doubled the following year. It didn't matter how much it was, such a feat surely wasn't possible? Aviators thought it was. Blériot's rival, Hubert Latham, was the favourite to win. On 19 July Latham made his attempt but six miles from his destination he developed engine trouble and had to be rescued by a French destroyer.

On 21 July Blériot arrived in Calais. He had to be patient. The wind was too strong for a crossing, although it began to drop on 24 July. At 4:15 am on 25 July, in front of an excited crowd, Blériot made a short trial flight. Once the sun had risen, he took off in earnest. Poor visibility plus no compass meant that for ten minutes of his flight, Blériot didn't know where he was, let alone if he'd make it. Then he saw the English coast and followed it until he spotted Charles Fontaine, a correspondent from *Le Matin*, waving a Tricolour to signal a suitable landing spot. Blériot made a rough landing and did some damage to his plane but he was uninjured.

Thirty-six minutes and thirty seconds. Unbelievable.

The *Daily Mail* took Blériot to the harbour where he met his wife, and then to the Lord Warden Hotel. Blériot had become a celebrity. Thousands waited to greet him the next day when he arrived at London's Victoria station. His plane was taken to London and displayed in Selfridges on Oxford Street where it was seen by 12,000 people over four days.

This was the year of the plane and Louis wanted to be part of it. He'd somehow wangled his way onto the International Aviation Committee, which formed a company in September 1909, registered at 32 Piccadilly Circus—the same address as Louis's other business concerns. The IAC planned to host the first English aviation races and announced meetings near London in October. Precisely where was unclear, and when a journalist turned up at their offices, he was told the chairman didn't want to give his name or the names of any of the promoters, although six aviators—three English and three French—had promised to take part. The IAC was organised by William Casper and Franz Reichel, sports editor of *Le Figaro*, who had recently taken charge of the arrangements for a similar show in Spa, Belgium, with Frank Harris, a friend of Louis's, as chair of the committee, Charles Holland Hastings and Hugo Martens. [i]

Harris was an Irish writer and publisher who'd spent much of his life in the US where he'd run away to at the age of thirteen.[ii] After a variety of jobs, including as a construction worker on the Brooklyn Bridge, Harris moved to Chicago and worked as a hotel clerk and eventually a manager. He left Chicago to become a cowboy in Kansas and then trained as a lawyer. Moving to England in 1882, Harris became a journalist and an editor of a series of London papers. He was part of Oscar Wilde's circle and one of his biographers.[iii]

Harris knew everyone. Wilde apparently said to him, 'Yes, dear Frank—you have dined in every house in London—once.'[2]

Frank Harris was an objectionable little man. He was sallow as a gypsy. He had bat ears, dark hair with a crinkle in it that grew low on the forehead, and a truculent mustache. People remarked on the richness of his bass voice. His charm was great, particularly for the opposite sex. He had the gift of gab to a sublime degree and a streak of deep scoundrelism that was the ruin of him.[3]

Frank Harris... had the crippling disqualification that he told the truth,

---

i Known as an explorer, Hastings was often remembered for going bankrupt in 1904 after recruiting African natives to create a Somali village for the Bradford Exhibition.
ii Born James Thomas Harris.
iii In 1922 his book *My Life And Loves* which detailed this period of his life was published— at least, it detailed his sex life during this period and mentioned his writing activities. The book was banned in several countries for decades.

as Max Beerbohm remarked, only 'when his invention flagged'.[4]

He caught the money–grubbing fever of the time. He'd speculate in anything.[5]

And he dressed to be noticed: 'One does not meet Frank Harris; one collides with him.'[6] When Louis knew him, he was primarily a novelist. He was also a close friend of Aleister Crowley's having published much of his writing while editor of *Vanity Fair* between 1907 and 1909.[iv]

But we digress…

Soon it was announced that the first aviation event would take place in Doncaster and the second at Dunstall racecourse in Wolverhampton. And Blériot had agreed to fly. The problem was that someone else had got there first. The Aero Club of the United Kingdom had already sanctioned a meeting in Blackpool for 13-23 October. H E Perrin, club secretary, visited the IAC's offices but remained close-lipped about discussions. Eventually, on 6 October, the Aero Club announced they couldn't sanction the Doncaster meeting—it considered there weren't enough aviators to go round and called for the banning of the IAC's meetings. And it said that aviators who partipated in the Doncaster meeting would be disqualified from international competitions.

The argument blew up into one of those fights that only truly obsessed people understand. It was an attack on free enterprise said the IAC. No, said the Aero Club, the IAC was trying to overbid flyers already contacted for Blackpool. The IAC said they hadn't much choice about the date because it was simply when Doncaster was available. The French aviators said they didn't care one way or the other. People got indignant and then there was a row about who was actually in charge of the IAC event.

The argument reached court the same day Doncaster opened on 15 October. Caspar at first refused to say who was in the new syndicate, except that he'd met them at Spa. He admitted there'd been negotiations with Harris and Louis, saying they'd been given until the 14 September to come up with their promised cash. When they failed, he had to seek money elsewhere and had teamed up with a Mr Byron and Aubrey de Vere

---

iv In 1913, Harris became editor of *Modern Society* and was charged with prejudicing a trial after publishing an ongoing divorce case. When the judge noted, 'It seems to me you have a certain disdain for this court,' Harris famously responded, 'Oh, if I could only express all the disdain I have.' He received three months in prison for contempt of court. Shortly after his release he left London and never lived there again. He died in Nice in 1931.

Beauclerk (the Duke of St Albans).ᵛ Byron and Beauclerk now expected their share of any profits.[7] Louis, Harris, Hastings and Martens said it was their event. Louis had supplied an affidavit (he was in Wolverhampton to discuss a meeting planned for November) saying they'd agreed to share profits or losses equally. It became clear that Caspar was broke and his hotel bill had been paid by Martens. Caspar was accused of trying to con the original investors so he and his friends could share the profits. With the case convened at such short notice, there was general confusion and the exasperated judge appointed an interim receiver to keep control of the money over the next week.[8]

In Doncaster rain poured down accompanied by a blustery wind. That morning, all the crowd saw was four machines doing engine runs in front of the grandstands. One machine was damaged in the wind. There was much excitement when a telegram arrived saying the receiver was to take the gate money received that morning. Late afternoon, Colonel Cody's monoplane slid across the ground for a quarter of a mile and then stopped. The crows turned their attention to watching Princess Louise Schleswig-Holstein and Earl and Countess Fitzwilliam who'd arrived to watch the event. It was still raining.

The weather improved on the second day so some flights took place, although high winds meant a pause for the 70,000 spectators in the early afternoon. Monday attracted 50,000 people, although they had to wait until the afternoon to see any flying. The remainder of the week was the same—long pauses because of bad weather and short flights accompanied

---

v Charles Victor Albert Aubrey de Vere Beauclerk, 11th Duke of St Albans (26 March 1870 – 19 September 1934) was a godchild of Queen Victoria and Albert, Prince of Wales and inherited his father's titles in 1898. He was descended from Charles II and Nell Gwyn in the male line and via his mother he was a direct descendant of the American Indian princess Pocahontas (Rebecca Rolfe). After a visit to Australia he fell prey to attacks of fever and came to believe that his father and stepmother were conspiring against him, that his stepmother was trying to poison him, and that the family doctors and lawyers were in league with them. After he ran up debts and ended up in court, his father agreed to pay them on condition that he went to India. Beauclerck contracted dysentery and on his return was bent on a lawsuit against his father for the loss of his hair. In 1899, he boarded his then dead father's yacht and fired at the captain with a revolver, urging the rest of the crew to take up arms against a gang of (invisible) conspirators. He was bound and taken into custody under an urgency order. Beauclerck spent the rest of his life as a 'Chancery lunatic' at Ticehurst House private asylum in East Sussex. It was widely assumed that he had gone on an extended cruise around the world. On his death, many newspapers were under the impression that he'd been living in retirement on his Lincolnshire estate, Redbourne (which had been sold in 1917).

by multiple accidents. Doncaster council extended the event by two days to make up for it.

In the end, the money didn't matter. Although 160,000 people had visited, even with Doncaster council's £5,000 to cover expenses, the meeting made a loss of £ 8,000—maybe less surprising when you realise the appearance money for the flyers totalled £11,600. Negotiations with Wolverhampton council broke down before Doncaster had ended. The Aero Club demanded letters of apology—and received some. Other aviation groups emerged and the Aero Club slowly lost their monopoly.

Although the IAC continued until 1916, Louis's involvement from then on goes unrecorded. And he was constantly beset by hassles beyond his control. Earlier that year he'd lent his accountant, Isaac Coop, some money to help him get a business off the ground. On 30 October Coop appeared in court for not having complied with a maintenance order. His wife and children had been forced to rely on friends while Coop had 'plenty of money for drinking'.[9] Louis didn't want any more bad press so he promptly sacked Coop.[vi]

At this point, Louis switched gear completely and directed his energy towards some of the multiple spiritualist and psychic groups he hadn't joined. He had to make careful choices. Unlike astrology, which was primarily a middle-class London interest, and palmistry, which was popular amongst high society (although much less popular than it had been), spiritualism in England had a history of being a northern, working class activity.

The easiest way of ensuring he mixed with the right class of spiritualists was to arrange events himself. Louis took advantage of his relationship with the *American Register* to host events on psychic phenomena, the first being a lecture by a Mr Mitras on psychic control at the *Register's* reception rooms on 2 October 1909. Once the aviation fuss had died down, Louis gave talks himself. In December 1909 he spoke under the banner of the London Occult Society on 'Numbers the secret of life's mysteries' and 'A distinguished audience [was] held spellbound for two hours by a remarkable lecture'.[10]

The Society had been hosting lectures since the late 1880s (occult royalty such as A E Waite of the Golden Dawn had spoken there in 1887). Its president had been A F Tindall, who was also behind the London Spiritualist Federation and was involved with the National Spiritualist

---

vi The following year, Coop was in court again, as he never paid his maintenance, and ended up serving two months.

Federation. It was a diverse organisation, although heavily Christian in focus. Interestingly, Tindall, a teacher of music correspondence courses (no, I don't know exactly how that worked), claimed Helena Blavatsky as one of his spirit controls. Tindall had died in July 1909, but by then the Society had taken on a life of its own. Of course, some reorganisation was inevitable after Tindall's death, and the secretary received inquiries for tickets at 32 Piccadilly Circus—coincidentally, Louis's business address.

Unsurprisingly, 1910 was a quiet year for Louis. He was broke, after all. The society events he attended were of the larger kind where anyone who purchased a ticket could get in. For example, in July he was at the American Ambassador's reception for Independence Day amongst three or four thousand others.[11] But Louis was no longer top of anyone's guest list, no longer offering flowing champagne and no longer buying pianos at the drop of a hat. He had some income, but he'd had to severely tighten his belt.

Not that he wanted anyone to know this, of course. Indeed, according to Louis he lent Captain Arthur de Courcy Bower £500 to take to Monte Carlo. Bower was a convicted fraudster who'd been sentenced to six months hard labour in 1904. In January 1911 he was reported to have won the maximum payout eighteen times in a row and to have broken the bank five times on a visit to Monte Carlo.[vii] According to Louis, Bower had gone to see him after he'd left his wife and fallen in love again. And he needed money.

> 'We have just time to reach your bank before it closes; bring your cheque book and come with me.' There was such a pathetic look in his eyes I could not refuse. We went to the bank, got the money, and a few hours later I saw him off on the night train for the Continent. 'Good-bye,' he said. ' You will have your five hundred back within a week and another five hundred profit.'[12]

Two weeks later the story of Bower's success hit the papers and Louis received a bank order for £1,000. At least, that's Louis's version—he also said that Bower had used his numerology system to win. In fact, Bower had won £250,000 using his own system in which he had five assistants engaged in placing maximum stakes. The money was spent in a year or two. Bower made a hobby of spending money like water, and he did remarry, but not the woman he'd earlier fallen in love with—he chose a millionairess who supplied him with even more money to spend.

---

vii Despite popular belief, he didn't inspire the popular song 'The Man Who Broke the Bank in Monte Carlo', as that pre-dated his adventure by twenty years.

On balance, spiritualist groups were much more welcoming to Louis at this time, and on 20 January 1911 he spoke on 'The Occult Significance of Numbers' at the Salon of the Golden Key.[13] [viii]

The Salon was an unashamedly upmarket spiritualist group. It didn't host séances, but offered talks where people discussed how important a variety of occult factors were. You didn't have to mess with potentially dangerous spiritual practices and you could be sure of sitting next to the right sort of people (despite the assertion that ordinary people could attend): 'When the psychic, door is open, it is well that the undesirables, if they do not seek help to progress, should be shut out.'[14]

Meetings took place at the home of Hugo and Flora Ames.[ix] The Salon had been founded in May 1909 based on their *Book of the Golden Key: an idyll and a revelation being a message from the so-called dead*.[15]

> At no time in our studies have we ever read anything so utterly and entirely unconvincing... it is a diary of a sham temperament finding a reincarnated lover in a man of sham cleverness, and both pouring forth their dull and uninteresting souls... the language in which it is written is of the sham grandilqouent style and its hopeless absurdities will provide several hours of almost continuous laughter...[16]

Flora (born Hayter), a romantic novelist who wrote under the name of 'Mrs. Beresford', was in her second marriage in 1908 when she eloped with Hugo Ames.[x] A former British Embassy attaché in Washington, Ames had become a journalist. In 1907 he'd become bored with married life and started spending more time away from home.[xi] He told his brother, 'I am going to America shortly on a lecturing tour with regard to some cult that I have started.'[17] [xii]

Flora took advantage of her husband's absence to set off with Ames in October 1908 on a tour around the US to lecture on the purity of divorce laws—which is almost the definition of irony. While in Idaho, Ames

---

viii This is different to the Society of the Golden Key, run by the same people—that was a guild for political debate.

ix Real name Hugh Ames. At 14 Lexham Gardens in Kensington.

x She'd divorced Arthur Forbes Montanaro (later the governor of Sierra Leone) in 1895 and two years later married Charles Northesk Wilson Montanaro.

xi He'd married Kate Palmer in 1896.

xii This may have been the Order of Sir Galahad, which Ames had founded and which became associated with Francis Vane's Order of World Scouts—a grander and more chivalrous movement than Baden-Powell's Boy Scouts movement that sought universal brotherhood.

received a (fraudulent) divorce and Flora and Ames married in California, returning to England and marrying for a second time (presumably, to be on the safe side) in London in January 1911.[xiii]

Ames 'took himself very seriously indeed, and I had some difficulty in persuading him that there was no reason why other people should do so' said one journalist.[18] But other people did, including Louis. The Golden Salon met every Friday night and he was certainly at its reception at the Piccadilly hotel in May. So was Baroness Epstein—maybe she and Louis had made up by then.[xiv]

Louis now said he'd always been into spiritualism. He'd been to many séances and had plenty of stories. Now firmly implanted in London, Louis moved his business address to the Total Insurance Buildings in Mayfair and is listed in the phone directory as having nine phone lines, so presumably was leading an active business life.[xv] Loewy was now working in the City and had an address in Kensington as well as in Lancashire. Whether Louis had any further dealings with him, or, indeed, any contact at all, is unknown, but he could easily have done so.

It didn't matter how low he lay, Louis's name kept popping up in court cases. In May 1911 he was mentioned in a hearing for Irene Osgood's divorce case.

Osgood had married her second husband Robert Harborough Sherard in 1906—they met when he was working as her literary secretary. The couple moved to Guilsborough Hall where Osgood enjoyed riding and had much of her land laid out as a plantation for birds. Great-grandson of the poet Wordsworth, Sherard was also a writer and had been a friend of Oscar Wilde—he was his first biographer. He was also a heavy drinker. Cracks emerged in their marriage from the start and the couple were soon locked in fight after fight. Osgood charged Sherard with cruelty.

She went to bed and locked the door. Suddenly she heard a dreadful noise and the breaking of glass, and the sound of a

xiii Ames's wife petitioned for divorce in 1912 on grounds of desertion, bigamy, and adultery. The following year both Flora and Ames pleaded guilty to bigamy and were imprisoned for six months. Once released, they married.
xiv I've unfortunately been unable to find out much about the Baroness—except that she became famous for walking her Siamese cat on a lead through Regent's Park as reported in the New York Times (17 August 1913, p. 5) and elsewhere.
xv The 1911 census records him as living at 17 Alexander Mansions, 15 Marylebone Road, with his valet William Fortescue and his Italian cook, Angele Toggio, although it oddly describes him as 39. He signed the record as correct. Surely Louis wasn't worried about getting older? His friend John Taylor, recorded as a journalist, was visiting him that night.

body falling on the floor. The respondent then came through the music room, and began knocking at her door... Witness—I really don't care to repeat the names I was called... they included such expressions as... 'I am going to kill you and beat out your brains.'[19]

It was a mavellously scandalous story. They separated, reconciled, fought and separated again. Osgood swore at him (reportedly saying things like 'damn' and 'bounder' although she probably said, much, much worse). They hit each other and both claimed to have insanity in their families—presumably implying they might have insanity in themselves. 'Mr Sherard denied that he ever seized his wife by the throat and tried to strangle her.'[20] And Sherard was wildly jealous. He sent a telegram to Jean-Joseph Renaud who'd been a guest at Guilsborough Hall saying. 'You are the rottenest cad in the world. I spit in your face. Send your seconds.'[21] That might not have been his best idea. Renaud was an Olympic fencer as well as an author, but there doesn't appear to have actually been a duel.

As Osgood pointed out in court, she barely knew Louis. However, Sherard got it into his head that the two of them were carrying on together and sent Osgood a telegram warning her off Louis.

He is... an international swindler... and he has ruined two American women at a boarding establishment in Paris and in his absence was sentenced to five years penal servitude. Then he came to London, and recently was bankrupt...[22]

Sherard added that Louis had tried to get £150,000 out of Osgood. The couple were finally divorced in 1915, but not before Sherard sued Osgood, saying he'd been responsible for writing their most recent books.

Even more social doors had closed against Louis. It was as if he'd gone back in time, reading hands and making wild predictions in the hope that one would stick. In June 1911 he met with W T Stead, who was worried because back in 1897 a palmist had predicted that Stead would die in 1912 at the hands of a mob. Louis was no good at cheering him up.

I have gone over very carefully the impression of your hand... judging from it and from your date of birth in the Sign of Cancer, otherwise known as the First House of Water... any danger of violent death to you must be from water and nothing else. The most important months for you to avoid travelling in are December and next April of 1912. Very critical and dangerous for you should be April 1912, especially about the middle of that month.[23]

Hopping from séance to séance, Louis attended one in July with Charles Bailey, the Australian medium who claimed with the help of his spirit guide Abdul that he could apport live items such as fish, crabs, turtles, coins, stones and antiques. Bailey had been exposed as a fraud in France in 1910 when he'd produced two live birds, unaware that the dealer he'd bought the birds from was present. Apparently, he'd hidden the birds in the 'unpleasant end of his alimentary canal'.[24] But Bailey also had many supporters, including Louis.

The psychic world was Louis's world. In December he spoke at a meeting of the London Spiritualist Alliance on 'Personal Experiences of Psychic Phenomena in India, America and Other Countries'.[25] He didn't claim to have psychic skills himself, stepping neatly around the question when it was asked, but he did claim to have experienced a lot of psychic phenomena.

> Cheiro, the physiognomist and astute homme du monde, was no
> clairvoyant. In his heart he knew this as well as I myself did. But
> it was his profession to pose and assume. And, truth to tell, he did
> the posing and assuming remarkably well.[26]

Louis was gathering his stories in preparation for his first memoirs, a process that never ended as several versions appeared serialised in newspapers and in book form over the years. *Cheiro's Memoirs. The reminiscences of a society palmist* appeared in May 1912.

According to his own account, in February 1912 a man arrived to see him dressed in a black coat with a cape thrown across his shoulders and sporting such a beard and moustache 'of the Vandyke style which matched a handsome head of blond hair'.[27] He also spoke in a foreign accent and carried a large roll of music. Louis commented he looked like Shackleton, the Antarctic explorer and his visitor removed his false beard and wig. 'Well,' he said, 'as you evidently don't tell these things by the face you may as well know now that I am Shackleton.'[28]

Cynical people might say that Louis recognised him.

Louis was back at the London Spiritualist Alliance in April and repeated the talk he'd given back in December—or perhaps he added a few new experiences. He'd recently been in Spain to attend to some business matter or another and had met with an accident that had left him confined to his bed for two months. But like everyone, he'd heard the news—the *Titanic* had sunk after striking an iceberg on 14 April and Stead had been one of the more than 1,500 passengers who'd perished. His death was a severe blow to the world of spiritualism. Stead had been travelling to take part in a peace congress at Carnegie Hall at the request of President Taft. Apparently, he'd chatted throughout the eleven-course meal that fateful night, telling thrilling tales, including one about the cursed mummy of the British Museum, before going to bed at 10:30 pm. After the ship struck the iceberg, Stead helped several women and children into the lifeboats and gave his life jacket to another passenger. He was seen clinging to a raft but the cold forced him to release his hold. His body was never recovered. The Spiritualist Alliance stood for a moment's silence to honour Stead before Louis began his talk.

And he wrote for the *International Psychic Gazette*, the journal associated with the International Society for Psychical Research.[xvi] Under the leadership of Annie Besant, this society had been planned since October 1909 when it was announced in the *Occult Review* that it already had a membership of a thousand and premises were being sought. The plan was to create an upmarket competitor to the Society for Psychical Research which would operate on the basis of a club. In addition to rooms for séances and psychic experiments, there would be accomodation and meals. Life membership would cost fifty guineas (equivalent to over £4,000 today) if you wanted to use all the facilities.

It finally opened at 22a Regent Street on 29 May 1911, opposite the statue of Eros in Piccadilly Circus at the heart of London, surrounded by shops, theatres and restaurants. This was the address of numerous clubs and societies over the years, including the Anti-Vivisection Society, the London Spiritualist Alliance, and the Society for American Graduates. Plans had been drastically down-scaled. There were no bedrooms and rather than operating as a private club, it was a spiritualist society managed by George G Knowles, who'd already managed clubs in the same building.

The Society boasted 500 members and was quite smart, although spiritualist experiments took place in the cellar. Above this was a lecture hall and library, a dining room and kitchens with a cook (strictly vegetarian), writing rooms and smoking rooms. Afternoons and evenings were filled with lectures, music, drama, readings and discussions, often interrupted by a drawing-room tea: 'There is no other place where theosophist can drop in for chat with a hypnotist, where spiritist can compare notes with a psychologist,

---

xvi In later years, this became the Delphic Club.

or where a phrenologist can run the risk of lunching with a mesmerist.'[29]

It's unknown whether Louis was actually a member (chances are, he at least had a friend who was), but he spoke there on 10 May, introduced by Annie Besant. 'Like Madame Blavatsky she always urged me to become a member of the Theosophical Society,' said Louis, 'but rightly or wrongly, I always stuck to my idea of the 'lone wolf'.'[30] Besant probably asked everyone to join the Theosophical Society, having been its president since 1907.

At the end of May, Louis wangled an invitation to a séance performed by Etta Wriedt, an American direct voice medium—Louis's favourite kind. In direct voice, spirits use the medium's ectoplasm to form an artificial larynx so they can speak independently of the medium's vocal cords. A trumpet was often used to amplify the voices. Many sceptics claimed that direct voice mediums were expert ventriloquists. This private circle had already met with Wriedt twice before Louis attended: '"Cheiro" had visits from two friends and his sister; the latter addressed him in very affectionate tones by his Christian name… Someone tried to etherealise, but it was faint.'[31]

Wriedt had been part of Julia's Bureau, the institution founded by W T Stead in 1909 for free communication with the beyond. She was exposed as a fraud in 1912 by the physicist Kristian Birkeland when her skills of speaking Norwegian were revealed to be sadly lacking as she could manage no more than 'yes' or 'no' in response to questions. Her spirit voices were attributed to Wriedt speaking through a hidden telescopic aluminium tube. Other accounts describe her speaking in languages she didn't know and said that numerous spirit voices could be heard simultaneously at her séances. Maybe this doesn't matter—Louis was convinced.

And then oddly, in summer 1912 Louis accepted an engagement to read his poems at the Pleasure Gardens in Folkestone. He performed at least twice as a support act to opera singer Jeanne Jomelli.[xvii] Apparently, his recitations went down well. And he was back lecturing at the Spiritualist Alliance on 24 August where he showed off some of his slides.

No longer working as a palmist, Louis probably wasn't too worried by the call to clear the West End of fortune tellers in September 1912. The number of fortune tellers in London had risen rapidly and an estimated six to seven hundred were working there. The Metropolitan

---

xvii On 27 July and 3 August.

Police issued an order that fortune tellers within their jurisdiction had to remove words such as 'palmist', 'clairvoyant' and 'astrologer' from their doorplates, window signs and other public advertisements. Such adverts placed them at risk of being convicted under the Vagrancy Act.

The *Daily Mail* gleefully reported what was going on and it was probably at the paper's suggestion that Louis wrote his letter of support for taking legal action against low-class fortune tellers.

> Very few of those who had flaring advertisements in the streets of London had any credentials or proper training, and consequently brought whatever they practised... into disrepute and discredit... I shall, therefore, in the true interests of all occult studies gladly welcome a strict police supervision over all those practise such things.. such supervision will in the end raise the standard of students and professors...[32]

It was as if he'd forgotten how he started out. But 'Cheiro' was no longer the celebrity he had been, neither was Louis as happy as he had been. 'I do not like myself... I regard my own personal entity as the heaviest cross that my spirit could have been called upon to bear...'[33]

But he soldiered on. In early 1913, Louis was in Vienna where he was discussing an invention of some sort, presumably with interested investors. While there he visited 'Princess Zisky', who claimed to be a direct descendant of the father of the late Emperor Nicholas of Russia. (The Russian court weren't convinced, hence why she was in Vienna.) The Princess went everywhere with her pet cobra, Tanitha, in a basket, believing the snake was the reincarnation of a Hindu god. Presumably minus the cobra, Louis and the Princess wandered to the Cathedral of St. Stephen where the Princess manifested a vapoury cloud that took on the shape of a woman. Louis took her word for it that this was Empress Elizabeth of Austria.

Obviously, he had to be mentioned in some court case or another, and this year it was in March when 'Madame Ziska' was summonsed for telling fortunes on Oxford Street. She claimed to be Cheiro's wife, which worried Louis enough to get a solicitor to write to the papers on his behalf to say he'd never been married and had never met Madam Ziska—who in reality was the American Ray Drummond.

A side-effect of Louis appearing in the papers was that Edith Halford-Nelson obtained his current address. She'd only been back in England for three days after her family had forced her back, worried that her sheikh was spending all her inheritance and not having heard anything from her for some time. Edith ended up in court in a dispute about her money and found she had been embezzled out of £10,000. She consulted a solicitor about getting her daughter back, but was advised that the law in Tunisia being what it was, her Arab husband could claim the child as his and it was impossible.

Despite what was going on in her life, Edith found time to write to Louis. He immediately responded suggesting she called to visit the next day at nine in the evening. Edith was bothered that his handwriting looked different, so she decided to take her maid with her. When the servant let them in, Edith's maid said the place gave her the creeps and she thought they should leave. Maybe the servant was listening because on his reappearance he said the maid should leave. She did and Edith was taken to see Louis.

> I stood blinking in the half light against which the man was standing holding out his hand to me in greeting. He stood, a powerful figure, with shoulders so bent that his head jutted forward in a peculiar crouching movement that suggested more than ever a cobra about to strike. His hair was nearly white. Surely this bent, sinister figure could not be what had once been the beautiful Cheiro? And suddenly I realised it was...[34]

Louis had put on weight since Edith had last seen him, and doubtless he looked older. But photographs make it clear his hair was far from white and he was still remarkably good looking. Anyway, he hugged Edith and asked her what she'd been up to. Edith proceeded to tell him about her time in Tunisia and Algeria in excruciating detail. Finally, once she'd detailed her doomed love affair, Louis asked her if she loved the man she'd been going on about.

> 'Love?' I echoed 'What do I know of love? What have you done to me that I have ever known it?'
>
> 'Little fool, you should have stayed with me, then all this would never have happened. I would have guarded you from it, locked you from it...'[35]

And then Edith noticed a stone was missing from Louis's ring, She pointed it out and he said, 'Yes, *I have lost Eternity*.'[36] Apparently, this was symbolic of wars to come. They talked until midnight and then Edith told Louis he no longer had any power over her.

'Ha, ha—you are not afraid of me any more! I have no power over you any longer? Then if I have not, someone else *has*. Who is it—who is it?' He hissed the words like a snake. 'Tell me his name—tell me—tell me—*I'll kill him!*'[37]

He shook Edith and she fell back at his release, knocking her head against a table.

I remember a sudden sharp pain and then his arms lifting me very gently, and his voice murmuring regrets and endearments. When I opened my eyes he was looking down at me, frowning and anxious; my hands were pressed against his chest...[38]

Edith saw Louis several more times and they did a lot of meaningful gazing and some psychic experiments as before. But this time their positions were reversed. Louis pleaded with her to stay with him and Edith said she had to return to Africa. She said that in past incarnations Louis had been her father to which he responded they were bound together by a silver thread. Despite dramatic pleas from Louis saying that Edith belonged to him, she was adamant. She was going back to Africa. 'You *cannot* go, you belong to *me*,' said Louis.[39]

Edith refused to comply. Immediately afterwards, she had a breakdown and ended up in a nursing home. Louis sent her a bunch of roses with a note saying he'd gone to Paris. As soon as she was well enough, Edith also went to Paris where she saw Louis for the final times when she passed him on the street. He was dressed in a top hat and accompanied by a very young man.

I heard him saying to his companion:
'She is a medium—a very wonderful medium,' to which the boy answered with a strange petulant eagerness:
'Then *why* don't you do it—what are you waiting for?'
'She is delicate—much too delicate—I would kill her.' As he said these words, I was passing them, walking as if I were asleep. The boy cried out bitterly:
'She doesn't know you!'
'Oh, yes she does. *Oh—yes—she—does.*'
I had walked on a few paces, turning as Cheiro repeated his words. He was standing a little apart from the boy. He was smiling. All the old tyranny had gone from his eyes; they were dark, with tenderness, love—farewell.[40]

Anyone else would simply have said 'hello'. After this encounter, Edith left for Tunisia.[xviii]

More mundanely, Louis was discharged from bankruptcy in May due to saying he'd been offered an appointment dependent on his discharge—presumably, a directorship, although it's unclear what business it related to.

On balance, the remainder of 1913 looked as if it was going to pass much the same as the last. Louis organised a few occult lectures and lectured occasionally, including at the Spiritualist Alliance and the London Occult Society.[xix] By the end of the year, Louis was ordering séances like the rest of us order pizzas. He was so impressed with Susannah Harris's skills at producing manifestations that he immediately arranged to attend five more (at one of these, his mother spoke to him). Indeed, he wrote a letter to the *American Register* in December 1913 giving her address and pointing out she'd be available in London after Christmas.

Susannah Harris was from Columbus, Ohio where she'd been pastor of a spiritualist church before moving to England. A direct voice medium, her control was a child, 'Harmony'. She was hugely popular at the start of World War I. Harris was accused of fraud on several occasions, including in Holland in 1914. However, many also defended her as genuine and it wasn't until 1920 that the Norwegian Society for Psychical Research published its unfavourable report about her séances.

But Louis's frequent assertion he didn't join societies was proven to be tosh from an unexpected direction in 1914. The A∴ A∴ (*Argenteum Astrum* or *Silver Star*) was a magical order organisation founded by Aleister Crowley in 1907.[xx] Presumably, Frank Harris had introduced Louis to Crowley with whom Louis exchanged several letters during 1913 and 1914. By the time Louis joined, Crowley had given up on the A∴ A∴ as his main means of promoting Thelema, his brand of esotericism, and it was a small organisation with only a few well-off, society adherents. In 1914 there were thirty-eight members, although most of them hadn't paid their subscriptions—including Louis who owed £4 4s. Maybe he

---

xviii In later years, Louis probably read about her in the papers. In 1933 the Corsican bandit Andre Spada was tried for murder. Edith had befriended him when trying to write his biography, although she denied they had been lovers. Apparently, Spada had escaped detection by living with Edith while dressed as a woman. When accused of being his accomplice, Edith fled to a convent. Thousands watched when Spada was guillotined in June 1935.

xix On 24 April and 4 December.

xx Membership involved a series of initiations, involving Theravada Buddhism with Vedantic yoga and ceremonial magic and was based on the Qabalistic Tree Of Life, following the sephirot up the tree in reverse order.

only *said* he was going to join and didn't actually follow up.

From time to time, Louis got dressed up and went out on the town. In about June 1914 he received a phone call from Mata Hari inviting him to join her for dinner at the Savoy. They were joined by a French politician who Louis had met in his newspaper days in Paris, back in 1903. But the important thing was that Mata Hari was still stunning.

> I can only say that if ever an angel had come down to earth and got dressed by Parisian masters of art—it was the woman who entered the room at that moment... She did not walk—she glided across the carpet... Her glorious eyes—made no doubt more brilliant by an extra drop of belladonna—shone with a radiance almost divine.

There was lots of chat about achieving international peace, and they had a nice dinner.

Back in the real world, Edith may have left Louis's life, but another woman had arrived. In *Real Life Stories*, Louis mentions that in early spring of 1914 he was staying with his wife in the Queen's hotel in Exeter. An odd thing to say, considering it would be several years before he married. That 'wife' was Katie Hartland.

Katie in 1929

CHAPTER
FIFTEEN

Indeed, Cheiro, the mystery of the world is the visible, not the invisible.[1]

*L*OUIS VAGUELY SAID HE'D RECONNECTED with Katie in about 1912, which is probably accurate. A hint of Katie appears in 1911 when her son Jack is recorded in the census as a boarder in Grassington, Yorkshire. There's no record of Katie, but thousands of women are unrecorded in the 1911 census. As part of their protest against the government's continued refusal to grant women the vote, the suffragettes had organised a mass boycott. Some women stayed away from home on census night, while others hid from the enumerator or refused to give any information.

By now, Katie had no close family remaining in her home town. Her father had died in 1893, her brother Thomas had died at sea in 1910 and her brother James had emigrated to Canada in 1908. Katie's mother was running a boarding house in Kensington, where she lived with Katie's aunt Felicia. By 1913 Katie was living under the name of 'Kathleen Mena Hartland' at 7 Acacia Road, in St John's Wood, which was her address until at least 1918.[2] It was a little over a mile from where Louis lived.[i]

Although it was easy for Katie to pop round to Louis's for a cup of tea, life suddenly became very, very different in July 1914.

The Great War came on, hurling doom and destruction across the world… Suddenly a gun in the far-off distance gave the alarm

i From 1911 to 1914, Louis was living at 17 Alexandra Mansions, Marylebone Road.

that a Zeppelin had been signalled. Then another and another boom, people began to rush past us with frightened faces, street lights went out one after the other. London drew over her shoulders a mantle of darkness, waited and hoped for the best. Cannon in the nearer barrages to London were already booming incessantly. Their circle of protecting shrapnel and bursting shells seemed to pierce the sky from all points of vantage. Defending aeroplanes roared over the now silent city. Taxis, omnibuses, carriages, people had run to shelter.

My taxi-driver refused to go further. I had to get out and make my way home as best I could. I had reached my door, and groped with my latchkey to find the lock. As I entered, I looked upward to the black sky above me. Far away at an enormous height, like the flash of a falling meteor, I caught sight of an aerial torpedo tearing downwards—then the increasing roar that such engines of destruction make. I stood rooted to the spot.[3]

For those so inclined, new business opportunities had arrived when war became imminent.[ii] In December 1913 Louis became involved in the company Oil Processes, based in Canada.[iii] It purchased distillation rights from Flax Limited, another Canadian company Louis was involved with. They were managed by Liverpudlian Albert Harvey who'd been a dry goods merchant before selling insurance. At different times, he'd made a fortune from his ventures and declared bankruptcy.

Flax sought to make money from the work of American chemist Nat Harris Freeman, who sorely needed cash. Freeman had been living in Brussels before arriving in the UK in November 1913 with £450 in cash and two cars. His idea was to take easily available kerosene (lamp oil) and use his method of distillation to create cheap fuel for internal combustion engines. Freeman soon established a plant at Chartridge Grange, Chesham, Bucks and began negotiations with Flax. Part of their agreement was that Freeman had to satisfy Sir Oliver Lodge, Flax's technical adviser.[iv]

---

ii Hamong and Cie and the Anglo-French Herald Motor Company were formally dissolved by 1916.

iii Based in Ottawa, its remit was to work on processes for distilling crude oil and to find methods to transform kerosene into petrol, and despite being registered in Canada, the company was operated from the UK, only holding the minimum of legally required meetings in Canada.

iv Lodge had been the president of Flax before Harvey. The other directors included Captain Geoffrey Lubbock (his family owned Robarts, Lubbock & Co. bank which

The problem was that Freeman's interest lay in research. Although he thought his method would work in the long run, that was useless for making money in the short term. Experiments and negotiations continued throughout 1914 by when everyone was desperate for motor fuel. Freeman had built a new laboratory and considered that if someone built a refinery, he could deliver 30,000 gallons of fuel daily. But he was a chemist and said dismissively that building refineries was out of his remit, so he continued to perform experiments, draw diagrams and accept any money that came his way. When the financial problems were too big to ignore, Freeman blamed the directors for taking large dividends. But Freeman also owned shares in Flax and received other payments in addition to his £4,000 annual salary. By early 1917 investors had lost over £300,000 and Oil Processes and Flax Ltd were wound up.

Louis was also a director of a syndicate which attempted to sell munitions to the government in 1915. Christopher Addison, then an MP, recalled:

> We persistently turned down an attractive offer of millions of shells from a certain group, well known to us as the Threadneedle Syndicate. This group consisted of a jeweller in Hatton Garden and two colleagues in New York, neither of whom possessed either works or machinery...[4] the Secret Service has given me an informative dossier on them.[5]

One of the Syndicate's directors was Baron Robert Oppenheim, a London and Paris banker who had such a shady reputation that in 1916 the US prevented him entering owing to charges of 'moral turpitude'.[6] Oppenheim was renowned for establishing the South African Selati Railway Company in 1892 with his brother Eugene. The contract had been secured through liberal bribes and the work then contracted out to the British company Westwood and Winby, who completed the first 80 km of track to the Sabie River (now Skukuza) in 1894. The Oppenheim brothers merrily cooked the books, cashing in false expense claims and arbitrarily hiring subcontractors while attempting to cover their tracks. In 1895 the scandal was uncovered and the brothers were found guilty by the Belgian courts and sentenced to prison. Over a million pounds had gone into the pockets of politicians and businessmen. Tools were downed and it took fifteen years before work resumed—the line wasn't completed until 1912. More recently, in May 1914 Eugene Oppenheim

---

merged with Coutts and Co. in 1914) and Admiral Sir Alfred Leigh Winsloe.

had been arrested at the First National Amsterdam Bank in New York on embezzlement charges.

Another director was Archibald Campbell Mitchell-Innes, past director of a railway company in British Colombia and an enthusiastic golfer. Before going to Canada he'd been declared bankrupt in 1902. Things clearly didn't go smoothly for him there as Mitchell-Innes was advertising for work in 1910, but he became a director of the Pioneer Oil Company in British Columbia in 1914.

The syndicate was a failure from the start and was wound up in . The Barons Oppenheim continued to feature in the papers, and delightfully a 1917 account described how Robert never wore underwear and frequently lent Eugene his shirts, socks and ties—he was attempting to prove Eugene was penniless, but how it helped to announce his lack of underwear is unclear.

These were Louis's friends. But they weren't Cheiro's.

Cheiro was more interested in messages from the beyond. One reached him on 5 June 1916. It had been over twenty years since he'd predicted that Lord Kitchener would die suddenly. Shortly before Kitchener went abroad, Louis said he'd been with him at the War Office, and Kitchener had said that if anything happened to him, he'd send Cheiro a sign.

> I and a number of my friends were seated in the large music-room of my country house. It was an informal sort of gathering...
> At one point conversation languished, and finally ceased for a space... During the temporary silence, we were startled by the loud crash of some object falling heavily in the north end of the room. Upon Investigating, we found the cause a large oaken shield, on which the arms of Great Britain wore painted, and which had been accustomed to hang on the wall. It appeared to have been hurled off its nail, thrown some distance into the room, and was lying on the floor—broken into two parts. As I picked it up, I observed that the shield had broken through those parts representative of England and Ireland.[7]

The clock struck eight. This was an omen! It was the moment when Lord Kitchener had perished in the Hampshire. Well, almost. It went down at about 7:30—close enough for Louis. 'I have often asked myself since,' Louis said, 'did Lord Kitchener remember, and was the broken shield his message to me as he passed over?'[8] Who knows?

In November 1915 Cheiro's *Palmistry for All* was published to lacklustre reviews. Maybe his heart was no longer in palmistry.

Susannah Harris was still his favourite medium. During the War, her reputation was enhanced by her fundraising for the British Hospital for Mental Disorders and Brain Diseases—in 1915 she donated her fee for séances to the hospital. On 13 May 1917 Louis attended one of his many séances with Harris. Also present was Felicia Scatcherd (who'd helped W T Stead set up Julia's Bureau and who was editor of the *Psychic Review*), Dr Hector Munro and 'Mena Dixon-Hartland'—Katie.[v]

In what became known as the 'Kildare-street Club case', after some less than interesting messages, a spirit visitor said he wanted to send a message to his father. When asked who he was, the spirit replied:

> 'I am an officer recently killed at the front in Flanders; my name is...'
>
> We could not hear the name very distinctly, so after some repeated efforts to get it, we said: 'Well, leave the name alone for the moment and try to give us the message.'
>
> Speaking very slowly at first, the spirit said, 'My father lives near Dublin; you will find him at the well-known club there.'
>
> A gentleman present asked: 'Which club do you mean?'
>
> The spirit replied: 'The Kildare-street Club; you know it well, and you also know my father.'[9]

It transpired that the spirit wanted someone to let his dad know he was fine. Unfortunately, he was unable to voice his name clearly. Louis decided to solve the mystery. He wrote to the Kildare Street Club with what he *thought* was the right name, only to have his letter returned. Then he realised there was a simpler way of going about such things and wrote to the Club secretary saying he was looking for a member whose son had recently been killed as he had a message for him. In response he received a letter saying, 'I have had a message from my son who was recently killed in Flanders, saying he had sent me a message through a medium in London, that he had difficulty in getting the name and address through but he wanted to give me a test.'[10] Oddly, the man added that he came from an old French family that had married into the Hamon family, suggesting he and Louis were related. Louis accepted what the man had

---

v The addition of 'Dixon' to her name may have been a simple error on the part of the journalist who originally wrote about the case in the *Psychic Gazette*. The Dixon-Hartlands were a prominent family and Sir Frederick Dixon Dixon-Hartland was an MP from 1991 to 1909. There is no connection between this family and the Hartlands Katie had married into.

written to him as proof of clairvoyance and of Harris's skills.

In about 1916, Louis had moved to 13 Nottingham Terrace, Marylebone Road. He'd also bought Green Isle, in Henley on Thames. Only a short distance from the station, the house was on an island by Marsh Lock, reachable by a wooden bridge. Here Louis hosted his many séances.

> It was the afternoon of Monday, the 8th of October, 1917. Boom! Boom! of the guns protecting London. Crash! Crash! of splinters of shells falling on the roofs we were in the middle of an air-raid in the worst days of the War.
>
> We had had little rest for the four previous nights and were beginning to feel the strain on our nerves from the want of sleep. I turned to my wife and said: 'We can do no good here: suppose we take the train to our country house and have a rest for at least a few days. There is a train at 6 o'clock—in an hour we shall be at all events out of this awful din.'[11]

You haven't missed anything so don't bother leafing back. Louis wasn't married in 1917, but in writing the many accounts of his life, he appears to have become muddled. In any event, it sounds as if he was living with Katie when the telephone rang and a voice said, 'Will you let me come up to your house? I am alone here in my rooms and terribly upset with the raids of the last few nights. Do let me come.'[12]

No name is given for this medium, although Louis says, 'The voice was that of a woman, one of the very many remarkable mediums I have come across' so it may have been Susannah Harris.[13] In any event, Louis suggested she packed a bag and joined him and Katie. They picked up two other friends and departed for Green Isle. That evening, they were watching the sun go down as they waited for dinner to be served. The medium wanted to show her gratitude and:

> She had hardly finished speaking when we noticed that the flowers in the central vase on the dining table had begun to move—the table was fully twenty feet from where we were sitting—the movement soon became very decided; several roses appeared to be lifted out of the bowl and fell on the polished oak table. For a few moments we sat and watched without speaking. Then to our amazement the roses slowly, but steadily, moved across the table till they reached the place mats at each place where we were going to sit.[14]

The medium gleefully said that this showed the spirits were pleased that Louis had invited her to stay. She was so grateful that she promised them a séance every evening. Later that evening, the medium lived up to her promise and manifested a floating light that said to Louis, 'I am Edith Cavell… who was, as of course you have read, executed in Brussels.'[15]

Louis took the light's word for it and asked what she wanted. She told him she wanted to get a message to a doctor Louis knew. Sensibly, Louis asked why she didn't speak direct to the doctor—after all, Louis was unlikely to see him in the near future. He was told that he'd be with the doctor at nine the next morning and so Louis said if that was the case, sure, he'd pass her message on. And then they got on with doing something more interesting and he forgot about it.

The next morning Louis woke with a sore throat. He sent for the doctor who couldn't find anything wrong and offered Louis some morphine. Then Louis remembered the events of the previous evening and passed on the spiritual message.

'What! What!' said the doctor. 'Have you gone mad?'[16] He told Louis he was experiencing hallucinations. Louis persisted and repeated some personal information the spirit had told him. The doctor promised to return that evening.

That evening everyone gathered for another séance. At the last minute, the doctor arrived and joined them. The spirit spoke to him and floated a flower from across the room to land on his hand. Everyone was impressed and signed a piece of paper to say so.

Louis may have called Katie his 'wife' but he'd demurred from actually marrying her.

> I did not approve of it [marriage], at least not for myself, for many reasons… I loved independence more than anything else in the world… I had in me that material that makes one a rebel against conventionality… I led an unusual life which would have been painful for any ordinary woman to follow—the life of a rolling stone, ready at a moment's notice to go anywhere in the search of material for my own particular study. Lastly, I did not understand why two persons had to be tied together by law…[17]

That was about to change. Louis claimed that shortly after the War it was announced in the *Daily Mail* that he had double pneumonia and he wasn't expected to live. Reading this, Katie rushed to London to care for him.

I had a long, hard fight for life; she nursed me night and day. Those little hands proved they could be useful as well as beautiful. We took a voyage to the Mediterranean to make my recovery complete. One day on the return journey to England I had a good look at the lines of my own hand. I saw I was approaching the date when marriage was marked for me late in life. I went down to the writing room and wrote my resignation to the Anti-marriage Society, to which I had belonged for nearly thirty years. For fear I might weaken in my resolution, I gave the letter to my future wife to post and we were married on my return home.[18]

Which is lovely. And completely made up. No such announcement appears in the *Daily Mail*. It isn't impossible that such an announcement appeared elsewhere, but I've been unable to find one.

Katie said she was a widow—although she'd looked for Henry, and even taken out adverts, there was no trace of him and she'd been told he'd been lost at sea—despite that being odd for a clerk who worked in Manhattan. She couldn't have looked very hard as he continued to work for steamship lines and had remained in New York—plus his brother and sister were still alive. However, Henry had married Harriet Pendleton Treat in 1918 so he probably wouldn't have worried had he known about her marrying Louis.

With the War, people had become more demanding about the legitimacy of names and passports were mandatory in the UK from 1914. Louis dropped the name 'Warner' and adopted the name Count Louis Hamon by deed poll on 16 August 1918.[19] [vi]

He could now claim, hand on heart, that he truly was a Count. Katie married the Count on 15 April 1920 at St Heliers, Jersey.

---

vi Prior to this, he was calling himself 'Count Louis William le Warner Hamon'.

The mummy's hand

Katie and Louis at Prospect in 1924. Getty Images.

CHAPTER

SIXTEEN

The count is a very clever talker and has a fund of interesting stories.[1]

O NE WAR HAD ENDED, BUT IN IRELAND another had just begun. January 1919 marked the start of the Irish War of Independence and the birth of the Irish Republican Army (IRA), who sought the establishment of a republic, the end of British rule in Northern Ireland, and the reunification of Ireland. They were ready to fight to force the British government to negotiate.

Louis had decided Ireland was the place for his new business.

To be fair, Louis wasn't acting on a whim. He'd long been planning to take advantage of something Ireland had a plentiful supply of—peat. Traditionally, peat was cut by hand and left to dry in the sun to use as fuel. But there were now far more efficient ways of preparing it, and by-products were being discovered with new scientific methods no-one had foreseen. Or if we take Louis's word for it, long forgotten ancient methods had come to light that could change the fuel supply forever. He was referring to what he'd discovered in the Vatican Library back in 1901.

> Some of the recipes and formulae in the manuscript had descended, copy by copy, from documents in the destroyed Library of Alexandria; and these again may have come from Greek and other origins dating as far back as B.C. 2,000… I was very much interested in scientific records, particularly in the matter of fuel… They did not contain anything of actual use in modern science, the terminology not being of our period. They were, largely, connected with the speculations of the old Egyptians as

to fuel that would melt metal, and so forth. But there was in them the material that led me to think along a fresh track about fuel and to invent a hardened peat, made in blocks like coal, that gave out very intense heat and left almost no dust at all.[2]

He claimed to have spent £45,000 experimenting on ways in which to produce fuel from peat that would be as efficient as coal, although much cheaper. Louis never explained how he came by such skills, beyond reading ancient manuscripts, but it may not be a coincidence that Nat Harris Freeman continued his research throughout the 1920s, primarily on fuel production and distilling gases from carbon fuels, and took out numerous patents. And one of Louis's patents was taken out jointly with renowned chemist Thomas H (Henry) Byrom, chief analytical and research chemist of the Wigan Coal and Iron Companies and and co-author of *The Physics and Chemistry of Mining*, which focused on coke manufacture and the recovery of coke by-products. This man knew his fossil fuels.

Before he got going, Louis had visited Dublin in August 1917. He was having tea and toast in a restaurant when an old Irish peasant woman asked him the time; she was about to miss her train so Louis offered her a lift.

She had a return third class ticket, I put her in a compartment. As I said good-bye and turned away, the woman leaned out of the window, and in a very soft voice called me back. With a sweet smile she said: "'Cheiro,' my dear, I am so glad you did not recognize me. It gives me implicit confidence in my disguise.' For a moment I was dumbfounded. It was none other than Mata Hari.[3]

No wonder he was dumbfounded. According to Louis, Mata Hari was picked up by a German submarine which took her to Spain after which she returned to France and became a dancer again. No, she didn't. Hari's last performance was in March 1915 and she was arrested in Paris in January 1917, although she wasn't executed until October. Louis insisted he'd foretold her execution—or at least that she'd die violently—but she was willing to accept her fate.[i]

In reality, Louis was looking at bogs.

In 1919 he bought 173 acres of bog land at Moorock, a mile from Ballycumber in County Offaly, renowned for its extensive bog and peatlands which make up a fifth of its area. He then erected a corrugated

---

i Edith's retelling of the story places Louis at the scene of Mata Hari's execution, which is clearly silly.

iron building and fitted it with machinery for making briquettes. Four days after his wedding, Louis took out a patent for his method of producing fuel, giving his address as 30 Elgin Road in central Dublin.

Katie and Louis moved into Prospect House in Ballycumber from where he could oversee his new factory on the edge of the Bog of Allen. Louis still took his mummy's hand with him wherever he went and one day in 1920 he noticed that:

> The hand, which was as hard as ebony and tobacco-brown, had changed position. The index finger was pointing towards the ceiling. I squeezed it and the finger gently gave way under the pressure. The next day, I felt the hand again. The flesh was tender and, to my amazement, there were drops of blood on the joints.[4]

The flesh had become soft as if the hand were alive! And in May 1921 it turned red. It must have been an omen.

Whatever the omen was, Louis didn't let it stop him from registering the Artificial Coal Company (Hamon Process) in Jersey in November 1920. Amongst the directors was Montague B Parker, the director of China Clays Ltd and the Paris Ritz hotel.[ii] Parker was mainly known for his Indiana Jones style expedition back in 1911 when he was searching for the treasures of Solomon's Temple. A former officer in the Grenadier Guards, Montague Parker had met a Finnish Bible scholar called Valter Juvelius, whose research told him that the Temple artefacts were located in Jerusalem in a secret passage under the Temple Mount. But he couldn't afford to mount an expedition. Parker agreed to help and raised £50,000—equivalent to several million pounds today. The sponsors would receive their share of the findings.

With well-thought out bribery, Parker obtained the permit he needed and a blind eye from officialdom. Digging went slowly and didn't produce anything. Back in London, Juvelius hired an Irish medium—an unidentified 'Mr Lee'—who studied the documents and sent directions to the team about suitable locations. When Parker was told to search the long water tunnel, he employed two mining engineers who'd worked on the Metropolitan Railway, the first line of the London Underground. He also persuaded Père Louis-Hughes Vincent of the Sainte-Etienne École Biblique

---

ii The other directors were financier Francis Taylor, F W Cooper, the assessor to the Corporation of Manchester; H Milner Willis and A T M Jones from Jersey. Although Louis held less than half the shares, he was a director for life, and to all intents and purposes it was his company.

in Jerusalem to join the team and guide them through the water channel where the medium had told them they'd find a secret passage to lead them to the treasure. They cleared the tunnel but found no secret passage. Lee told Parker to start work on the Temple Mount itself. After several nights of clandestine digging failed to yield results, the medium advised them to dig in the Cave of the Spirits.[iii] There was an ancient tradition there was a shaft within the cave that led to treasure. In April 1911, Parker began his search and the caretaker of the site called the police. The story spread that Parker had made off with the Crown of Solomon, the Ark of the Covenant and the sword of Muhammad.

Parker and his men managed to get out of the city. When the police finally reached them, Parker said he didn't have any of the treasures and invited the police to his yacht that afternoon to check. Before they could do so, Parker promptly sailed away. Who the Irish seer was that assisted Juvelius (or whether he truly existed) is unknown. But there weren't that many Irish seers around at the time, and Louis certainly knew these people.

The problem was that once Louis had set up the factory and workshops, with nearby huts for the workers to sleep in, it was almost impossible to make money. The Anglo-Irish Treaty of December 1921 had created two new political entities: the Irish Free State of twenty-six counties which was a dominion of the British Commonwealth, and Northern Ireland, made up of six counties which remained part of the United Kingdom.

The Dáil (Irish parliament) had been split about accepting the Treaty, and when Eamon De Valera resigned as President, his supporters refused to recognise the Irish Free State. The IRA split into two factions, and the government of the Irish Free State issued directives that its opponents were to be called 'irregulars' in an attempt to delegitimise the republican campaign. As the War of Independence ended, the Civil War began in June 1922.

Everything was at a standstill. Transport was difficult, to say the least. Roads were often blocked and bridges blown up. Property and businesses were attacked and country houses were particular targets—many were burned to the ground. 'No insurance company would entertain a risk on property in Ireland in those troublesome days,' pointed out Louis.[5]

Exasperated, Louis and Katie returned to London in May 1922, leaving the factory under the control of its manager, Mr McCauley. While they

---

iii The cave under the Even Shetiya, the Foundation Stone in the centre of the Dome of the Rock from which, by tradition, Muhammad had ascended to Heaven and on which two thousand years earlier, Abraham had prepared to sacrifice his son Isaac.

were absent, the kitchen maid, Mary Digan, let Irregulars into Prospect to sleep and provided them with food. She told Louis what she'd been doing and he said, 'I am delighted, as they are a protection to the house.'[6]

It wasn't the first time this had happened, after all. 'They used,' Louis said, 'to come into the house very often when we were upstairs in our own room. We could not prevent them.'[7]

He didn't try very hard. When asked (superfluously, when events are considered) if he was on good terms with the Irregulars, Louis diplomatically said, 'I hope I was on good terms with everybody.'[8] When pressed, he denied being in 'active sympathy' with them—clearly, providing accommodation and food wasn't 'active.'[9]

In early August, McCauley met Louis in London to discuss staffing problems and recent financial difficulties. McCauley returned to Ireland with instructions to sack the unmarried workmen. Rather than simply processing peat for fuel, Louis had decided they should also work on converting peat into carbon for gas masks.

Ominously, the mummy's hand had softened again and was producing blood. Louis said he was worried that if he told anyone they wouldn't believe him, so he obtained sworn depositions from an engineer and chemist who confirmed that the hand had softened. The chemist restored the hand to its hard condition by using a solution of pitch and shellac.

A week after McCauley's return, on 15 August, the factory's caretaker Michael Daly, closed his wooden hut seven yards from the factory and went to Ballycumber for provisions. Two hours later, at about 10:30, he returned to find the place ablaze. He did nothing to report the fire and seek help, saying he wanted to 'preserve his life' and he didn't believe there was anything that could be done.[10] Shortly afterwards, Macauley also returned from wherever he'd been, and they watched while the factory buildings and much of the machinery was destroyed, along with 800 briquettes stored there.

The Irregulars had done it. That's what Louis said, although there were also rumours that disputes with his workmen were behind the arson. Or maybe he'd ordered the fire. The IRA never said they were responsible, although they never denied it, either. The factory was closed down.

A few months later, at midnight on 19 October, three masked and armed men visited Prospect. One said, 'I am very sorry, Count, to have to come like this and annoy you, but our orders have got to be obeyed. We have been sent here tell you if you persist in making attempts to save the machinery at the burnt-down factory you will have some of your men shot, and if you still further persist you will burned out of Prospect.'[11] They must have been the most polite IRA members ever.

POLITE IRISH RAIDERS. VERY SORRY FOR YOU BUT HAVE TO BURN YOU OUT.[12]

Louis argued, saying it was a shame it was to throw so many men out of work and asked for a chance to save some of the machinery, but the men refused, one saying, 'The more damage we can do the more this alien Government and the English Government at its back will have pay, so I give you fair warning if you make any attempt to save any of these machines or part of the factory.'[13]

The man then said to Katie, 'You have heard what I have told the Count, and I have given you fair warning, and hope you won't be fool enough to go against our orders.'[14]

Louis didn't tell anyone about the men's visit, claiming that to do so might have turned the Irregulars against him. It was too dangerous. But he gave up the idea of the factory—it was time to pack everything up so they could return to London. Shortly afterwards (Louis claimed it was on Halloween), Louis looked at the mummy's hand and said to Katie, 'I cannot bring my mind to pack it in that state.'[15] They decided to cremate the hand once the servants were in bed.

Before I placed the relic on the fire the countess recited one of the prayers from the *Egyptian Book of the Dead*.[16]

Thy flesh have I given unto thee,
They bones have I kept for thee,
Thy members have I collected,
Thou art set in order;
Thou seest the gods,
Thou settest out on thy way,
Thine hand reaches beyond the horizon
And unto the holy place where thou woudst be.[17]

Louis dropped the hand, along with its velvet cushion and ebony stand, onto the fire. Long white flames shot upwards and the perfume of the embalmer's spices filled the room. Louis and Katie watched until only a red glow remained and then set off for bed.

Then this tremendous thing happened. The outward glass doors of the porch burst with a crash.[18]

We thought it was a raid, for the raiders had already burned down a neighbouring factory.

Then, as we stood staring like frightened children, the great oak doors within the porch bent inwards. A moment later they were thrown wide open.

We could see the passion flowers in the porch. Amid them appeared the head and shoulders of a woman. On her head were the beaten gold beetle wings, with the snake, the royal emblem, in the middle. As she advanced into the firelight a girdle she wore blazed with jewels. Arms developed. She bent close over the fire as we held our breath. A moment later, standing upright and facing us, she raised her arms, and held two hands above her head. Then slowly she receded. We followed across the hall, not because of courage, but because we were fascinated. We reached the porch, in the shadow of the passion flowers, and gradually she faded, her beautiful eyes intent upon us, vanishing last.[19]

They collected up the calcified bones and packed them carefully. One day, Louis hoped to return them to the Valley of the Kings.

On 6 November, some (maybe the same original polite ones) Irregulars turned up and told Louis and Katie it would be best to leave the next afternoon as they were going to blow up the railway bridges and no more trains would be running to Dublin for some time. Louis took their word for it and readied himself to catch the next day's midnight boat from Kingstown harbour.

Travelling at such short notice meant that the only available carriage was filled with officers and soldiers belonging to the new Irish Free State, who were armed to the teeth as an attack was expected on the barracks that night. Louis rammed his cases into the overhead luggage racks. He soon nodded off, despite the soldiers launching into a raucous round of 'It's a long way to Tipperary'. Waking up, Louis glanced at the case containing the mummy's hand and decided the label was moving too much. Despite protests from the soldiers, he insisted his cases were put on the floor. The moment that was done, the train came to a violent stop and the other luggage tumbled down. They looked out of the window to see Liffey junction terminus was on fire—but there was a greater danger:

Far away in the distance one could hear the roar of an engine rushing towards us on the same track. In another second we saw it in the distance, tearing like a mad thing, under a full head of steam, directly towards where our train was standing. Men threw themselves on their knees and prayed; others white as death seemed turned to stone.[20]

Rebels had uncoupled the engine of the Galway mail train waiting in the terminus, opened the throttle and sent it in their direction.

> And then the miracle happened—the railway points... were closed only a hundred yards ahead—the swaying monster swung over to the Liffey track, crashed through a freight train on the siding, finally smashing itself against a concrete wall some ten miles away at the end of the line.[21]

Louis and Katie solicited the help of a couple of soldiers and walked into Dublin with their luggage. Before long they were on their way back to England.

Shortly after their return, they learned that George Herbert, the Earl of Carnarvon, who had sponsored Howard Carter to dig for seven years in the Valley of the Kings, had finally found Tutankhamen's tomb and planned to enter it. Louis wrote to Carnarvon telling him to be careful.

This was the year of the mummy. Everyone was talking about mummies. People had long been fascinated by them—in the early nineteenth century, surgeons unwrapped mummies in front of an appreciative audience and no-one worried about suffering ill effects. But the curse associated with mummies became fixed in global consciousness in 1923, when Carnarvon died from blood poisoning and pneumonia on 3 April, only six weeks after the lost tomb was opened and its treasures revealed.

The story came about because Carnarvon had signed an exclusive deal with the Times to report on the findings inside the tomb. This meant the other papers had no story to tell while the world wanted to read about mummies and ancient treasures. So they focused on what they could report. Multiple stories became associated with Carnarvon's death. The lights of Cairo flickered and failed as he died and his three-legged dog Susie, back in England, howled mournfully and dropped dead.

Immediately, the British Museum was inundated with mummy memorabilia offloaded by guilty tourists fearing they'd been cursed. Stories were told about how archaeologists and their loved ones had died due to the mummy's curse—from suicide, accident or exotic disease.

One of these was Thomas Douglas Murray, who'd travelled down the Nile in 1865 and bought back a mummy case from Luxor before returning to Cairo. While near the pyramids, Douglas Murray went quail shooting, slipped over and shot his own arm off. Although he survived, he'd always be associated with the curse. As a spiritualist and a member of the Ghost Club, which had strong connections with the Society for Psychical

Research, Douglas Murray was ideally placed to spread the story of a curse.

The mummy case (the 'unlucky mummy') had been donated to the British Museum in 1889 after reputedly causing numerous misfortunes, including nasty tricks performed on visitors to the Egyptian Rooms. The story was debunked again and again, and the British Museum issued a statement denying it had ever possessed a mummy, coffin or cover that had been involved in, or connected to any unusual events.

Given that Louis had been carrying a mummy's hand around for decades, claiming it was cursed, it would have been extremely odd if he hadn't said anything. Opportunistic as ever, Louis sold stories about his mummy's hand to newspapers in Britain, America, Australia and France multiple times from 1923 to 1926. Other newspapers picked up his stories and repeated them. He even claimed to have known Douglas Murray and to have read his palm (as Douglas Murray had died in 1912, he could neither confirm nor deny such a meeting, but it had never been mentioned before).

At the end of February 1923, Katie left for a few weeks in New York and Louis returned to Ireland. Presumably, he planned to stay for a while as he bought himself an Irish terrier—records show he was granted a dog licence on 31 March 1923. That same day Louis was also present to oversee the auction of 20,000 boxes of turf stored at his works.

On the day of the auction a gang turned up to loot what they could. Fortunately, a few Irregulars were hanging around to make sure things ran smoothly and they soon stopped that by showing off their revolvers. A few weeks later, in May 1923, the Irregulars capitulated, although they neither surrendered their arms nor disbanded, However, it was too late to save Louis's business.

Back in London, Louis had gone into partnership with Arthur de Courcey Bower, setting up a financial company. Bower had fallen on hard times. He'd spent time in prison after being made bankrupt and in 1924 was fined for being drunk and throwing ink on a woman's clothes (there'd been a spate of similar crimes that year and it was hinted that Bower was behind all of them), although he apparently gave up drinking after this episode.

> Grace Whitehouse… said that on Saturday evening Bower looked at her, and then deliberately threw a bottle of ink by the side of her. The bottle broke on the kerb, and the ink splashed her shoes, stockings, and coat… She asked Bower what he was going to do, and be pushed her aside, mumbled something, and walked away…. Bower said that the splashing was quite unintentional. He had met Watt, an old friend, selling matches, and invited him

to have a drink. He afterwards bought a bottle of ink to fill his fountain pen, so that he could take Watt's address. After filling the pen he threw the bottle away, without noticing that anyone was near... Edward Bacon said that he saw Bower take the bottle from his pocket, pour some ink over Watt's hand and deliberately throw the bottle in front of Miss Whitehouse and her companion. When Miss Whitehouse spoke to Bower, he pushed her aside so violently that witness had to catch her to save her from falling.[22]

Bower was probably a lost cause. Maybe dealing with him was detrimental to Louis's health because he suffered a heart attack in June 1925.

As the spirit passed out of my body I appeared to see... a man robed like a Lama making passes over me with his hands. His words formed in my mind that my life would be given back to me as it had been once before in a Buddhist temple in India... The Lama seemed to say, 'For the second time you will be restored to life, when the third time comes—you will not come back.' After some considerable period... the doctor at my bedside thought he detected a slight movement in the heart, then steadily it got stronger and stronger, and to the amazement of those present I came back to life.[23]

Obviously, he slowed down after this and began to take things easier.

Not in the least. He did, however, dissolve his partnership with Bower just before Christmas 1925. On 2 January 1926, Bower visited Louis and Katie at their home at 4 York Terrace Mews. Penniless, he returned to the single room he rented in Hampstead, and that night he collapsed and died of a heart attack. Louis sent a wreath to the funeral.

Louis still hadn't given up the idea of making money from peat. He conducted (or had conducted for him) several experiments that focused on by-products. In case anyone questioned how hands-on he was, Louis took kept bottles of interesting looking liquids in his study to show off, and he tried to drum up support for a new peat venture whenever he could. This included meetings with Sir Horace Curzon Plunkett, the Anglo-Irish agricultural reformer and politician, who took him seriously enough to conduct enquiries into 'Hammonite' (the 'activated carbon' made from peat), and referred to Louis as a 'peat fiend'.[24] And Lady Angela Forbes, the socialite and novelist, recalled that at a dinner party hosted by Major Geoffrey Lubbock:

He brought a sample of the new fuel with him, and whilst we were at dinner the fire was left to go down, leaving when we came back only a few dying embers. Almost directly the new coal was added, a beautiful blaze resulted, which gave out far more heat than that from ordinary coal. It appears to be very cheap to produce, and if it were possible to develop it on a large enough scale would make us very independent of coal strikes, but I suppose some technical hitch will arise. The bye-products were also wonderful, and we were shown slabs of material which would replace asbestos for building purposes at an infinitely lower cost.[25]

In January 1926, Louis set up a factory in Norfolk and made arrangements for Hammonite to be produced at a factory in Swinton, Yorkshire. Everything ceased when the Ministry for Finance agreed to hear Louis's claim for compensation for the fire of August 1922. The hearing opened in April 1926 when Louis was asking for £34,073. By June his claim had dropped to £12,960.

That there'd been a fire and property had been destroyed was clear. The question was who was responsible? If it was the Irregulars, as Louis claimed, under whose orders? Could it have been an accident? After all, there was a smithy near the factory and the workmen smoked.

Mr Lupton, who acted for the prosecution, focused on demolishing Louis's credibility—and he'd done his homework. Producing a copy of Confessions, he described how Louis had spent several years as a palmist, saying, 'I am… strictly accurate in describing him as an adventurer. He was a gentleman who engaged in hazardous enterprises for the greater part of his life.'[26] Then he added. 'You were not candid when you did not tell me anything about this precarious occupation.'[27] Louis testily responded. 'There was nothing precarious about it. I earned more money than many of you barristers.'[28]

Those watching settled back to enjoy themselves amidst the general laughter. Lupton said he'd received a photograph of Louis from Scotland Yard with a report. The irritated judge told him the report couldn't be considered unless someone from Scotland Yard was going to appear to verify it. Louis added, 'Have I committed any crime that I should come here to hear a report of Scotland Yard read?'[29]

When the financial scandal of 1909 was inevitably raised, Louis insisted he'd never been charged and anyone could make a complaint—it didn't mean they were right. He'd left Paris in the normal scheme of things, several months after the complaint was made—a clear lie—and he was tried in his absence, hence the fine and sentence of thirteen months that Lupton mentioned (or the case was never tried and Lupton had misunderstood as French law was different—Louis suggested both). Louis's counsel complained that this line of questioning was 'highly irregular and most improper'—probably to shut Louis up as much as anything.[30]

Judge Roche asked Lupton to stick to what was relevant but Lupton insisted that Louis's credibility was relevant. When Lupton produced a copy of Louis's baptismal certificate, Louis accepted it was his but added that his father had traced his family back to his aristocratic heritage. When his right to call himself a count was questionned, Louis said, 'I am entitled to it For the past thirty years I am only known by it. I have got to sign all legal documents, as you will see by the deed poll, under that name.'[31] Louis produced his paperwork, and when its validity was challenged, he insisted that his solicitor had advised it didn't need to be registered (which was true) but in any event, he *had* registered it in Lisburn.

In summing up, Judge Roche reminded everyone that Louis used to read palms (as if they'd forgotten), adding, 'I am quite sure that he had given satisfaction, or at any rate pleasure, to a great many people by telling them what they wanted to know, and some what they might not have expected to hear... But according to his book a good deal of it turned out to be true.'[32]

The judge, 'entertained grave suspicions as to the applicant himself being responsible for the injury,' but felt compelled to award compensation, because it hadn't been proved that Louis was responsible for the fire: 'The case was full of suspicion, but suspicion was not enough.'[33]

Louis was awarded £7,037 with a reinstatement clause attached. The case went to appeal in 1928. The High Court was divided and subsequently the Supreme Court allowed the appeal and dismissed Louis's claim. He never mentioned peat again.

Cheiro in 1920s

Cheiro in 1930s

CHAPTER
SEVENTEEN

Many people will doubtless ask, 'Who is Cheiro?' He is already known to thousands as the greatest living student of the Occult.[1]

FTEN LEAVING HIS BUSINESS INTERESTS IN IRELAND to take care of themselves during the 1920s, Louis spent much of his time in London writing. He didn't languidly produce an occasional poem or article—he went into a writing frenzy.

It started with a series of articles for the *Sunday Illustrated* in 1923. Excited announcements heralded their appearance from September, although the articles didn't feature until the next month. Many of the tales were rehashed, but they hadn't been told for a long time. Some were new and would later enter Cheiro's mythology. Whichever way you looked at it, Cheiro was back!—well, almost. Even allowing for hyperbole, the stories were popular. The *Sunday Illustrated* reported a:

FLOOD OF APPEALS TO 'CHEIRO.'
Readers Ask Famous Seer to Help and Advise Them.
WOMEN'S PATHETIC LETTERS.

That the astounding confessions of 'Cheiro' which began in last week's Sunday Illustrated have captured the interest of the public has been proved in every conceivable way. The stream of requests, by telephone, telegram and messenger, from newsagents for additional supplies, told its own tale. But 'Cheiro' has also been inundated with letters from readers who are in trouble or in despair. Hundreds upon hundreds of these have arrived during the week at the offices of this paper... and have been forwarded to the famous seer at his private residence… Almost without exception the writers, after congratulating Sunday Illustrated on securing such a unique feature, beseech 'Cheiro' to break his rule and give them a professional appointment.[2]

The *Illustrated* featured a photo of three women attempting to sort the many letters, surrounded by posters advertising the series. But despite many letters 'telling pitiful tales of struggles against adversity', Cheiro wasn't resuming his practice; it didn't matter how much money you offered.[3]

ON THE TRACK OF 'CHEIRO.'
Run to Earth By People Anxious to Have His Help.

Londoners have found a new pastime. On Sunday amateur sleuths were 'sleuthing' all over the place—on the 'buses, in the Underground, and in the principal thoroughfares. They were looking for 'Cheiro,' the wonderful palmist and seer, who is contributing his amazing reminiscences of noted men and women to this paper. The searchers were trying to find him with the aid of his photograph. Three men, each carrying a Sunday Illustrated, followed 'Cheiro' from the Savoy Hotel on Sunday. Dashing for the Underground, he spotted a passing omnibus, and by boarding it managed to elude his pursuers… 'All the way home,' he stated, 'I was dogged by people who pleaded for interviews, with the result that a journey which should have taken only twenty minutes occupied two hours. I have no desire to be a spoil-sport, but I should take it as a favour if those who recognise me outside would refrain from pursuing me in this fashion,' added 'Cheiro.'

Far from being a has-been, Cheiro could clearly sell papers. And to prove he was no 'spoil-sport', he was happy to sell what he could produce. For example, from February 1924 a series of articles entitled 'Secrets of the Future' appeared in *The Age,* in Melbourne, Australia and in 1925 the *Daily Telegraph* in Sydney announced a long discussion on numerology with: '13 is not unlucky: Cheiro explodes absurd superstition.'[5] In Britain the *People* carried a series of articles about astrology in 1926 and 1927, covering the zodiac signs of towns and cities, lucky numbers, numbers and health, numerology and horse racing, and the occult meaning of jewels, amongst other similar subjects. This also resulted in a flood of letters, some enclosing money which Louis scrupulously returned.

Louis also busied himself writing books. *Cheiro's Book of Numbers* appeared in 1926, to be followed by *Life, Love and Marriage, Read Your Past, Present, and Future* and *Cheiro's World Predictions* in 1927. *True Ghost Stories* and *Cheiro's Year Book for 1929* followed in 1928, with another yearbook the following year.

World Predictions received the most attention. Meticulously listing potential wars and earthquakes, Louis told his readers they were in the midst of the Age of Aquarius and Russia would become the 'most dreaded power in modern civilization... until her armies will be wrecked by a combination of powers, including Great Britain and Germany, on the plans of Armageddon.'[6] The US would also be involved in this war and the 'Israelites will see all the ancient promises fulfilled, becoming a great and dominant nation which will exert a beneficial influence on the rest of mankind.'[7] Occultists commonly made predictions that Jews might take over the world soon, but in general they thought it was a bad and worrying thing. It was exactly what everyone needed, according to Louis, and he was in favour of it.

Writing of the then Prince of Wales, Edward VIII, Cheiro said:

> Rumours say that Queen Mary, and, in a lesser degree, King George, have worried themselves seriously over this problem of the Prince, who may be fond of a light flirtation with the fair sex but is determined not to settle down until he feels a grande passion, but it is well within the range of possibility, owing to the peculiar planetary influences to which he is subjected, that he will in the end fall a victim of a devastating love affair. If he does, I predict that the Prince will give up everything, even the chance of being crowned, rather than lose the object of his affection.[8]

Louis also scripted a set of short films. They were produced and directed by Anglo-Indian Gerald Barton Savi, the son of the novelist E W (Edith Winifred) Savi (he took up writing crime novels himself in the 1930s). Eight episodes of *The Language of the Hand* were released by United Films for distribution from January 1926. They fundamentally offered the same material as in Louis's palmistry books—diagrams explaining the techniques of palmistry and details of celebrity readings.

> Interspersed with these main features are short acted scenes picturing such subjects as 'Cheiro' reading King Edward's hand, Queen Elizabeth consulting her palmist, and a mother reading the hand of her child... The acted bits, although they add a touch

of variety, are also rather a mistake, as they tend to cheapen a production which is intended to be taken very seriously.[9]

Working so hard meant Louis needed to get away sometimes. In January 1927 he and Katie set sail for Los Angeles.[i] They arrived in California on 17 February, but Louis couldn't simply take a holiday. He wanted to check out the possibilities of making more palmistry movies. That didn't lead anywhere, despite his clutching letters of introduction from stars such as Douglas Fairbanks and Lillian Gish which were enough to open doors for him and Katie. Never mind, he had a thoroughly marvellous time. 'When I undertook the journey I was prepared for wonders and miracles and I was not disappointed,' he said. 'I expected difficulties and marvels almost beyond belief. They confronted me.'[10]

The following year, Louis sold a set of articles to the *People* about his trip, saying, 'I have just returned from an extended tour of California, during which I have explored Hollywood and Los Angeles and done all that a man may to study the intimate life of the most-talked-about colony in the world… In so doing I have had unique opportunities to obtain inside information.'[11]

This inside information comprised standard fare about film stars of the day—not all of whom Louis actually met. For example, one article explained how he'd managed to see a cast of Rudolf Valentino's hand, allowing him to ramble on about him.[12] Another about Lillian Gish could easily have been cobbled together from press releases.[ii] Louis claimed that he approached Paul Bern, the director, screenwriter and producer, who was interested in producing a series of palmistry films but Metro-Goldwyn-Mayer turned down his proposal.

Louis had the sense to realise that sex sold, and discussed midnight orgies that no longer happened and violent deaths and attacks—which presumably also no longer happened, but it was nice to mention them.

> A conspicuous case was that of Art Jennings, a young comedian from Vaudeville… He jumped from twenty dollars to three hundred a week and lost his head. His midnight orgies were notorious; but when he had exhibitions of Bacchanalian nymphs upon the beaches, the authorities warned him. He took no notice

---

i Louis and Katie were accompanied by Harriet Robb, their servant who was planning to stay in Los Angeles as her sister lived there. The shipping records meticulously record that Louis was 5 foot 10¾ to Katie's 5 foot and they both had green eyes.
ii Which appeared on 25 June 1928.

and in due course he was conducted to the train and barred from California. He fell back into a medium vaudeville career and died at an early age…

Many of the stories were hushed up, but while I was in Hollywood I learned the true facts from friends who had lived through the early days and had taken an active part in the cleaning-up of the city.[13]

Louis also pointed out the existence of luxurious hotels with heated swimming pools and huge dining rooms where you could go star-spotting. And the many opportunities for riding, playing golf and tennis, or taking life more quietly with a round of bridge. It was easy to guess how he and Katie had spent their time.

Faced with a whole new audience of glamorous people who were notoriously superstitious, Louis couldn't resist becoming Cheiro again and reading as many palms as they'd let him. He finally returned to England at the end of July.

At least some of his spare time was spent at Masonic lodges. Louis is recorded as attending a meeting of Drury Lane Lodge in October 1927 (he'd he changed his name to Louis le Warner Hamon in 1925) and in November 1928 he was advanced to the position of Mark Master Mason at the Dramatic Mark Lodge. Both lodges were made up of musicians, actors and other entertainers.

Cheiro's work was made easier by a man who'd begun life answering to the name of Harold Thropp.[iii] Son of a hardware manufacturer, Thropp had long dreamed of becoming an astrologer but he'd sensibly joined the York and Lancaster Regiment as a second lieutenant at the start of World War I. He hastily married Ellen Catley in 1916 and their son Edward was born three months later (they had three more children). After the war, Thropp was determined to pursue his dream of becoming a professional astrologer. But 'Thropp' wasn't the name of a famous astrologer—or a famous anything, really. So he was reborn as R H T Naylor (later, he dropped the T).

By 1919 he was running Memphis Occult Products in Derbyshire and selling horoscopes. In 1922 Naylor lived in Harrogate from where he offered horoscopes 'free from pseudo mystery or ambiguity.'[14] He also had an office in New Bond Street, and before long he'd sold Memphis Occult Products and moved to London. By 1923 Naylor also ran a bookshop in Oxford Street. At least, he often sold books from his 'salon' on the fourth

---

iii His birth was registered as Richard Harold Naylor—Naylor was his mother's surname.

floor along with a selection of incenses, jewellery and 'requisites of every kind for the student of occultism and astrology'.[15]

It was about this time that he met Louis and began to act as his agent (which may at first have been a grand description for collecting his mail). Naylor was gaining a reputation amongst astrologers and spoke at meetings of the London Astrological Research Society.

Maybe maths wasn't Louis's strong point, or perhaps he found it boring. In any event, his *Year Book for 1929* contains the credit 'Astronomical and astrological computations by R. H. T. Naylor'. The book was successful enough for a second edition to appear in 1930 which Naylor also collaborated on. Naylor also appears to have been working for the London Publishing Company, based at 42 Museum Street, which published Louis's books.

In early 1929, Naylor was also selling Cheiro's *Arcana of Astrology*, described as 'The only personal introduction Cheiro will ever give in his secrets' and 'A course of 10 confidential lessons (in MSS) teaching the methods and embodying the great experience of this world famous Seer'.[15][iv] No records exist to attest to the popularity or otherwise of these lessons, except that advertisements quietly disappeared later that year.

As if to make sure he covered all possible bases for his writing, Louis also contributed to pulp fiction magazines. The American *Ghost Stories* featured supernatural fantasy and occult fiction mixed with semi-fiction or pseudo-factual articles. At least three of Louis's stories appeared—'A Bargain with a Spirit', 'The Haunting Horror of the White Bat' and 'Nurse Cavell Speaks'.[v]

Maybe Katie was feeling left out with Louis spending so much time writing, although she helpfully designed the cover for *True Ghost Stories* and *World Predictions*. In any event, she worked on her own novel and *Outlawed for Love* appeared in January 1929.

> The publishers announce that they have their possession a sworn affidavit from a person who played one of the principal roles in this remarkable story… the incidents related by Countess Hamon are true… Countess Hamon relates the tale simply and tenderly, and the descriptive passages are full of colour. If all Mexican bandits are anything like the ones she describes, then the outlaws in this delightful country have been badly maligned.[17]

---

iv 'MSS' is an abbreviation for manuscript.
v In October, November and December 1929.

And then Louis narrowly missed the chance to go down in history as the man who changed astrology forever—the man credited with inventing the horoscope column.

Princess Margaret (younger daughter of the future King George VI) was born on 21 August 1930 and when the *Sunday Express* was preparing its issue for 24 August the news was already old. The editor decided to give the story a fresh angle by publishing a story about the Princess's horoscope. Arthur Christiansen, the entertainment editor of the Express who was responsible for the decision to hire Naylor later wrote: 'John Gordon [the Express editor] suggested, "Get Cheiro (then the greatest name in the astrology business) to do a horoscope of Princess Margaret." But Cheiro was of all places in Cairo that week, which was lucky for R H Naylor, one of his assistants, who undertook the assignment.'[18]

On 24 August 1930, Naylor's article appeared. Almost as an afterthought, Naylor added predictions and comments based on readers' dates of birth. A flood of appreciative letters persuaded the Sunday Express to commission a feature 'Were You Born in September?' for the following week. And Naylor's success was secured when a million readers read his prediction that British aircraft were in serious danger and the BBC announced that the R01 airship had crashed that day in northern France. He became famous overnight.

> Naylor and his horoscopes became a power in the land. If he said that Monday was a bad day for buying, then the buyers of more than one West End store waited for the stars to become more propitious.[19]

Naylor introduced his readers to Sun signs as a character type, featuring Mr and Mrs Taurus, for example. He didn't write a twelve-sign horoscope column in the format we're used to until 1936 when it appeared in *Prediction* magazine. And Naylor wasn't the first to use this format—or to introduce astrology columns to newspapers. That doesn't matter. As far as everyone was concerned, Naylor invented the horoscope column. One by one, the national press took up similar features.

And Naylor realised what he'd done. 'In 1930 I commenced a series of Astrological articles which have entirely altered the orientation of the public mind towards Astrology. I am aware all this sounds egotistical and perhaps boastful, but it so happens it is true,' he said, modestly.[20]

The following year was busy for Naylor. The Filmaphone company struck a deal with him for exclusive recordings of *What the Stars*

Foretell—a free horoscope was offered with every purchase. And instead of contributing to Cheiro's predictions, Naylor issued his own yearbook in 1933.

Although he achieved instant fame, Naylor continued to work as a consultant astrologer from an office in New Oxford Street. But in 1931 he abruptly left Ellen and set up home with Phyllis Poulton who immediately started describing herself as Phyllis Naylor. Ellen filed for divorce and in 1933 Lord Merrivale, who granted the decree nisi, said, 'A somewhat absurd description has been given of the husband's occupation. I see he describes himself an author and publisher'.[21] The divorce gained scant press attention as few people knew Naylor's real name.

But what did Cheiro care? He'd moved to Hollywood.

INTERLUDE

ASTROLOGY

Cheiro is well aware that to cast a horoscope requires a precise time of birth and hard work and skill to interpret it. Those with such skills are not only adept at offering a truthful description of your character, they can also make predictions with unswerving accuracy.

Most people want something simpler. They don't have time to spend hours making mathematical calculations. Fortunately, it's possible to read character and disposition by your period of birth, and the meaning of the number of the day on which you're born.

What you need to remember is that the first seven days of the period is overlapped by the period that comes before it. It comes into full power after that seven days and then gradually loses strength.

For example, the zodiac sign of Capricorn begins on 21 December but as it's overlapped by the 'cusp' of the previous sign (Sagittarius), it doesn't come into its full power until about 28 December. It's then in full strength until 20 January, after which it loses its strength over the next seven days, being overlapped by the 'cusp' of the incoming sign— Aquarius. So if you're born between 20 January and 27 January, you have characteristics of both Capricorn and Aquarius.

If you're born during this period, you may often be misunderstood. As a thinker and reasoner, it's natural for you to head a business organisation. You are independent and high-minded in all you do and hate being beholden to anyone else. Being in control is important to you, but your odd ideas of love, duty, and social position can make others view you as strange and you find it hard to get on with other people. A plain speaker, you often make the mistake of choosing the unpopular cause and supporting the underdog. Your responsibilities weigh heavily on you and your worries can cause you ill health. A lack of self-confidence may hold you back although you will offer practical aid to those who suffer. Should you follow a religion, you need to guard against becoming fanatical, Often feeling lonely and misunderstood, your home and family life can be very troubled.

Should you be one of Cheiro's more illustrious clients, he may interpret your full horoscope alongside a palm reading. He did so for Lord Kitchener.

> Born as he was in what is called 'the Cusp of the first House of Air' in the Sign of Gemini, and entering into the first House of Water, the Sign of Cancer, also House of the Moon and detriment of Saturn—taking these indications together with the cabalistic interpretation of the numbers governing his life—and the position Jupiter would be towards his sixty-sixth year, that his death would be by water...[1]

Indeed, Lord Kitchener was on a ship bound for Russia when it struck a German mine and sank on June 5, 1916.

Cheiro is always happy to offer insight into the lives of royalty and other prominent figures, whether they ask or not.

> On the day of his birth, June 3, 1865, at 1.18 am, London, Aries, the House of Mars, and significator of England... was rising... [2]
>
> King George V. was born ... on the 'cusp' of the Sign of Gemini, the Sun being only 2.21 of the next Zodiacal Sign of Cancer.
>
> The Regal sign of the planet Jupiter is almost in mid-heaven in the Ninth House, and in a powerful position to Aries the Zodiacal Sign governing England. Thus, even when he was a sailor and a second son—with no expectation that he would come to the Throne as his brother the Duke of Clarence had every right to expect to reign—the promise of the planets was, that he should have Regal position and be destined to wear a Crown. Mars is King George the Fifth's ruling planet in the House of Aries (England's Sign). From these astrological influences he received kingship and the natural dignity that well becomes him as a Monarch.[3]

When it comes to the fate of countries and nations, Cheiro pays close attention to the movements of the planets. He has his own methods, which he doesn't want to share, although he might be persuaded to teach them to you for a fee—especially if you're a woman.

As Cheiro will tell you, we're now in the Age of Aquarius, the New Age, and this is the time for women to come into power. Something he heartily approves of.

CHAPTER
EIGHTEEN

It would never do to take him as seriously as he does himself.[1]

ATIE'S SON JACK had been studying at the Royal Academy of Music, a short distance from his home with Katie and Louis at 4 York Terrace, Park Square, in a beautiful Regency apartment near Regent's Park. He also spent some time at Trinity College, and it seems that Louis had dropped in a good word in for him as he'd sung for Hamilton Harty as well as in William Harty's (Hamilton Harty's father) choir—apparently he was a 'fine tenor.'[2]

'My son and husband were inseparable because both had psychic powers,' Katie said. 'Although my son was untrained, he had second sight and could foretell happenings in the next few months in the family circle.'[3]

Psychic he may have been, but primarily Jack was an organist, and now his studies were over, he was seeking work. He was soon the organist at the Blessed Sacrament Catholic Church on Sunset Boulevard in the heart of Hollywood.

Katie, Louis and Jack arrived at San Pedro on 4 August 1929, accompanied by Katie's aunt, Felicia Purnell and Boston-born (1872) Grace Kuhn. She'd been in England since June 1908 and as an American living overseas, she'd had to apply for a passport annually after the War. In March 1916 Louis supplied her with a reference from his company Flax, and in 1918 she gave her address as 30 Elgin Road, Dublin—where Louis's companies and patents were registered. On the 1930 US census she's described as a 'cousin' with no indication as to who claimed her as their cousin. Whatever the relationship was, it was a close one as she moved in with Katie and Louis. Also living with them was their English butler William Darcy and his wife Mary, their cook. A few weeks later, Leslie Stuart, Louis's agent, followed them.

It's comforting to know that Louis's eyes were still powerful—the shipping records record him as having 'agate' eyes while everyone else had to be satisfied with grey or brown.

This time, Louis planned to stay in the US. Described as a 'British yachtsman and scribe'[4] he 'held a citizenship declaration in his hand as he climbed down off the Dollar liner President Garfield and inhaled the delicious aroma of his new homeland.'[5] He'd almost become an American citizen forty years previously, he said, but he:

> Went away to cover the Chinese-Japanese war and never got back to complete his patriotic obligations... Two years ago he and the Countess were here, hobnobbing with film royalty, and fell in love with the place. They have sold their properties in London and are 'coming out practically bare,' they said, although a ship clerk recalled they have eighty or more pieces of luggage.[6]

Louis wanted to make films. Not about palmistry, but more excitingly, 'For the first time in history... the real India is to be filmed.'[7] Louis's plan was to produce a picture in the independent states of Mysore and Bikaner. One of his many meetings with the Maharajah of Bikaner took place shortly after the First World War when the Maharajah was in London accompanied by 'a regiment of his best troops, together with a hundred of his trained fighting elephants'.[8] That consultation had gained Louis a gold cigarette case with his name engraved on it and a carpet. Of course, Louis gave the impression that they'd met in India.

> Hamon lived in India for several years, was known as a White Brahman and has entry to the estates and palaces of the maharajahs of the above named Indian states, as well as the friendship and co-operation of their majesties... They are willing... to co-operate with me to the fullest extent in the filming of various rites, ceremonies and sports, such as wedding feasts, elephant hunts and other matters.[9]

Louis never made a film about India. He didn't make a film at all, although he kept saying he would. It was what you did in Hollywood, after all. No-one can say he didn't try. He churned out screenplay after screenplay, registering nine for copyright in 1934—amongst them a treatment of Katie's novel. The remainder sound like exactly the sort of screenplays you'd expect: *Cagliostro, the great lover, Rameses the Great, The Disappearance of Marianne Delorme* and *Revenge; a Russian drama.*

As soon as they'd settled into their Santa Monica house, in September Louis and Katie hosted a house-warming party—the first of many such parties. Amongst their hundred-or-so guests was Jack's close friend American-born Frank Perkins who had been a student with him and had recently returned to the US. Louis, Katie and Jack attended Perkins' wedding in April 1930 to English-born Louisa Banning.

Life wasn't only about parties. Louis planned to spend one day a week reading palms for $100 a time or $50, depending on the source—point being, he wasn't cheap. He didn't have to be. Despite the multitude of people who could sort out your destiny in Hollywood, there was plenty of demand.

> Scratch a movie star and you'll find a patron of the mystic mumbo-jumbo... The Beverly Hills are full of fortune-tellers... In businesslike offices, glib individuals work out destinies in columns of cold figures. Spirit controls named Oscar and Pocahontas haunt the incense-laden corridors of some of the old apartment buildings... Lots of contracts are signed on days pronounced auspicious by the seers... there are players who will work only for those companies whose astral vibrations are sympathetic to their own... The dean of mysticism and all-around, catch-as-catch-can champion in the decathlon of occultism is Count Louis Hamon...[10]

And he met movie star after movie star, including Marion Davis, Tallulah Bankhead, Ramon Navarro, and Douglas Fairbanks. But it was the parties that made the press. After all, 'Cheiro was always a welcome guest and if it were noised [*sic*] abroad that an extraordinary successful hostess had snared him to her soirée, every person invited inevitably turned up.'[11]

> Don't forget... to address the Count and Countess Hamon by their titles when they greet you! Just because the Count happens also to be Cheiro, who can read your horoscope and your palm in a way to make you scared to be in the room with him, don't forget and say, 'Hello, Chei!' or anything crude like that![12]

Amongst the guests that night were Mrs Sam Goldwyn, Theda Bara and her husband, Peg Talmadge and other Hollywood royalty. Jack and Frank Perkins played the piano while Katie and Louis regaled the journalists with tall tales.

The Countess claimed they sent a Cheiro book to the queen of England... [Katie said] 'But of course, royalty is not allowed to accept presents from anybody. The book was returned to us next morning—but with the word that the Queen had sat up for hours reading it!'...

We stayed very late to hear the Countess' son and Mr. Perkins play, and suddenly there appeared in the drawing-room the handsome Spanish maid who had served us so delightfully all evening. She was all brightened up after drinking stimulants which she had obtained in some mysterious manner, and she wanted to do a Spanish dance for us. The Countess laughed good-naturedly. It would take a Countess, we decided—or a picture star—to carry off a thing like that...

'What wonderfully interesting, brilliant people!' we decided, as we wended our way homeward.[13]

Every Sunday afternoon, the Hamons threw their house open for one of their salons, usually filled with lots of musicians. One of their most famous guests was Hamilton Harty, by then extremely famous. He conducted at the Hollywood Bowl in August 1931 and the following week Katie and Louis took him on a sightseeing tour.

While Louis and Katie threw parties and treated going out to for meals with film stars as a career move (for example, Louis dined at the Roosevelt hotel with Anita Loos and John Emerson in December), Jack had more than enough opportunities for work—far more than he'd have had back in England. He spent three years as a member of the Hollywood Bowl Choral Association and sang in an open-air theatre which held 27,000 people, and he worked as a voice teacher to Hollywood stars.

Of course, Louis couldn't completely leave his past behind. People still sought him out for his occult connections, including the Australian Major W H Cross, a mining engineer whose past was littered with arrests for theft and embezzlement. When serving in India in 1917, he'd been court martialled for dishonesty and the police kept a close eye on him due to his shady reputation. In 1921 he'd fled to Tibet to avoid charges of deception pending in Calcutta, calling himself Mr Brown and immediately launching into new scams. In 1924 the Swiss tourist department asked the British legation whether he was genuine in claiming to be an agent of the Dali Lama as he'd recently completed a lecture tour collecting for Tibetan medical institutions… the list goes on.

He described himself as a businessman who during his time in Mongolia had met 'many of those Masters who have drunk deep of the eternal writings of Occultism that have flowed and are still flowing since the earliest dawn of civilization,' and that 'in those Tibetan monasteries on 'the roof of the World' where so few strangers are allowed to enter, as far back as I can remember I have heard the name of "Cheiro" spoken of with respect and admiration.'[14] Cross didn't really know Louis, although he'd translated some of his books into Chinese.

> But where was this man to be found, that was the question? While turning this point over in my mind, an incarnate Abbot in the Monastery of Toussoun Nor, announced to me one day, that one of monks had been sent to California to find a man whose occult vibrations were of such a high order that perhaps he might be the Seer I sought and whom they also wanted to find for a purpose of their own. This Abbot told me that I would recognize the man in question, not only by his high vibration but by an extremely old Carved image of a Chinese Buddha which would be found where he lived.[15]

He could have read the Los Angeles papers or asked anyone in Hollywood where Louis lived. They'd have pointed him in the right direction, maybe even offered him a lift while filling Cross in on how Louis was doing.

> His long reputation as an oracle has been sensational…. And now he is living in Hollywood!… I had met Cheiro once before… What had puzzled me then was his rich Irish brogue. And now I was again hearing it and listening to the newest predictions of this huge, bluff fellow, tall, stalwart, wide as a grand piano…. the hair atop his massive head is graying, but he teems with the high animal zest of a young football player… Immensely alive eyes and an easy, dignified voice and manner. A healthy vital sorcerer, this man! No sinister, cadaverous Merlin.[16]

Katie, on the other hand, was 'plump with red hair.'[17] Anyway, using mystical methods, Cross ended up on Louis's doorstep.

> We were standing before the gates of an old-world-looking house surrounded by over two acres of gardens and half concealed

by palms and beautiful trees in one of the principal avenues of Hollywood, California. Walking up the avenue of flowering trees, I entered and was received by a man who closely resembled the photographs of 'Cheiro' I had seen in his books... I asked: 'Have you a Chinese Buddha here?' Asking his date of birth I then tested his vibrations by the Chinese tablets I had with me. I found they were higher than those of any man I had ever met, indicating that the man before me must a reincarnation of some unusual person of some far-distant past.[18]

Cross stayed on in California and became a regular visitor, even giving talks at some of Louis's parties, and was present at Katie's birthday party in May 1931.

Edith Halford Nelson claimed that Louis was the master of a Rosicrucian lodge and that in his final years he drew up plans for a temple intended for a ritual he used where he wore grand jewelled robes and communed with the dead. However, when Wilfred Talbot Smith phoned him to seek his help in organising OTO (Ordo Templi Orientis) activities in Los Angeles at Aleister Crowley's suggestion, Louis said he was too busy. Smith was annoyed as Louis wasn't living up to his obligations (although he didn't clarify what these obligations were) and had apparently said some not nice things about Crowley. Louis pointed out that he was a freemason and that conflicted with the OTO's practices. Smith phoned him a second time, but it made no difference.

It's true that Louis was busy—he spent most of his time writing. His tall tales regularly appeared in *Ghost Stories* throughout 1930 and 1931, and *When were you born* was published in 1930, *Fate in the Making* and *You and Your Hand* in 1931, *Confessions: Memoirs of a Modern Seer* (a compilation of his newspaper memoirs—a further version of his memoirs appeared in the Daily Express in 1933) in 1932, *Real Life Stories* in 1934, *Mysteries and Romances of the World's Greatest Occultists* in and *You and Your Star* in 1936. He also wrote for journals and magazines on a wide range of subjects, including an article on genealogy for *The Ancestor* magazine. Although Louis's books sold well, reviews tended to be lukewarm, at the best—sometimes, they were tetchily disapproving as in one review of *Confessions*: 'The palpable errors in this book are very, very numerous.'[19]

It was hard to keep up, so it was no wonder Louis employed a ghostwriter. Olga Rosmanith was a London journalist who produced numerous short stories for the *Daily Mail* and published sensational novels in the 1950s.[i] She stayed with Louis and Katie in 1930 and commented, 'Cheiro was a repository of star secrets which would make a very startling book since he knew things the gossip mongers never found out and was ethical and kept them secret.'[20] However, Rosmanith didn't write a startling book:

> He was ill and had a deadline of two books of memoirs and palmistry. I offered to write them for him if he would teach me his science. So I was living in his house (to work at nights) in 1930 and met the people who came there. I met Paul Bern and Jean Harlow together, for they came to him for counsel. I loved her at once, a darling girl and nothing like her screen image of hard-boiled brassiness. Pure acting and very good.[21]

Rosmanith is credited with supplying the drawings and diagrams in *You and Your Hand*. The 'memoirs' would have been *Fate in the Making*. Although Rosmanith didn't mention her involvement in Louis's work until 1971, the trip was a success for her on more than one level. While staying with Louis, she met the composer Edward Nies-Berger—he wrote the soundtracks of several films, including *The Bride of Frankenstein*—who she later married.

What did Katie do while Louis was so busy? She retreated to her laboratory they'd installed in their house to conduct some scientific research.

> Having a decided talent for geology, botany, and chemistry in later years she has devoted her time to the study of pests that injure plant life in various parts of the world. In such research work she has been extraordinarily successful, having been invited by Governments of many countries to assist them in their fight against insect plagues of many kinds. She has recently written an exhaustive treatise on the cause of the widespread destruction of the coca plantations in South America, and has pointed out how this destruction might be prevented and the plants brought back to their original productiveness.[22]

That Louis wasn't short of money and easily able to fund such ventures is attested to by the fact that Leslie Stuart sued him for $56,000 in

---

i Grace Olga Rosmanith Roxburgh married Archibald Hall Brown in 1918 and also wrote under the names of Olga Hall-Brown and Olga Roxburgh. A taste of her novels can be viewed at Sarah Boyle, 'My love-Haunted Heart', https://hauntedhearts.wordpress.com/category/unholy-flame-by-olga-rosmanith/ [accessed January 2021].

1931—equivalent to almost a million dollars today. Stuart (born Thomas Barrett) was the son of the composer Leslie Stuart (Thomas Augustine Barrett), who was well known for his musical comedies, especially *Florodora* (1899), and numerous popular songs.[ii] Leslie Stuart junior also appeared in films for the Goldwyn studios.[iii] He knew how Hollywood worked and he described himself as a picture producer. Stuart claimed he'd accompanied Louis to the US to act as his business manager and said the contract they'd signed in December 1926 entitled him to twenty-five per cent of receipts. Louis said no such contract existed. To refute Stuart's claim that he acted as business manager for several authors and film stars, Louis's attorney Roger Marchetti summoned a number of actors and producers, including Mary Pickford.

No celebrities testified in the end as Stuart settled out of court for $250. The following year he attracted attention when he drove his 1911 Rolls Royce (valued then at $20,000) from Hollywood to Victoria, British Columbia. He clearly wasn't broke, although this skirmish might partly explain why Louis's planned films were never made.

Much of Louis's time was occupied by speaking at events or attending book signings. With the rate he churned out books, there was plenty of opportunity for those.

> 'Every Man's Fate Is Written On His Forehead'—OLD ARAB PROVERB. COUNT LOUIS HAMON known the world over under his professional cognomen of 'CHEIRO' insists that this is really true… The public is incited to hear Cheiro relate some of his unusual experiences. He will also autograph his books…[23]

> CHEIRO The World-famous Seer will lecture personally at 3pm… All persons having a special 35 cent tea luncheon (with service) will be welcome to hear the lecture.[24]

Louis was also available for fund-raising events and private luncheons. Plus he spoke at occult gatherings whenever he could wangle an invitation—that wasn't difficult as he was a popular speaker.

---

ii Leslie Stuart Junior's sister acted under the name of May Leslie Stuart (born Mary Catherine Barrett, 1886–1956) in operetta and musical comedy from 1909 to 1915, often performing with her father. She also appeared in silent movies and is most remembered for her role in The Second Mrs Tanqueray (1916).

iii Including *Bonds of Love* (1919), *The Profiteers* (1919), *Lord and Lady Algy* (1919), *Mr. Fix-It* (1918), *The Secret Code* (1918), and *A Diplomatic Mission* (1918).

Cheiro, the internationally famous palmist, lectured... to a crowded hall... Every seat was taken and more were brought in, set up, and immediately occupied... He spoke throughout without notes, without gestures and without raising his voice, yet he reached each person in his audience. This man has by his sincerity and constant labors, lifted palmistry from the obscurity into which it had fallen.[25]

Louis was a headlining guest at an astrological banquet hosted by Manley P Hall in July 1932. Leading lights of the astrological world such as Mark Jones and Myrna Loy were present, and it was clearly an upmarket affair as in addition to speeches, you could dance to the orchestra under the new moon.[26] And he continued to teach classes at his home—at least one afternoon and one evening class a week, although he announced in May 1936 he planned to stop. He didn't.

If you couldn't make it to one of his classes, talks or signings, or you didn't move in the right sort of circles to be invited to one of his parties, there was no need to fret as you could turn the knob and listen to Cheiro on KNX radio during summer 1932, when he'd explain what tomorrow meant to you—and presumably, to lots of other people.

Louis and Katie didn't venture far from home until summer 1933— he and Katie were granted American citizenship in August 1933, so that may have been related. But in May 1933 the press reported that 'Within a month he is leaving for South America, but confidently predicts from the lines in his own hand that he will return.'[27]

The lines were correct. Louis and Katie took a two-month cruise to Peru and Ecuador at the end of May 1933. That Louis had to be careful while waiting for naturalisation is supported by a note on the ship's records that his movements were to be reported to the Irish Free State—being an assumed IRA supporter made him worth watching. In any event, this trip supplied Louis with a whole new talk—one on sun worshippers in South America.

In October 1934 Louis and Katie took another cruise, this time to Mexico. But living the high life had taken its toll on Louis's health. He suffered a minor heart attack in August 1930, and in November 1932 had to send his apologies to the California State Spiritualist Association where he was due to be their guest speaker at a banquet. And a bout of flu led to his cancelling his appointments in April 1933.

The biggest problem was he'd developed diabetes. In November 1935 he wrote to H G Wells care of Charlie Chaplin asking for the address of the *Diabetic Journal*.[28] Wells was staying with Chaplin at the time, as everyone in Hollywood knew. And Chaplin lived next door to Mary Pickford, so it was hardly complicated for Louis to find the right address. Wells's secretary responded saying that a letter addressed to 'The Diabetic Society, London' would reach the right people.

Even Wells's powers could only extend so far. Louis lived for less than a year after he wrote this letter.

Cheiro in 1933

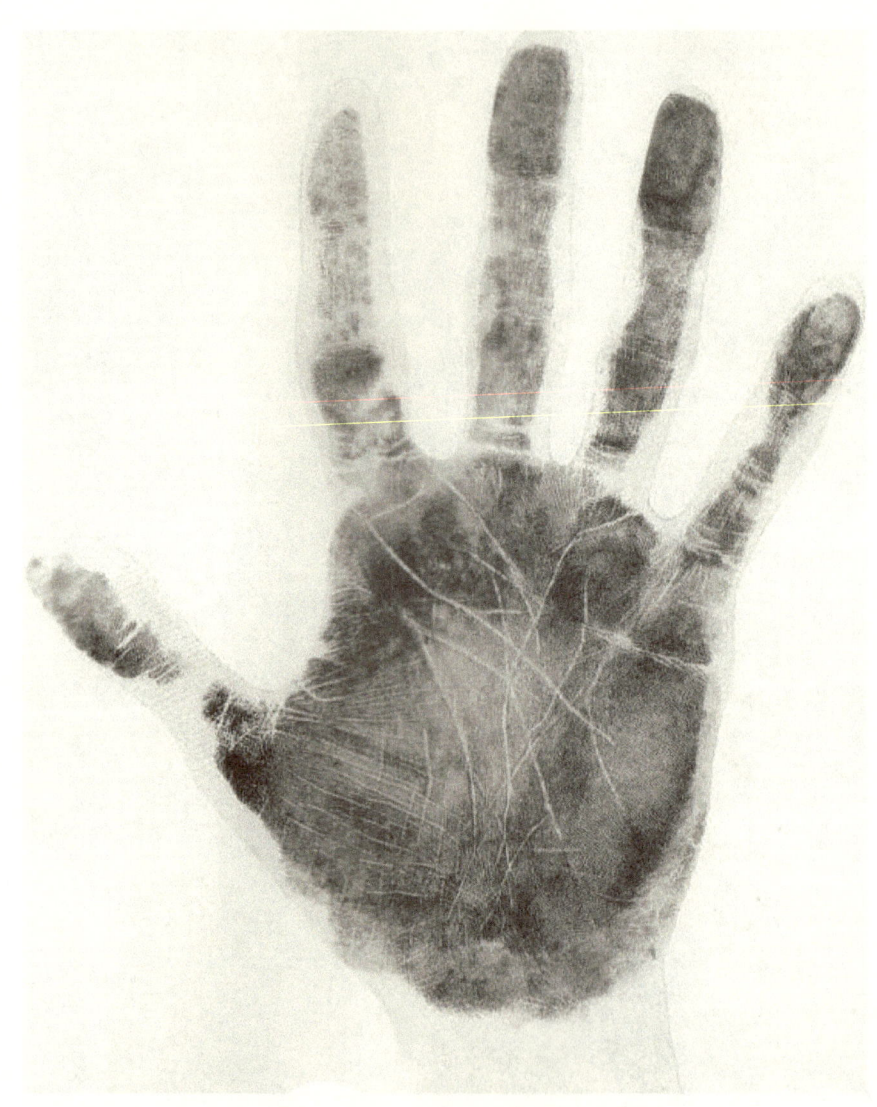

Cheiro's right palm

CHAPTER

NINETEEN

The most amazing man I have ever known was my husband. This is an estimate not born of natural and forgivable prejudice but one arrived at only after consideration.[1]

AGREEING WITH KATIE, Thomas James said Louis was the 'most handsome man and the best conversationalist' he'd ever met.[2] At the ripe old age of ninety-one, James died on 8 October 1936. Fascinated by the occult, James had run the London Publishing Company, which published the majority of Louis's books. He'd also collaborated with Louis in writing his books, especially *Confessions*. It isn't clear how far this collaboration extended, but it was no secret that he'd also heavily edited *World Predictions*. It appears James had a hand in much of Louis's writing after he met him in around 1916. As James was breathing his last, Edith Halford-Nelson was in France when:

> I began to suffer from a violent pain in my right side. After several days and nights of intense pain I awoke… to find that the pain had left me, but that I could not move, and was suffering from the peculiar 'malaise' which heralds the commencement of psychic visions.
>
> A familiar form stood at the foot of my bed. Cheiro. He looked older, heavier, his hair was quite white, and his stoop, which had already been so pronounced, was accentuated. He was, in fact, a very old man, but his eyes still held their force and beauty. They smiled to me now, as a father would smile in the joy of reunion with a long-lost and very dear child. He nodded as if contented and, still smiling, in an adieu which I felt that he was suggesting was only temporary, he turned away, folding his hands behind his back in the old familiar way, and still looking over his shoulder, disappeared.[3]

She didn't receive conformation of Louis's death until several days later. He must have been thinking about her. Whether Edith truly saw Louis in his final moments is unknowable. But what didn't happen was the collapse into madness and poverty often described:

> In about 1930, his powers suddenly failed, and his friends and clients deserted him. He fell into depression and suffered setbacks. He wrote books to make a meager living. In 1936, he was found by Hollywood police babbling incoherently on a sidewalk. They took him to a hospital, but he died en route.[4]

Louis's health had begun to fail in June and his heart problems meant that at the end he passed into a coma. However, first he extracted a promise from Katie—his ashes were to be buried alongside Katie's and Jack's when their time came to leave the world. Apparently, Louis predicted the exact moment of his death, but then Katie would say that. Edith Halford Nelson said it too, adding that Louis's friend Howard Dangerfield (who she said was his constant companion for many years) told her that Louis briefly woke from his coma on his final night to say, 'I am happy. I have seen my Teacher.'[5]

On the night of Louis's death, one of his students, Frances Kernan, an astrologer who taught for the Church of Light in Hollywood, was present. Katie was also there and Louis was attended by an English nurse, Edith Phelan, who said, 'I'm a registered nurse… I've seen hundreds of people die, and I don't believe in spooks. I came to this house four days before the patient passed away. I didn't know his name when the doctors called me.'[6] She added:

> In the last hour, I went outside his room and sat at the head of the stair, reading. Suddenly, they began to creak as though an army of people were coming and going. My hair stood on end, although I'm never easily impressed by such things. I switched on the floodlight at the head of the staircase. Nothing was visible there. Yet, I could have sworn scores of feet were moving on those steps. At the last moment, the whole house was filled with an overpowering fragrance of flowers. There were none in the room, and none outside. Yet we all smelled it, and could still smell it in the morning.
>
> [At about midnight] I noted that he was sinking rapidly. I went in and told his wife and Mrs. Francis Kernan, who were in the house, that he couldn't last long. They were just asking me

how long I thought his strength would hold out when the clock struck: one. My wrist-watch showed 12:15. I thought nothing of it, except that perhaps the big clock on the stairs was wrong. Twice again, at about 10-minute intervals, it struck one. He died at 1:05 by my watch.[7]

Edith (despite not being there) offered a more evocative description. Louis's dog began to howl and:

In his death chamber Cheiro lay with his face illuminated as by a light from within; it was calm and beautiful, with the strange beauty of youth that Death at times returns to faces. As the pulse of life waned the unearthly light of his face increased. The footsteps mounting the stairs paused now at the door of the room, but when the door was opened, there was no one to be seen, yet these footsteps were heard to advance towards his bed, a host of invisible Messengers, till the whole room was felt to be crowded with their unseen Presence—great spirits, Masters, who had come to claim one of their own, and to escort him to his well earned rest.[8]

News of Cheiro the Wonderful's death appeared in the papers the next day, along with Phelan's account of the strange phenomena surrounding it.

Mrs. Phelan was frankly puzzled. She said she could not deny the evidence of her own senses. Nor could she believe them.[9]

Even the skeptics were somewhat at a loss to account for this weird, free show, if it was a show. Their best guess is that perhaps a sort of occult Chamber of Commerce, composed of all the leading professional Hollywood mystics, decided that it would be good advertising for the business if everyone would put on his best tricks that night. It is hoped that Cheiro was not too preoccupied with dying to enjoy it.[10]

Katie collapsed with exhaustion and Louis's funeral was arranged by his attorney, George Nilson. On 10 October Louis was cremated while Masonic rites were celebrated to aid his passing. If we are to believe Edith, Louis lay on a bed of roses, and 'I Hear You Calling Me' was sung by a Hollywood star followed by more songs and music.[11]

Beautiful women—roses—roses—roses. Yes, it was a fitting and triumphant adieu to the man they had known as 'a great lover', 'a very remarkable man', 'The World's Greatest Seer'; the great and beautiful soul had passed on, was far away, mounting the heights in the safe company of his own.[11]

A few weeks later, Cheiro again appeared in the newspapers when on 10 December 1936 the world gasped as King Edward VIII abdicated to marry Wallis Simpson, a twice-divorced American socialite. Cheiro's 1927 prediction had been spot-on.

He was still Cheiro the Wonderful.

Katie pointing out Cheiro's prediction

POSTSCRIPT

Once she'd recovered, Katie wasted no time in setting up a séance. Unfortunately, she couldn't make contact with Louis—perhaps it was too soon. 'I am expecting my husband to converse with me as soon as he has recovered from his last fatiguing illness,' she said haughtily in late November.[1] Whether or not Katie was successful in contacting Louis from beyond the veil, Edith later reckoned she was. She'd been ill and ended up in a nursing home but had recovered with Louis's help.

> Cheiro, a blue ethereal Cheiro, leant over me, showing me gently caged in his hands a little wounded bird. Its feathers were ruffled, its right side and wing maimed and bleeding, but it nestled contentedly in the refuge of his hands. Cheiro said to me: 'My poor little ruffled bird. My beloved child.'[2]

Edith decided to go to Bournemouth for a change of air. There she attended the Church of the Confraternity run by Mabel St Clair Stobart. In years gone by, Stobart had been a suffragist and had created and commanded all-women medical units to serve in the Balkan Wars and the First World War, becoming the first woman to achieve the rank of Major in any national army. In later life, she became a spiritualist and applied her skills to running a church and writing books and articles.

During a séance after a church service, Edith was told she'd been rescued by 'a great spirit who on Earth was a dominating character and a very remarkable man'.[3] And at the séance she received a message from a handsome elderly man with magnetic eyes who told her to continue the work she and Louis had begun many years ago. Shortly afterwards, Edith attended another séance with the same medium. He was full of messages from Louis, telling Edith to look after her health, and promised, 'If you call me I *will* come—you will always be—my child.'[4] The medium collapsed and Edith felt herself enveloped in a soft blue light—the light was Louis and his arms were around her.

In the popular version of events, shortly after Louis's death, Katie returned to England where she lived out her life in poverty, scratching for a living and selling her possessions to get by. It's true that although Louis had left everything to Katie, it didn't amount to much. And probate wasn't granted on his English estate until 1948 and she did sell her things at auction—some of her clothes and shoes are held by the Museum of London. She planned to write a book about the later years of Louis's life, but if she did so, she never managed to sell it to a publisher. However, she was more worried about bananas.

In January 1937, clutching Louis's ashes and accompanied by Jack and her aunt Felicia, Katie sailed to Jamaica. Back in Hollywood, she'd worked out a process to preserve bananas for long periods without losing their vitamins. She and Louis had apparently been planning to go to Jamaica before he fell ill so she could advance her research. 'It is delightful here,' she declared.[5]

Banana export was a major problem for Jamaica. Huge amounts were ruined through being in cold storage while being shipped. Katie's method allowed bananas to ripen before shipping, meaning more vitamins. According to Katie, Japan and an unnamed country had already expressed interest in her method, and if her process was adopted, there'd be work opportunities for Jamaicans who'd recently been repatriated from Cuba.

A few weeks later, Katie returned to England to sort out Louis's affairs and to be in London for the upcoming coronation of George VI in May. She also hoped to interest the Colonial Office in her method. Jack remained in Jamaica and became organist to St Luke's church as well as playing with the Jamaica Symphony. In December 1937 there was a fire in Katie's flat at Half Moon Street when a toy burst into flames in the servants' quarters in the basement. Still hard at work, Katie shifted from bananas to making biscuits for use in food shortages saying, 'My partner and I, working 16 hours a day, lived three days on four-and-a-half of these biscuits and nothing else.'[6] Katie's partner was Denys Shoppee, a Royal Navy officer.

What exactly happened with Katie's inventions is unknown. But she was distracted by a case that came to court in February 1938 in the US. When Louis died, Katie commissioned sculptor Djey el Djey (Djey

Owens) to make a death mask and cast of his hand to be used as the basis of a bronze bust she'd agreed to pay $2,500 for. Fearing that bits of Louis's skin and hair would remain attached to the mask, and her enemies (she never said who these were) would use them for black magic against her, she demanded the return of the working material. Katie won her case and no bust ever appeared.

Later that year, Katie moved to 'Fair View' in Chichester, along with Jack and Shoppee. Jack joined the Royal Army Service Corps early in the war and was later in the navy. After being bombed out, Katie returned to live in New York to live at 236 E. Fourth St, Brooklyn in July 1940.

It isn't clear precisely what had happened to Jack—Katie referred to him as an invalid and one source states he'd received a head injury when a hoarding fell on him and he spent time in in a mental institution.[7] What is clear is that Katie was short of money.

Katie looked up the name 'Hartland' in the New York telephone directory, called the number and reached a relative of her first husband, Henry Hartland, who gave her his address. She called him on 24 April 1941. Hartland was still working as a purchasing agent for a steamship line and was now living with his second wife, Harriet. Katie asked him for money to support Jack.

Two days later, Hartland arranged to meet Katie at a hotel. They apparently had a nice time and Katie blew him a kiss when he put her into a taxi with the support question still unsettled. But Katie didn't give up easily. She asked to meet Harriet who took her out for lunch. Katie told her about Louis's book *Confessions*, pointing out how she featured in it. The following month Katie served Hartland with divorce papers, claiming his second marriage constituted adultery. She wanted it annulled so he'd be forced to support her and Jack. On 22 June her plea for temporary alimony was denied.

The case reached court in October 1942. Hartland agreed he hadn't been divorced but said Katie's disappearance absolved him from blame. It turned out that Hartland was a hoarder, and he managed to produce the letters Katie had written to him before she'd vanished back in 1902. Louis's account of their relationship in *Confessions* was also produced as evidence. The judge ruled that Hartland's second marriage was valid because prior to 1922 it was unnecessary to obtain a dissolution decree. He also said Katie had wilfully abandoned him, and the situation was her fault. After all, she'd also remarried.

It didn't matter in the end. While Katie was in the US, Jack had sought out Irene Nuttall, who'd worked for Katie in Chichester and was now a nurse near her home in Meltham, Yorkshire. Jack arrived on her doorstep claiming he was homeless and owned no more than the clothes he stood up in. The Nuttalls took him in and he worked at a variety of odd jobs, including as a cement mixer, warehouseman, labourer and fire warden. The villagers liked him and called him 'the Count'. While Katie was in court in October 1942, Jack suddenly died of myocarditis and the villagers buried him at St Bartholomew's church.

Katie didn't return to England until April 1945. When she did so, she posted Louis's ashes to George Pogson, the undertaker in Meltham. 'In an elm casket, with a tiny brass plate reflecting in the afternoon sunlight, they were laid to rest beside the remains of the countess's son.'[8] Katie died in 1969 and her ashes were also buried alongside.

Edith's account of her experiences with Louis, *Out of the Silence*, was also published in 1945. Edith was 'one of the original Cheiro girls' said one reviewer—the stories of the other Cheiro girls must remain untold.[9]

> 'Miss Nelson relates that on one occasion she sojourned with a Sheikh in Africa. When she left the sheikh's family broke up the earthenware. Perhaps like other things in the house, it was a bit cracked already.'[10]

Edith oddly completely ignores Katie's existence, and she said, 'I do not think that Cheiro was a great lover, or that he ever cared sufficiently for any woman to place her desires before the realization of his own ambitions. There were times when he allowed nothing to stand in the way of his ambition, when all barriers were swept aside by a will that was literally inhuman.'[11]

She would die herself the next year. Maybe Edith was a bit cracked, but it seems fitting to give her the last word. She'd have liked that.

> He could be the delightful companion and friend—the clever practical business man—the society favourite—even the showman; yes, he appreciated the glamours attached to success, and all the prestige and influence it brings, but he was not spoilt by it, for he of all men knew this glitter for what it was worth.[12]

To Edith, Louis was 'the one man in my life to whom I had given my allegiance, the one man of whom I felt no shame in admitting as my master.'[13] And it was Cheiro of whom Edith said until her dying day:

> I hear you calling to me out of the silence.[14]

BOOKS BY CHEIRO

The following lists Cheiro's books in date order of publication. All were consulted in writing this book, apart from those marked by an asterisk, which I was unable to access. They were published under the name of Cheiro except where otherwise indicated. Numerous later editions exist of all titles. In addition, some books were repackaged and appear in compilation form, particularly in editions in the US and India. Many of these are pirated editions. It is impossible to trace all such editions as many do not appear in libraries and new ones continue to appear.

Cheiro's Book of the Hand (London: Record Press, 1892).
Cheiro's Language of the Hand (London: Nichols and Company, 1897).
(Also credited to Leigh Warner, Count de Hamong, Comte de Hamong and Louis Hamon in different editions.)
If We Only Knew, and other poems (London: Chatto and Windus, 1895).
(Also as Count de Hamong, L. Hamon and Louis Hamon).
*A study of destiny (London: Saxon and Company, 1898). (*As Leigh de Hamong. US title *The Hand of Fate.*)
A Guide to the Hand (London: publisher not identified, 1898). (As Leigh de Hamong. Sometimes credited to Count de Hamong.)
* *Practical Palmistry* (London: publisher unidentified, 1904).
Cheiro's Memoirs: The Reminiscences of a Society Palmist (London: Rider, 1912). (Also credited to Louis Hamon.)
When were you Born? (London: Herbert Jenkins, 1912).
Palmistry for All (London: Herbert Jenkins, 1916).
What I read in Lord Kitchener's hand (London: publisher not identified, 1916).
* *What your hands reveal by Cheiro* (Sydney: Zam-buk Co., 1920).

Cheiro's Book of Numbers (London: London Publishing Company, 1926). (Also credited to Louis Cheiro.)

Life, Love and Marriage (London: London Publishing Company, 1927).

Read Your Past, Present, and Future. Teaching the study of the hand by pictures as on the cinema (London: London Publishing Co, 1927).

Cheiro's World Predictions (London: London Publishing Company, 1927).

True Ghost Stories (London: London Publishing Company, 1928).

Cheiro's Year Book for 1929 (London; Hollywood : London Publishing Company, 1929).

Cheiro's Yearbook[s] for 1929 [and] 1930. (London: London Publishing Company, 1929).

Fate in the Making. Revelations of a lifetime (New York; London: Harper and Brothers, 1931).

You and Your Hand (Garden City, New York: Doubleday, Doran and Company, 1931).

Confessions: memoirs of a modern seer (London: Jarrolds, 1932).

Real Life Stories (London: H. Jenkins, 1934). (By Count Louis Hamon.)

Mysteries and Romances of the World's Greatest Occultists (London: Herbert Jenkins, 1935).

Cheiro, You and Your Star (London: Herbert Jenkins, 1936).

Also used throughout was Halford Nelson, Edith, *Out of the Silence* (London: Rider, 1944).

The majority of these books are in my personal collection.

ENDNOTES

CHAPTER 1

1 *Irish Society* (Dublin), 23 September 1893, p.26.
2 *St. Albans Daily Messenger* (Vermont), 6 August 1910, p. 1.
3 *Sketch* (London), 5 July 1893, p. 18.
4 *Toronto Saturday Night* (Toronto, Canada), 22 December 1900, p. 15.
5 *Coventry Evening Telegraph* (Coventry), 14 October 1936, p.3 and *Buffalo Commercial* (Buffalo, New York), 19 May 1894, p. 10.
6 *Saint Paul Globe* (Saint Paul, Minnesota), 26 January 1898, p. 2.
7 *Buffalo Commercial* (Buffalo, New York), 19 May 1894, p. 10.
8 *The London Forum* (London), November 1934, p. 345.
9 Edith Halford Nelson, *Out of the Silence* (London: Rider, 1945), p. 61.
10 *Brownville Sun* (Brownville, Nebraska), 4 Feb 1898, p. 8 and multiple later advertisements.
11 Oscar Wilde, *A Woman of No Importance*, Lord Illingworth, Act 3.
12 'Twentieth Century Squires', *Time*, 10 December 1951.
13 Cheiro, *Confessions: Memoirs of a Modern Seer* (London: Jarrolds, 1932), p. 26. Most sources claim 525 CE.
14 *Dublin Weekly Nation* (Dublin), 15 April 1899, p. 11; *Toronto Saturday Night* (Toronto, Canada) 22 December 1900, p. 15; Stuart Cumberland, *That Other World; Personal Experiences of Mystics and their Mysticism*, London: Grant Richards, 1918), p. 105.
15 *Borderland* (London), October 1897, p. 446.
16 'A bit of seaside England came to Wicklow's coast', *Irish Times* (Dublin), 2 March 1999.
17 On Mary Warner's death certificate.
18 For example, *Chicago Tribune* (Chicago, Illinois), 1 July 1909, p. 1 and *Altoona Tribune* (Altoona, Pennsylvania), 23 September 1910, p. 6.
19 Cheiro, *Confessions: Memoirs of a Modern Seer*, p. 22.
20 *The Sunny South* (Atlanta, Georgia), 21 April 1894, p. 23.

CHAPTER 2

1 *Blackburn Standard* (Blackburn), 19 November 1898, p. 8 quoting *Homeland*.
2 Cheiro, *Confessions*, p. 28.
3 Cheiro, *Confessions*, p. 28.
4 Cheiro, *Confessions*, p. 31.
5 Cheiro, *Confessions*, p. 32.
6 *Akron Daily Democrat* (Akron, Ohio) 6 July 1894, p. 3.
7 *Light* (London), May 1912, p. 212.
8 *Akron Daily Democrat* (Akron, Ohio), 6 July 1894, p. 3.
9 *Hornellsville Weekly Tribune*, (New York), 13 July 1894, p. 6.
10 *Light* (London), May 1912, p. 212.
11 *Chicago Tribune* (Chicago, Illinois), 9 August 1890, p. 1.
12 Cheiro, *Language of the Hand* (London: Nicholls and Co., 1897), p. 4.
13 Cheiro, *World Predictions* (India: Sagar Publications, no date), p. 215.
14 *Los Angeles Times*, 9 August 1931, p. 20. *In Cork Constitution*, 9 March 1896, p. 6 he claimed that this 'Britisher' was 'General Roberts'.
15 Willy Reichel, *An Occultist's Travels* (R. F. Fenno, 1908), p. 194.
16 *Los Angeles Times*, 9 August 1931, p. 20.
17 *Portsmouth Evening News* (Portsmouth), 8 February 1924, p. 5.
18 *Belfast News-Letter* (Belfast), 12 October 1888, p. 6.
19 *Belfast News-Letter* (Belfast), 4 March 1889, p. 2.
20 '1890 Belfast Street Directory', Lemon Wylie, https://www.lennonwylie.co.uk/Lcomplete1890.htm [accessed March 2021].
21 Cheiro, *Real Life Stories*, (London, Herbert Jenkins, 1934), p. 11.

CHAPTER 3

1 *Morning Post* (London), 5 May 1888, p. 4.
2 *Akron Daily Democrat* (Akron, Ohio), 21 July 1894, p. 4.
3 Cheiro, *Cheiro's Memoirs: The Reminiscences of a Society Palmist* (London: Rider, 1912), p. 9.
4 Cheiro, *Reminiscences*, p. 12.
5 *Art of Chiromancy*, 1475 by Johann Hartlieb.
6 Cheiro, *Confessions*, p. 27.
7 Cheiro, *Reminiscences*, p. 16.
8 *Akron Daily Democrat* (Akron, Ohio), 21 July 1894, p.4.
9 Cheiro, *Confessions*, p. 27.
10 Cheiro, Confessions, p. 37.
11 Louis Hamon/Cheiro, *Mysteries and Romances of the World's Greatest Occultists* (London: Herbert Jenkins, 1935), p. 172.
12 Cheiro, *Mysteries and Romances*, p. 175.
13 Cheiro, *Mysteries and Romances*, p. 177.
14 'Keeley's Secrets', *Theosophical Siftings*, Volume 1 (London: Theosophical Publishing Society, 1888).
15 *London Evening Standard* (London), 15 June 1899, p. 3.
16 *South London Press* (London), 11 July 1891, p. 2.

17 Marshall P Wilder, *The Sunny Side of the Street* (New York and London: Funk and Wagnalls, 1905), p. 295.
18 Programme for *Arrah-na-Pogue*, personal collection.
19 *Bury and Norwich Post* (Bury St Edmunds, Suffolk), 29 December 1891, p. 3.
20 *Stage* (London), 24 December, 1891, p. 10.
21 *The Era* (London), 23 April 1892, p. 7.
22 *The Era* (London), 11 June 1892, p. 7.
23 *Daily Telegraph and Courier* (London), 10 June 1892, p. 3.
24 *Clarion* (London), 11 June 1892, p. 5.
25 *Pall Mall Gazette* (London), 10 June 1892, p. 3.
26 *Daily Telegraph and Courier* (London), 10 June 1892, p. 3.
27 *Washington Post* (Washington), 13 January 1909, p. 1.
28. Cheiro, *Confessions*, p. 33.
29 *The Era* (London), 23 Jul 1892, p. 6.

CHAPTER 4

1 Oscar Wilde, 'Lord Arthur Savile's Crime: A Story of Cheiromancy', *The Complete Works of Oscar Wilde*, (London: Galley Press, 1987), p. 169.
2 Cheiro, *Reminiscences*, p. 9.
3 Cheiro, *Confessions*, p. 147.
4 Cheiro, *Confessions*, p. 147.
5 Cheiro, *Confessions*, p. 147.
6 'Lord Savile's Crime', 1887.
7 Blanche Roosevelt, *Stage Struck*, 1884; *Life and Reminiscences*, 1885.
8 Cheiro, *Confessions*, p. 152.
9 Cheiro, *Confessions*, p. 195.
10 *Sunday Illustrated* (London), 21 October 1923, p. 14.
11 Maria Popova, 'Oscar Wilde's Stirring Love Letters to Lord Alfred "Bosie" Douglas, *brainpickings*, https://www.brainpickings.org/2013/07/15/oscar-wilde-love-letters-bosie/ [accessed February 2021].
12 Sheridan Morley, *Oscar Wilde* (London: Applause, 1997), p. 169.
13 *Daily Telegraph* (Sydney, NSW), 23 May 1925, p. 19.
14 *Sketch* (London), 5 July 1893, p. 18.
15 *Chicago Tribune* (Chicago, Illinois), 9 February 1896, p. 33.
16 *Toronto Saturday Night* (Toronto, Canada), 22 December 1900, p. 15.
17 *St Louis Post-Dispatch*, (St Louis, Missouri), 19 November 1893, p. 24.
18 *Sketch* (London), 5 July 1893, p. 18.
19 Cheiro, *Reminiscences*, p. 85.
20 *Derry Journal* (Londonderry, Northern Ireland), 21 August 1893, p. 6.
21 *Middlesex Courier* (London), 27 October 1893, p. 7.
22 Cheiro, *Confessions*, p. 51.
23 Cheiro, *Confessions*, p. 52.
24 Cheiro, *Confessions*, p. 52.
25 Cheiro, *Confessions*, p. 52.
26 Cheiro, *Confessions*, p. 52.
27 *Sketch* (London), 5 July 1893, p. 18.

28 *Sketch* (London), 5 July 1893, p. 18.
29 Cheiro (ed. S. Aryanam), *Reading the Secret Language of the Hand* (New Delhi: Orient Paperbacks, 2006), Ch. 14 (no page numbers).

CHAPTER 5

1 Advertisement in the *Times* (Philadelphia, Pennsylvania), 26 August 1894, p. 7.
2 Cheiro, *You and Your Hand* (St Albans: Gainsborough Press, 1932), p. 291.
3 Cheiro, *You and Your Hand*, p. 292.
4 H. Merian Allen, 'Who was Who?', *The Sewanee Review* Vol. 26, No. 4 (Oct., 1918), p. 436.
5 *Daily Telegraph* (Sydney, NSW), 8 August 1925, p. 2.
6 *Daily Telegraph* (Sydney, NSW), 8 August 1925, p. 2.
7 *Indianapolis Journal* (Indianapolis, Indiana), 14 January 1894, p. 10.
8 *Red Lodge Picket* (Montana), 16 December 1893, p. 2.
9 *Australian Star* (Sydney, NSW), 23 July 1894, p. 5.
10 *The Sun* (New York), 11 June 1894, p. 3.
11 *Evening World* (New York), 14 0ctober 1893, p. 4.
12 *Red Lodge Picket* (Montana), 16 December 1893, p. 2.
13 Marshall P Wilder, *The Sunny Side of the Street*, p. 290.
14 Marshall P Wilder, *The Sunny Side of the Street*, p. 290.
15 Cheiro, *Reminiscences*, p. 111.
16 *New York World* (New York), 26 November 1893, p. 18.
17 Cheiro, *Reminiscences*, p. 113.
18 *Light*, 31 June 1911, p. 293.
19 *Daily Telegraph* (Sydney, NSW), 8 August 1925, p. 2.
20 Cheiro, *You and Your Star* (London: Herbert Jenkins, 1936), p. 420.
21 *Daily Telegraph* (Sydney, NSW), 8 August 1925, p. 2.
22 *Daily Telegraph* (Sydney, NSW), 8 August 1925, p. 2.
23 *Sun* (New York), 11 June 1894, p. 3.
24 *Sun* (New York), 11 June 1894, p. 3.
25 *Akron Daily Democrat* (Ohio), 6 July 1894, p. 3.
26 *Strand Magazine* (London), Vol. II (Jul-Dec 1891), p. 196.
27 *Strand Magazine* (London), Vol. II (Jul-Dec 1891), p. 196.
28 Albert Bigelow Paine (ed.), *Mark Twain's Notebook* (New York and London: Harper Brothers, 1935).

CHAPTER 6

1 *Evening Star* (Washington), 11 April 1896, p. 10.
2 *Buffalo Enquirer* (Buffalo, New York), 16 January 1896, p.5
3 Cheiro, *True Ghost Stories* (London: London Publishing Company, 1928), p. 220.
4 'Notes on books', *British Medical Journal*, 9 September 1893.
5 Cheiro, *True Ghost Stories*, p. 222.
6 Cheiro, *True Ghost Stories*, p. 226.
7 Cheiro, *True Ghost Stories*, p. 237.
8 Cheiro, *True Ghost Stories*, p. 241.
9 Cheiro, *True Ghost Stories*, p. 251.

10 Syed Tariq Javed, *Horus the Astro-Palmist*, https://horusastropalmist. wordpress.com/2016/07/ [accessed January 2021].

11 *Buffalo Evening News* (Buffalo, New York) 10 September 1897, p. 5.

12 *Sketch* (London), 1 September 1897, p. 30.

13 *Boston Post* (Boston Massachusetts), 12 May 1895, p16.

14 *Boston Post* (Boston Massachusetts), 12 May 1895, p.16.

15 *Arkansas Democrat* (Little Rock, Arkansas), 7 January 1909, p. 7.

16 *Buffalo Courier* (Buffalo, New York), 1 January 1896, p. 7.

17 *Evening Star* (Washington), 11 Apr 1896, p. 10.

18 *Boston Post* (Boston, Massachusetts), 12 May 1895, p. 16.

19 *Evening Star* (Washington), 11 Apr 1896, p. 10.

20 *Buffalo Courier* (Buffalo, New York), 1 January 1896, p. 7.

21 *Evening Star* (Washington), 11 Apr 1896, p. 10.

22 Cheiro, *Confessions*, p. 173.

23 Bradley Tolppanen, "'A Vulgar Yankee Impresario'—Churchill, Major Pond, and the Lecture Tour of 1900–1901', *Finest Hour*, No. 174, Autumn 2016 (International Churchill Society), https://winstonchurchill.org/publications/finest-hour/finest-hour-174/vulgar-yankee-bradley-tolppanen/ [accessed January 2021]

24 *Finest Hour.*

25 *Finest Hour.*

26 Karen Christino, *Foreseeing the Future: Evangeline Adams and Astrology in America* (Stella Mira Books, 2019), p. 54 quoting Adams, *Bowl of Heaven.*

27 *New York Times* (New York), 26 May 1895, p. 25.

28 Cheiro, *Confessions*, p. 173.

29 Cheiro, *Confessions*, p. 173.

30 *Boston Post* (Boston, Massachusetts), 12 May 1895, p. 6.

31 *Boston Globe* (Boston, Massachusetts), 11 May 1895, p. 2.

32 *Boston Globe* (Boston, Massachusetts), 23 June 1895, p. 21.

33 *Boston Post* (Boston, Massachusetts), Sep 15, 1895, p. 18

34 Josephine Anna Ingersoll, *Greenacre on the Piscataqua* (New York: Alliance Publishing Company, 1900), p. 3.

35 *Inter Ocean* (Chicago, Illinois), 3 August 1895, p. 10.

CHAPTER 7

1 *Atlanta Constitution* (Atlanta), 24 February 1896, p. 132.

2 *Boston Globe* (Boston, Massachusetts), 1 December 1895, p. 21.

3 *Boston Globe* (Boston, Massachusetts), 7 December 1895, p. 9 and *Buffalo Commercial* (Buffalo, New York), 2 January 1896, p. 8.

4 *Russell Record* (Kansas), 3 October 1895, p. 2.

5 Cheiro, *Confessions*, p. 175.

6 Cheiro, *Confessions*, p. 175.

7 *Saint Paul Globe* (St Paul, Minnesota), 19 January 1896, p. 14.

8 *Buffalo Evening News* (Buffalo, New York), 6 January 1898, p. 3.

9 *Chicago Tribune* (Chicago, Illinois), 12 February 1896, p. 5.

10 Cheiro, Confessions, p. 175.

11 *Lake Geneva Herald* (Wisconsin), 15 June 1872, p. 2.

12 *Atchison Daily Champion* (Kansas), 16 April 1876, p. 2.
13 *Herald and Mail* (Tennessee), 19 September 1891, p. 4.
14 *Boston Post* (Boston, Massachusetts), 12 May 1895, p. 16.
15 Karen Christino, *Foreseeing the Future*, p. 52.
16 Cheiro, *Confessions*, p. 178.
17 Cheiro, *Confessions*, p. 179.
18 *Buffalo Enquirer* (Buffalo, New York), 4 January 1896, p. 7.
19 Cheiro, *Confessions*, p. 183.
20 *Buffalo Evening News* (Buffalo, New York), 2 January 1896, p. 2.
21 *Buffalo Sunday Morning News* (Buffalo, New York), 12 January 1896, p. 7.
22 *Buffalo Enquirer* (Buffalo, New York), 10 January 1896, p. 7.
23 Cheiro, *Confessions*, p. 184.
24 Cheiro, *Confessions*, p. 187.
25 *Inter Ocean* (Chicago, Illinois), 21 February 1896, p. 7.
26 *Pensacola News* (Florida), 6 March 1896, p. 4.
27 Cheiro, *Confessions*, p. 204.
28 *Pensacola News* (Florida), 9 March 1896, p. 3.
29 *Saint Paul Globe* (St Paul, Minnesota), 8 February 1895, p. 4.
30 *Saint Paul Globe* (St Paul, Minnesota), 8 February 1895, p. 4.
31 *Pensacola News* (Florida), 3 March 1896, p. 3.
32 *Tampa Tribune* (Florida), 15 March 1896, p. 1.
33 Cheiro, *Confessions*, p. 210.
34 *Evening Star* (Washington), 27 April 1896, p. 6.
35 *Times* (Philadelphia), 26 April 1896, p. 9.
36 *Daily Telegraph* (Sydney, NSW), 27 June 1925, p. 4.
37 *The World* (New York), 24 May 1896, p. 32.
38 Cheiro, *Mysteries*, p. 185.
39 Fydell Edmund Garrett, *Isis Very Much Unveiled: Being the Story of the Great Mahatma Hoax* (London: Westminster Gazette, 1894).
40 Cheiro, *True Ghost Stories*, p. 95.
41 *Buffalo Enquirer* (Buffalo, New York), 18 June 1896, p. 3.
42 *The Era* (London), 27 June 1896, p. 10.
43 Cheiro, *True Ghost Stories*, p. 96.

CHAPTER 8

1 Halford Nelson, *Out of the Silence*, p. 46.
2 Halford Nelson, *Out of the Silence*, p. 20.
3 Halford Nelson, *Out of the Silence*, p. 20.
4 Halford Nelson, *Out of the Silence*, p. 20.
5 Halford Nelson, *Out of the Silence*, p. 21.
6 Halford Nelson, *Out of the Silence*, p. 21.
7 Halford Nelson, *Out of the Silence*, p. 21.
8 Halford Nelson, *Out of the Silence*, p. 21.
9 Halford Nelson, *Out of the Silence*, p. 23.
10 Halford Nelson, *Out of the Silence*, p. 24.
11 Halford Nelson, *Out of the Silence*, p. 28.

12 *Morning News* (Savannah, Georgia), 10 October 1897, p. 18.

13 *Kent and Sussex Courier* (Tunbridge Wells), 28 October 1896, p. 3.

14 *Pittsburgh Daily Post* (Pittsburgh, Pennsylvania), 10 October 1897, p. 19.

15 *Pall Mall Gazette* (London), 6 November 1896, p. 11.

16 *Pittsburgh Daily Post* (Pittsburgh, Pennsylvania), 10 October 1897, p. 19.

17 *Morning News* (Savannah, Georgia), 10 October 1897, p. 18.

18 *Journal of the Society for Psychical Research*, Vol. VIII, 1897-8, p. 249.

19 *Westminster Gazette* (London), 28 April 1896, p. 1.

20 *Westminster Gazette* (London), 28 April 1896, p. 1.

21 *Sketch* (London), 16 February 1898, p. 7.

22 *Borderland*, October 1897, p. 416.

23 *Borderland*, October 1897, p. 416.

24 *Times-Picayune* (New Orleans, Louisiana),10 February 1897, p. 4.

25 *Morning Post* (London), 18 & 19 December 1896, p. 1.

26 *Sketch* (London), 28 October 1896, p. 9.

27 *New York Magazine of Mysteries*, October 1901, p. 190.

28 *Vancouver Daily World* (Vancouver, Canada), 9 January 1897, p. 1.

29 *Saint Paul Globe* (St Paul, Minnesota), 9 January 1898, p. 7

30 Halford Nelson, *Out of the Silence*, p. 32.

31 Halford Nelson, *Out of the Silence*, p. 25.

32 Halford Nelson, *Out of the Silence*, p. 26.

33 *Morning Post* (London), 24 October 1896, p. 5; *Morning Post* (London) 19 December 1896, p. 5; *Vancouver Daily World*, (Vancouver, Canada), 9 January 1897, p. 1.

34 C. H. Malcolm, *Poems* (Westminster: Roxburghe Press, 1897).

35 *Glasgow Herald* (Glasgow), 21 January 1898, p. 9.

36 Swami Vivekananda, Letter written 7 October 1896, *Complete Works*, Vol. 6 (Kolkata, India: Advaita Ashrama, 1989 , reprint, originally published 1907), p. 1618.

37 Vivekananda, Letter written to Josephine MacLeod 3 December, 1896, Vol. 8.

38 *Brooklyn Daily Eagle* (Brooklyn, New York), 4 November 1896, p. 5.

39 *Daily Republican* (Connecticut), 2 February 1897, p. 4.

40 *Morning Post* (London), 2 March 1897, p. 2.

41 *Cheltenham Examiner* (Cheltenham) 26 May 1897, p. 2.

42 Cheiro, *Confessions*, p. 117.

43 Halford Nelson, *Out of the Silence*, p. 28.

44 Halford Nelson, *Out of the Silence*, p. 29.

45 *Saint Paul Globe* (Saint Paul, Minnesota), 4 May 1902, p. 19. Although the news item clearly refers to this occasion, it oddly appeared in 1902 as if it had been languishing in someone's desk drawer for a few years.

46 *Chicago Tribune* (Chicago, Illinois), 11 November 1897, p. 7.

47 *Topeka State Journal* (Kansas), 9 December 1897, p. 5.

48 *Topeka State Journal* (Kansas), 18 January 1898, p. 8.

49 *Saint Paul Globe* (St Paul, Minnesota) 23 January 1898, p. 14.

50 *Inter Ocean* (Chicago, Illinois) 15 November 1896, p. 7.

51 *San Francisco Examiner* (San Francisco, California), 21 March 1898, p. 1.

52 *Truth* (London) 25 March 1897, p. 9.

53 *The Era* (London), 26 March 1898, p. 14.

54 *Edinburgh Evening News* (Edinburgh), 13 April 1898, p. 4.

55 *New York Journal and Advertiser* (New York), 19 July 1898, p. 11.

56 *New York Journal and Advertiser* (New York), 19 July 1898, p. 11.

57 *New York Times* (New York), 19 July 1898, p. 7.

58 *New York Journal and Advertiser* (New York), 19 July 1898, p. 11.

59 New York Times (New York), 20 July 1898, p. 7.

60 Kieran McNally, 'Catatonia: Faces in the Fire', *A Critical History of Schizophrenia* (London: Palgrave Macmillan, 2016), p. 68.

61 *San Francisco Examiner* (San Francisco, California), 5 January 1901, p. 1.

62 *San Francisco Examiner* (San Francisco, California), 5 January 1901, p. 1.

CHAPTER 9

1 Halford Nelson, *Out of the Silence*, p. 48.

2 *Gentlewoman* (London), 30 July 1898, p. 44.

3 *Glasgow Herald* (Glasgow), 10 March 1898, p. 10.

4 Review, 'Curse of the Yogi's Tomb: Cheiro, A Study in Destiny', *Irish Journal of Gothic and Horror Studies* 7 (December 20, 2009) https://irishgothichorror.files.wordpress.com/2016/04/ijghsissue7.pdf , p.49 [accessed March 2021].

5 Review, 'Curse of the Yogi's Tomb', p. 50.

6 Review, 'Curse of the Yogi's Tomb', pp. 50 and 51.

7 Louis Hamon, *Real Life Stories* (London: Herbert Jenkins, 1934).

8 *Morning Post* (London), 1 May 1897, p. 9.

9 *Westminster Gazette* (London), 3 February 1899, p. 4.

10 *Modern Astrology*, June 1928, p. 194.

11 *Astrology Quarterly*, Vol 18, No 3 (Astrological Lodge of London), 1944, p. 1.

12 *Morning Post* (London), 20 October 1899, p. 1.

13 Cheiro, *True Ghost Stories*, p. 81.

14 Cheiro, *True Ghost Stories*, p. 99.

15 Cheiro, *True Ghost Stories*, p. 75 .

16 Halford Nelson, *Out of the Silence*, p. 26.

17 Halford Nelson, *Out of the Silence*, pp. 52 and 26.

18 Cheiro, Confessions, p. 294.

19 Edith Halford-Nelson, *Desert Sanctuary* (London: Skeffington and Son, 1946), p. 118.

20 Cheiro, *Confessions*, p. 294.

21 John Cook Bennett, *The History of the Saints: Or, An Exposé of Joe Smith and Mormonism* (Leland and Whiting, 1842), p. 239.

22 *Light*, 17 June 1899, p. 283.

23 Halford Nelson, *Out of the Silence*, p. 43.

24 Halford Nelson, *Out of the Silence*, p. 44.

25 Halford Nelson, *Out of the Silence*, p. 44.

26 Halford Nelson, *Out of the Silence*, p. 44.

27 Halford Nelson, *Out of the Silence*, p. 45.

28 Halford Nelson, *Out of the Silence*, p. 45.

29 *Light*, 2 February 1901, p 59.

30 *South Wales Echo* (Cardiff), 14 June 1899, p. 4.

31 *Dundee Evening Telegraph* (Dundee), 2 June 1898, p. 3.

32 'R v. Callan 1898', Colonial Cases, Macquarie University, Sydney, Australia, http://www.law.mq.edu.au/research/colonial_case_law/colonial_cases/less_developed/tangier/r_v_callan_1898/ [accessed March 2021].
33 *Daily Telegraph and Courier* (London), 15 June 1899, p. 5.
34 Cheiro, *Confessions*, p. 136.
35 *Daily Telegraph and Courier* (London), 15 June 1899, p. 5.
36 *London Evening Standard* (London),15 June 1899, p. 3.
37 *Illustrated Police Budget* (London), 24 June 1899, p. 15.
38 *London Evening Standard* (London),15 June 1899, p. 3 and *Daily Telegraph and Courier* (London), 15 June 1899, p. 5.
39 Cheiro, *Confessions*, p. 136.
40 Halford Nelson, *Out of the Silence*, p. 53.
41 Halford Nelson, *Out of the Silence*, p. 53.
42 Halford Nelson, *Out of the Silence*, p. 53.
43 Halford Nelson, *Out of the Silence*, p. 53.

CHAPTER 10

1 *Buffalo Sunday Morning News* (Buffalo, New York), 27 January 1901, p. 4.
2 *Boston Post* (Boston, Massachusetts), 4 December 1899, p. 7.
3 *Buffalo Times* (Buffalo, New York), 22 April 1900, p. 3.
4 *Grantham Journal* (Grantham, Lincolnshire), 4 August 1894, p. 6.
5 *Dublin Daily Express* (Dublin), 15 May 1895, p. 4.
6 *St Louis Post Despatch* (St. Louis, Missouri), 23 August 1900, p. 11; *San Francisco Examiner* (San Francisco, California), 8 January 1900, p. 8; *Daily Ademorite* (Oklahoma), 13 April 1900, p. 4.
7 *North Adams Transcript* (North Adams, Massachusetts), 5 March 1902, p. 7.
8 *San Francisco Examiner* (San Francisco, California), 25 December 1898, p. 14.
9 *Newburyport Daily News* (Massachusetts), 29 March 1900, p. 1; *San Francisco Examiner* (San Francisco, California), 4 December 1898, p. 12.
10 *San Francisco Examiner* (San Francisco, California), 30 January 1899, p. 8.
11 *South Bend Tribune* (South Bend, Indiana), 8 May 1901, p. 1.
12 *Salt Lake Herald* (Salt Lake City, Utah), 25 October 1902, p. 3.
13 *Dundee Evening Telegraph* (Dundee), 10 July 1900, p. 3.
14 *Dundee Evening Telegraph* (Dundee), 10 July 1900, p. 3.
15 *Evening Express* (London), 13 September 1900, p. 4 and *St James's Gazette* (London), 6 September 1900, p. 12.
16 *Belvidere Daily Republican* (Belvidere, Illinois), 3 August 1900, p. 1.
17 Cheiro, *Confessions*, p. 114.
18 Light, 25 August 1900, p. 403.
19 *Star Tribune* (Minneapolis, Minnesota), 24 August 1900, p. 1.
20 *Daily Telegraph* (Sydney, NSW), 12 August 1925, p. 2.
21 Cheiro, *Reminiscences*, p. 59.
22 Cheiro, *Reminiscences*, p. 60.
23 Cheiro, *Confessions*, p. 105.
24 *Daily Mail* Atlantic Edition (London), 8 November 1923, p. 13.
25 Cheiro, *Confessions*, p. 249.

27 Halford Nelson, *Out of the Silence*, p. 25.
27 Cheiro, *Confessions*, p. 248.
28 *Toronto Saturday Night* (Toronto, Canada), 22 December 1900, p. 15.
29 Paris Morning Post (Paris), 14 September 1901, p. 1.
30 *Free Press* (Detroit, Michigan), 3 June 1901, p. 4.
31 *Brooklyn Daily Eagle* (Brooklyn, New York), 30 October 1942, p. 26.
32 *Brooklyn Daily Eagle* (Brooklyn, New York), 28 October 1942, p. 3.
33 *Brooklyn Daily Eagle* (Brooklyn, New York), 28 October 1942, p. 3.
34 *Daily News* (New York), 29 October1942, p. 76.
35 *Brooklyn Daily Eagle* (Brooklyn, New York), 28 October 1942, p. 3.
36 *Brooklyn Daily Eagle* (Brooklyn, New York), 28 October 1942, p. 3.
37 Cheiro, *Confessions*, p. 294.
38 *Brooklyn Daily Eagle* (Brooklyn, New York), 28 October 1942, p. 3.
39 *Daily News* (New York), 29 October 1942, p. 76.
40 *Inter Ocean* (Chicago, Illinois), 21 December 1902, p. 15.

CHAPTER 11

1 *Toronto Saturday Night* (Toronto, Canada), 22 December 1900, p. 15.
2 *Godey's Magazine*, November, 1895, p. 561.
3 *The Cornishman* (Cornwall), 22 October 1936, p. 4.
4 Cheiro, *Confessions*, p. 43.
5 *American Register* (London), 26 March 1904, p. 3.
6 Cheiro, *Confessions*, p. 46.
7 Cheiro, *Confessions*, p. 45.
8 *American Register* (London), 19 February 1905, p. 5.
9 Halford Nelson, *Out of the Silence,* p. 54.
10 Halford Nelson, *Out of the Silence,* p. 54.
11 Halford Nelson, *Out of the Silence,*, p. 54.
12 Halford Nelson, *Out of the Silence,*, p. 54.
13 *American Register* (London), 27 June 1903, p. 5.
14 *Evening Standard* (London), 8 May 1903, p. 5.
15 *Light*, 2 January 1904, p. 23.
16 *Light*, 2 January 1904, p. 23.
17 *Newbury Weekly News and Advertiser* (Newbury, Berkshire), 14 July 1904, p. 8.
18 *Richmond Palladium* (Richmond, Indiana), 8 January 1909, p. 3.
19 *St Louis Post-Dispatch* (St Louis, Missouri) 10 January 1909, p.25.
20 *St Louis Post-Dispatch* (St Louis, Missouri) 10 January 1909, p.25.
21 *Northern Chronicle and General Advertiser for the North of Scotland* (Inverness), 13 January 1909, p. 6.
22 *American Register* (London), 16 January 1904, p.4.
23 *Saint Paul Globe* (St Paul, Missouri), 10 January 1909, p. 25.
24 Bob Atchison, 'Travel Guides - St. Petersburg, Russia's Capital—1904 American Article', *Alexander Palace Time Machine*, http://www.alexanderpalace.org/palace/petersburgbayview.html [accessed March 2021].
25 Cheiro, *Mysteries*, p. 272.
26 Cheiro, *You and Your Star*, p. 85.

26 Cheiro, *You and Your Star*, p. 85.

27 Cheiro, *Confessions*, p. 292.

28 Daily Mail, 12 July 1904, p. 5.

29 *St James Gazette* (London) 19 August 1904, p. 13.

30 *London Daily News* (London), 6 October 1904, p. 12.

31 Cheiro, *Confessions*, p. 66.

32 Cheiro, *Confessions*, p. 251.

33 Cheiro, *Confessions*, p. 251.

34 Cheiro, *Confessions*, p. 252.

35 Cheiro, *Confessions*, p. 67.

36 Cheiro, *Confessions*, p. 70. 37 *Daily Telegraph* (Sydney, NSW) 17 June 1925, p. 4.

38 *Daily Telegraph* (Sydney, NSW) 17 June 1925, p. 4.

39 *Daily Telegraph* (Sydney, NSW) 17 June 1925, p. 4.

40 *Daily Telegraph* (Sydney, NSW) 17 June 1925, p. 4.

41 *Daily Telegraph* (Sydney, NSW) 17 June 1925, p. 4.

42 Cheiro, *Confessions*, p. 66.

43 Halford Nelson, *Out of the Silence*, p. 55.

44 Halford Nelson, *Out of the Silence*, p. 55.

45 *American Register* (London), 25 June 1905, p. 3.

CHAPTER 12

1 *Semi-weekly Billings Gazette* (Montana), 9 January 1909, p. 4.

2 Cheiro, *Confessions*, p. 294.

3 Cheiro, *Confessions*, p. 369.

4 *Los Angeles Times* (Los Angeles, California), 20 October 1929, p.150.

5 *Brooklyn Life* (Brooklyn, New York), 26 April 1902, p. 19.

6 *La Liberté* (Paris), 20 January 1909, p. 1.

7 *American Register* (London), 22 October 1905, p. 1.

8 *Daily Mirror,* 14 May 1906, p. 11.

9 Halford Nelson, *Out of the Silence*, p. 56.

10 Halford Nelson, *Out of the Silence,* p. 11.

11 Cheiro, *Confessions*, p. 71.

12 Ernest Bryham Parsons, *Pot-Pourri Parisien* (New York: Broadway Publishing Company, 1912), p. 15.

13 Bryham Parsons, *Pot-Pourri Parisien*, p. 16.

14 Bryham Parsons, *Pot-Pourri Parisien*, p. 18.

15 Bryham Parsons, *Pot-Pourri Parisien*, p. 20.

16 Bryham Parsons, *Pot-Pourri Parisien*, p. 21.

17 *Evening Express* (Wales), 26 May 1902, p. 2.

18 *Salisbury Times* (Salisbury), 23 May 1902, p. 2.

19 *Evening Express* (Wales), 1 August 1902, p. 4.

20 Bryham Parsons, *Pot-Pourri Parisien*, p. 78.

21 Bryham Parsons, *Pot-Pourri Parisien*, p. 79.

22 *American Register* (London), 29 December 1906, p. 8.

23 Bryham Parsons, *Pot-Pourri Parisien*, p. 105.

24 *Daily Telegraph* (Sydney, NSW), 10 June 1925, p. 4.

25 *Daily Telegraph* (Sydney, NSW), 10 June 1925, p. 4.
26 *Daily Telegraph* (Sydney, NSW), 10 June 1925, p. 4.
27 Cheiro, *Confessions*, p. 92.
28 Cheiro, *Confessions*, p. 91.
29 Cheiro, *Confessions*, p. 89.
30 Cheiro, *Confessions*, p. 91.
31 Cheiro, *Confessions*, p. 94.
32 Cheiro, *Confessions*, p. 95.
33 Cheiro, *Confessions*, p. 96.
34 *Truth* (Sydney, NSW) , 15 July 1951, p. 30.
35 *Truth* (Sydney, NSW) , 15 July 1951, p. 30.

CHAPTER 13

1 *Northampton Mercury* (Northampton), 21 June 1907, p. 5.
2 Cheiro, *Confessions*, p. 259.
3 Halford Nelson, *Out of the Silence*, p. 11.
4 *Chicago Examiner* (Chicago, Illinois), 7 January 1909, p.1
5 *Washington Times* (Washington), 7 January 1909, p. 9.
6 *San Francisco Examiner* (San Francisco, California), 17 January 1909, p. 57.
7 *Evening News* (Sydney, NSW), 17 Apr 1909, p. 3.
8 *St Louis Post-Dispatch* (Missouri), 10 January 1909, p. 25.
9 *Gazette* (Cedar Rapids, Iowa), 11 January 1909, p. 6.
10 *Hutchinson Gazette* (Hutchinson, Kansas), 9 January 1909, p. 4.
11 *Irish Standard* (Minneapolis, Minnesota), 16 January 1909, p. 5.
12 *San Francisco Examiner* (San Francisco, California), 17 January 1909, p. 57.
13 *Democrat and Chronicle* (Rochester, New York), 15 January 1909, p. 15.
14 *Hutchinson Gazette* (Kansas), 9 January 1909, p. 4.
15 *Fort Worth Star* (Texas), 10 January 1909, p. 13.
16 *Irish Standard* (Minneapolis, Minnesota), 16 January 1909, p.5.
17 *Irish Standard* (Minneapolis, Minnesota), 16 January 1909, p.5.
18 *Washington Post* (Washington) 8 May 1909, p. 1.
19 *Evening News* (Sydney, NSW) 17 April 1909, p. 3.
20 *Bryham Parsons* Pot-Pourri Parisien, p. 105.
21 *Altoona Tribune* (Pennsylvania), 23 September 1910, p. 6.

CHAPTER 14

1 Cheiro, *True Ghost Stories*, p. 90.
2 Anthony Clayton, *Decadent Westminster,* http://www.antonyclayton.co.uk/
Decadent.html [accessed March 2021].
3 Frank Harris, 'Introduction', *The Bomb*, http://public-library.uk/ebooks/16/7.
pdf [accessed March 2021].
4 *Time*, 21 March 1960.
5 Harris, *The Bomb*, p. 2.
6 Harris, *The Bomb*, p. 2.
7 *Manchester Courier and Lancashire General Advertiser* (Manchester), 16
October 1909, p. 7.

ENDNOTES

8 *Manchester Courier and Lancashire General Advertiser* (Manchester), 16 October 1909, p. 7.
9 *Yorkshire Post and Leeds Intelligencer* (Leeds), 1 November 1909, p. 3.
10 *American Register* (London), 4 December 1909, p. 7
11 *Daily Telegraph*, 5 July 1910, p. 15
12 Cheiro, *Confessions,* p. 309.
13 *American Register* (London), 29 January 1911, p. 4.
14 *Light*, 11 April 1910, p. 166.
15 *Book of the Golden Key* (London : K. Paul, Trench, Trübner, 1909).
16 *Tatler* (London), 1 September 1909, p. 16.
17 *London Standard* (London), 1 March 1912, p. 12.
18 *Truth* (London), 1 May 1912, p. 1088.
19 *Belfast Telegraph* (Belfast), 24 May 1911, p. 5.
20 *Dundee Courier* (Dundee), 27 May 1911, p. 5.
21 *Dundee Courier* (Dundee), 27 May 1911, p. 5.
22 *Daily Mail*, 27 May 1911, p. 3.
23 Cheiro, *Confessions,* p. 68.
24 Joseph McCabe, *Is Spiritualism based on Fraud?* (London: Watts and Co., 1920), p. 90.
25 *Light*, 7 October 1911, p. 470.
26 Stuart Cumberland, *That Other World: Personal Experiences of Mystics and Their Mysticism* (London: Grant Richards, 1019), p. 104.
27 Cheiro, *Confessions,* p. 133.
28 Cheiro, *Confessions,* p. 133.
29 *Dundee Courier*, 30 December 1911, p. 5.
30 Cheiro, *Mysteries,* p. 188.
31 *Light*, 3 August 1912, p. 410.
32 *Daily Mail* (London), 20 September 1912, p. 3.
33 *Light*, 4 May 1912, p. 211.
34 Halford Nelson, *Out of the Silence,* p. 66.
35 Halford Nelson, *Out of the Silence,* p. 67.
36 Halford Nelson, *Out of the Silence,* p. 67.
37 Halford Nelson, *Out of the Silence,* p. 68.
38 Halford Nelson, *Out of the Silence,* p. 68.
39 Halford Nelson, *Out of the Silence,* p. 71.
40 Halford Nelson, *Out of the Silence,* p. 72.
41 Cheiro, *Confessions,* p. 255.

CHAPTER 15

1 Oscar Wilde quoted in the appendix of Cheiro's *Language of the Hand.*
2 British telephone directory.
3 Cheiro, *Confessions,* p. 280.
4 Christopher Addison, *Politics From With In 1911 To 1918* (London: Herbert Jenkins, 1924), p. 80.
5 *Lincolnshire Echo* (Lincolnshire), 30 January 1934, p. 4.
6 *Los Angeles Herald* (Los Angeles, California), 22 December 1916, p. 17.
7 *Daily Telegraph* (Sydney, NSW), 20 May 1925, p. 5.

8 *Daily Telegraph* (Sydney, NSW), 20 May 1925, p. 5.
9 *Light*, 19 July 1917, p, 234.
10 *Light*, 19 July 1917, p, 234.
11 Cheiro, *True Ghost Stories*, p. 126.
12 Cheiro, *True Ghost Stories*, p. 126.
13 Cheiro, *True Ghost Stories*, p. 126.
14 Cheiro, *True Ghost Stories*, p. 127.
15 Cheiro, *True Ghost Stories*, p. 186.
16 Cheiro, *True Ghost Stories*, p. 186.
17 Cheiro, *Confessions*, p. 293.
18 Cheiro, *Confessions*, p. 294.
19 *London Gazette*, 25 December 1928, p. 8515 reports that the deed poll was enrolled on 20 December 1928.

CHAPTER 16

1 Halford Nelson, *Out of the Silence*, p. 73.
2 *Daily Mail* Atlantic Edition, 8 Nov. 1923, p. 13.
3 Cheiro, Confessions, p. 257.
4 Original in *French*. Author's translation. Repeat of report in *Le Matin*. 'La Fille de Pharon Revient Chercher apres des millenaires sa man mumifee', *Eon: Revue Initiatique*, January-March 1924, Paris, p. 64.
5 Cheiro, *You and Your Star*, p. 328.
6 *Irish Independent* (Dublin), 28 June 1926, p. 8.
7 *Irish Independent* (Dublin), 28 June 1926, p. 8.
8 *Irish Independent* (Dublin) 4 February 1927, p. 9.
9 *Evening Herald* (Dublin) 26 June 1926, p. 1.
10 *Evening Herald* (Dublin) 26 June 1926, p. 1.
11 *Ballymena Weekly Telegraph* (Antrim, Northern Ireland), 1 May 1926, p. 10.
12 *Ballymena Weekly Telegraph* (Antrim, Northern Ireland), 1 May 1926, p. 10.
13 *Ballymena Weekly Telegraph* (Antrim, Northern Ireland), 1 May 1926, p. 10.
14 *Ballymena Weekly Telegraph* (Antrim, Northern Ireland), 1 May 1926, p. 10.
15 Bundaberg Mail (Queensland), 12 April 1924, p. 14.
16 *World's News* (Sydney, New South Wales) 5 April 1924, p. 3.
17 *Waikato Times* (New Zealand), 29 April 1924, p. 3.
18 *World's News* (Sydney, New South Wales) 5 April 1924, p. 3.
19 *Queensland Times* (Ipswich, Queensland), 5 April 1924, p. 3.
20 Cheiro, *Real Life Stories*, p. 44.
21 Cheiro, *Real Life Stories*, p. 44.
22 *Halifax Evening Courier* (Halifax, Canada), 9 September 1924, p. 2.
23 Cheiro, *Confessions*, p. 16.
24 Kate Targett (transcribed), *1918 Diary of Sir Horace Targett*, http://www.nli.ie/pdfs/diaries_of_sir_horace_curzon_plunkett/1918_diary_of_sir_horace_curzon_plunkett.pdf [accessed March 2021].
25 Angela Forbes, *Memories and Base Details* (London: Hutchinson and Co., 1921).
26 *Irish Independent* (Dublin), 28 June 1926, p. 8.
27 *Wicklow People* (Wicklow), 1 May 1926 p. 3.

28 *Wicklow People* (Wicklow), 1 May 1926 p. 3.
29 *Wicklow People* (Wicklow), 1 May 1926 p. 3.
30 *Evening Herald* (Dublin), 26 June 1926, p. 1.
31 *Irish Independent* (Dublin) 28 June 1926, p. 8.
32 *Irish Independent* (Dublin), 5 February 1927, p. 5.
33 *Derry Journal* (Londonderry), 18 February 1942, p. 4 and *Irish Independent* (Dublin), 5 February 1927, p. 5.

CHAPTER 17

1 *People* (London), 3 January 1926, p. 1.
2 *Sunday Illustrated* (London), 14 October 1923, p. 2.
3 *Sunday Illustrated* (London), 14 October 1923, p. 2.
4 *Sunday Illustrated* (London), 21 October 1923, p. 2.
5 *Daily Telegraph* (Sydney, NSW) 22 July 1925, p. 7.
6 *San Francisco Examiner* (San Francisco, California), 2 September 1928, p. 40.
7 Cheiro, *World Predictions* (London: Herbert Jenkins, 1931), p. 87.
8 *Bioscope*, 3 September 1925, p. 43.
9 *People* (London), 29 May 1928, p. 7.
10 *People* (London), 29 May 1928, p. 7.
11 *People* (London), 29 May 1928, p. 7.
12 *People* (London), 17 June 1928, p. 7.
13 *Occult Review*, June 1922, p. 68.
14 *Occult Review,* July 1923, p. 77.
15 *Occult Review,*, May 1929, p. 3.
16 *Mid Sussex Times* (Haywards Heath, Sussex), 29 January 1929, p. 8.
17 Arthur Christiansen, *Headlines All My Life* (London: Heinemann, 1961), p. 65.
18 Christiansen, *Headlines*, p. 65.
19 *Prediction*, 1 May 1936, p, 162.
20 *Lincolnshire Echo* (Lincoln, Lincolnshire), 31 July 1933, p. 6.

INTERLUDE: ASTROLOGY

1 *Strand*, December 1916, p. 198.
2 *Sunday Illustrated*, 11 November 1923, p. 12.
3 *Cheiro's World Predictions* (London: London Publishing Company, 1927), p. 83.

CHAPTER 18

1 *Yorkshire Post and Leeds Intelligencer* (Leeds), 26 March 1932, p. 8.
2 *Chichester Observer* (Chichester), 10 December 1938, p. 5.
3 *Mail* (Adelaide, South Australia), 4 August 1945, p. 2.
4 *Mail* (Adelaide, South Australia), 4 August 1945, p. 2.
5 *Los Angeles Times* (Los Angeles, California), 5 August 1929, p. 26.
6 *Los Angeles Times* (Los Angeles, California), 5 August 1929, p. 26.
7 *Los Angeles Times* (Los Angeles, California), 17 September 1929, p. 30.
8 Cheiro, *You and Your Star*, p. 324.
9 *Los Angeles Times* (Los Angeles, California), 17 September 1929, p. 30.
10 *Enquirer and Evening News* (Battle Creek, Michigan), 31 May 1936, p. 20.

11 *Bordon Reporter* (Iowa), 23 February 1939, p. 10.

12 *Los Angeles Times* (Los Angeles, California), 20 October 1929, p. 150.

13 *Los Angeles Times* (Los Angeles, California), 20 October 1929, p. 150.

14 Cheiro, *Confessions*, p. 15.

15 Cheiro, *Confessions*, p. 15.

16 *Los Angeles Times* (Los Angeles, California), 31 January 1932, p. 95.

17 *Los Angeles Times* (Los Angeles, California), 28 July 1930, p. 48.

18 Cheiro, *Confessions*, p. 16.

19 *Yorkshire Post and Leeds Intelligencer* (Leeds), 26 March 1932, p. 8.

20 Beatrice Behlen, 'Countess Hamon—the last chapter', *Museum of London* (10 January 2011), quoted from *Liberty*, autumn 1971, http://www.mymuseumoflondon.org.uk/blogs/blog/countess-hamon-the-last-chapter/ [accessed December 2020].

21 Beatrice Behlen, 'Countess Hamon—the last chapter'.

22 Cheiro, *Confessions*, p. 296.

23 *Los Angeles Times* (Los Angeles, California), 18 October 1931, p. 46.

24 *Los Angeles Times* (Los Angeles, California) 17 June 1932, p. 26.

25 *Mill Valley Record* (California), 29 January 1932, p. 6.

26 *Los Angeles Evening Citizen News*, (California), 9 July 1932, p.8.

27 *Monrovia News Post* (California), 1 February 1932, p. 1.

28 '[Letter] 1935 November 25th, Hollywood [to] H. G. Wells/Louis Hamon', *Charlie Chaplin Archive, Cineceta Bologna*, http://www.charliechaplinarchive.org/en/collection/cerca/lettera-1935-november-25th-hollywood-a-h-g-wells-louis-hamon/search/actor:hamon-louis/page/1/view_as/grid [accessed March 2021].

CHAPTER 19

1 *Sunday Tribune* (Singapore) 18 June 1950, p. 8.

2 *Somerset Guardian and Radstock Observer* (Radstick, Somerset), 16 October 1936, p. 1.

3 Halford Nelson, *Out of the Silence*, p. 45.

4 Rosemary Guiley, *Encyclopedia of Magic and Alchemy* (New York: Facts On File, 2006).

5 Halford Nelson, *Out of the Silence*, p. 48.

6 *Ironwood Daily Globe* (Ironwood, Michigan), 9 October 1936, p. 1.

7 *San Bernardino Sun* (California), 10 October 1936, p. 2.

8 Halford Nelson, *Out of the Silence*, p. 48.

9 *Ironwood Daily Globe* (Ironwood, Michigan), 9 October 1936, p. 1.

10 *Minneapolis Star* (Minneapolis, Minnesota), 18 February 1940, p. 70.

11 Halford Nelson, *Out of the Silence*, p. 95.

POSTSCRIPT

1 *Daily Express* (London), 23 November 1936, p. 5.

2 Halford Nelson, *Out of the Silence*, p. 92.

3 Halford Nelson, *Out of the Silence*, p. 92.

4 Halford Nelson, *Out of the Silence*, p. 93.

5 *Kingston Gleaner* (Jamaica), 16 January 1937, p. 14.

ENDNOTES

6 *Evening Star* (Dunedin, New Zealand), 16 July 1938, p. 16.
7 Beatrice Behlen, 'Countess Hamon—the last chapter'.
8 *Daily Mirror* (London) 4 August 1945, p. 5.
9 *Daily Telegraph* (Sydney, NSW), 10 November 1945, p. 12.
10 *Daily Telegraph* (Sydney, NSW), 10 November 1945, p. 12.
11 Halford-Nelson, Desert Sanctuary, p. 17.
12 Halford Nelson, *Out of the Silence*, p. 28.
13 Halford-Nelson, *Desert Sanctuary*, p. 122.
14 Halford Nelson, *Out of the Silence,* p. 95.

SOURCES

Public records were checked wherever available. This included those relating to birth, death, marriage and travel, naturalisation and citizenship records and census returns. Searches were also made of street directories and phone books. Each record was verified through two or more sources. Initial searches were made on Ancestry.co.uk, with additional searches and verification of records made on Find my Past.com, and Myheritage.com.

Irish records were accessed via Irishgenealogy.ie.

Newspaper reports were accessed via the British Library Newspaper Archive, Newspapers.com, Newspaperarchive.com, Trove (Australian), Gallica (French) and UKpressonline. Searches were made in both English and French language publications.

Spiritualist and smilar publications were accessed via the International Association for the Preservation of Spiritualist Periodicals—isapsop.com.

Specific sources consulted for each chapter are listed below.

CHAPTER 1

'Ancestors of Russell Owen HJELM', *Rootsweb*, http://freepages.rootsweb. com/~rohjelm/genealogy/aqwg220.htm [accessed April 2020]
'Parish History', *St. Peter's Parish Bray*, https://www.stpetersparishbray.com/our-parish/parish-history/ [accessed April 2020].
'Turkish Baths built in 1859 in Bray, Ireland, as part of its Victorian seaside resort heyday. Replaced by a supermarket in 1980', *Ye Olde Buildings*, https:// yeoldebuildings.home.blog/2020/02/02/turkish-baths-built-in-1859-in-bray-ireland-as-part-if-its-victorian-seaside-resort-heyday-replaced-by-a-supermarket-in-1980-2/ [accessed April 2020].
Banks, T. C., *The Dormant and Extinct Baronage of England*, Vol 1 (London: Printed by T. Bensley for J. White, 1807).

Barry, Michael, 'Transport in 19th Century Dublin', *The Irish Story*, https://www.theirishstory.com/2014/03/06/transport-in-19th-century-dublin/#.XnoPvfn7SJA [accessed April 2020].

Belfast Mercury (Belfast), 10 August 1861.

Best, E. Joyce, 'The Hugeunots of Lisburn', Chapter V, http://lisburn.com/books/huguenots/huguenots_5.html, [accessed April 2020].

Borrowes, Erasmus D. Bart., 'The Huguenot Colony of Portarlington', *Ulster Journal of Archeology* (Belfast: Archer and Sons, 1858).

Boston Post (Boston, Massachusetts), 12 May 1895.

Buffalo Inquirer (Buffalo, New York), 11 January 1896.

Burke, Bernard and Burke, John, *A genealogical and heraldic history of the extinct and dormant baronetcies of England, Ireland and Scotland* (London: Scott, Webster and Geary, 1841).

Burke, John, *A Genealogical and Heraldic History of the Commoners of Great Britain and Ireland*, Vol. III (London: Colburn, 1836).

Cawley, Charles, 'England, Earls Created 1067–1102', *Medieval Lands*, (Foundation for Medieval Genealogy) http://fmg.ac/Projects/MedLands/ENGLISH%20NOBILITY%20MEDIEVAL.htm [accessed May 2020].

Comerford, Patrick, 'Beginning to explore the Victorian and Edwardian architecture of Bray', 16 August 2016, http://www.patrickcomerford.com/2016/08/beginning-to-explore-victorian-and.html [accessed April 2020].

Comerford, Patrick, 'The Royal Hotel in Bray stands on the site of the town's oldest hotel', 9 March 2018, http://www.patrickcomerford.com/2018/03/the-royal-hotel-in-bray-stands-on-site.html [accessed April 2020].

Cooper, Matthew Franklin, 'Martyr Helier the Hermit of Jersey', The Heavy Anglo Orthodox, 16 July 2019, http://heavyangloorthodox.blogspot.com/2019/07/martyr-helier-hermit-of-jersey.html [accessed April 2020].

Coventry Evening Telegraph (Coventry), 14 October 1936.

Davies, K.M., *Irish Historic Towns Atlas* (IHTA), no. 9, Bray https://s3-eu-west-1.amazonaws.com/assets.ria.ie/ihta/ihta-digital/towns-in-19th-century/bray/ihta-9-bray-text.pdf [accessed April 2020].

Davies, Mary K., 'Bray's Turkish Baths', *History of Ireland*, Nov/Dec 2007, https://www.historyireland.com/18th-19th-century-history/brays-turkish-baths/ [accessed April 2020].

Duchess of Celveland, *The Battle Abbey Roll* (London: John Murray, 1889).

Dugdale, William, *The baronage of England*, Early English Books https://quod.lib.umich.edu/e/eebo/A36794.0001.001/1:11?rgn=div1;view=fulltext [accessed April 2020].

Falle, Samuel (1854-1937), Dean of Jersey, 'Saint Helier - Saint Hélyi - Saint Hélier', *Societe Jersiaise*, http://members.societe-jersiaise.org/geraint/helier/falle.html [accessed April 2020].

Feist, Paul, *House of Goldsborough* (Lulu, 2011).

Fitchburg Sentinel (Fitchburg, Massachusetts), 6 May 1895.

Garner, William, *Bray: Architectural Heritage* (Ireland: An Foras Forbartha, 1980).

Gazette, The (Cedar Rapids, Iowa) 8 January 1909.

Herron, Kris, 'Ancestors of Montagu John Felton Durnford the first of this Durnford lineage to settle in Australia', 31 August 2014, https://edurnford.blogspot.com/2014/08/ [accessed April 2020].

Hodges, Figgis, *A Hundred Years of Bray and its Neighbourhood* (Bray, Ireland: 1907).

Holler, Michael G., 'Ancestors of Caden Michael Norquist', http://freepages.rootsweb.com/~mgholler/genealogy/Caden/a34.htm [accessed April 2020].

Jennings Lee, *Edward Lee of Virginia 1642—1892* (Philadelphia: 1895).

Larne Times (Antrim, Northern Ireland), 1 May 1926.

Lawless Lee, Grace, *The Huguenot Settlements in Ireland* (Heritage Books, 2008).

Lawlor, Chris, *Little book of Wicklow* (The History Press, 2014).

Little, Hannah Mary, 'Genealogy as theatre of self-identity: a study of genealogy as a cultural practice within Britain since c. 1850' (unpublished doctoral thesis, University of Glasgow, 2010).

McNally, Tom. 'Education in nineteenth-century Bray' in O'Sullivan, John, Dunne, Tony and Cannon, Seamus (eds), *The book of Bray* (Dublin: Blackrock Teachers' Centre, 1989).

Mill Valley Record (Mill Valley, California), 29 January 1932.

O'Laughlin, Michael C., *The Book of Irish Families, Great & Small* (Kansas City, MO.: Irish Genealogical Foundation, 2002).

Oxford Dictionary of National Biography (Oxford: Oxford University Press, 2012).

Polwhele, Rev. R., *The History of Cornwall*, vol. I (1816).

Prediction, July 1965.

Red Lodge Picket (Red Lodge, Mont.), 16 December 1893.

Richmond Palladium (Richmond, Indiana), 24 September 1910.

Shelley, Colin, 'Hammond Surname Meaning, History & Origin', *Selected Surnames Website*, http://www.selectsurname.com/hammond.html [accessed April 2020].

Sinclair, Mary, *The Sinclairs of England* (London: Trubner, 1887).

Sinclair, Thomas, *Sinclairs of England*, (London: Trubner and Co., 1887).

Smiles, Samuel, *The Huguenots—Their Settlements, Churches and Industries in England and Ireland* (Read Books Ltd, 2011).

St. Albans Daily Messenger (Saint Albans, Vermont), 6 August 1910.

Straits Times (Singapore), 1 February 1963.

Thomas, Thomas (rector of Aberporth, Wales), *Memoirs of Owen Glendower (Owain Glyndwr)*, (Wales, 1822).

Tout, Thomas Frederick, 'Fitzhamon, Robert', *Dictionary of National Biography*, 1885-1900, Volume 19 (London: Smith, Elder and Co., 1890).

Turner, James, 'Illegitimacy and Power: 12th Century Anglo-Norman and Angevin Illegitimate Family Members within Aristocratic Society' (unpublished doctoral thesis, Durham University, 2020).

Wace, Master, *The Chronicle of the Norman Conquest from the Roman de Rou* (London: William Pickering, 1837).

Weekly Irish Times (Dublin), 18 August 1894.

White, Brian, The Little Book of Bray and Enniskerry, (The History Press, 2016).

Wicklow news-letter (Wicklow, Ireland), 2 June 1860.

SOURCES

Williams, Kelsey Jackson, 'What's In a Name? Burke's Peerage and the Shape of British Genealogy', *A Scots Genealogical Miscellany*, 28 January 2014, http://scottishgenealogy.weebly.com/blog/archives/01-2014 [accessed April 2020].
Yeo, Sheila, 'The Grenville Family, *Yeo Family History* http://www.yeosociety.com/yeoroots/grenville%20family.htm [accessed April 2020].

CHAPTER 2

Albany-Decatur Daily (Albany, Alabama), 26 February 1924.
Altoona Tribune (Altoona, Pennsylvania), 23 September 1910.
Atlanta Sunny South (Atlanta, Georgia), 21 April 1894.
Australian Star (Sydney, New South Wales), 23 July 1894.
Belfast News-Letter (Belfast), 27 December 1887; 2 January 1888; 17 November 1888; 13 February 1889; 16 October 1889; 30 October 1888; 28 Sept 1889; 30 October 1889; 6 November 1889; 13 November 1889; 31 January 1890; 23 April 1890.
Belfast Telegraph (Belfast), 5 June 1909.
Chicago Tribune (Chicago, Illinois), 7 January 1909.
Cumberland, Stuart, *That Other World: Personal Experience of Mystics and their Mysticism* (London: Grant Richards, 1918).
Franklin Times (Pukekohe, New Zealand) 5 May 1924.
Greer, David, *Hamilton Harty: Early Memories* (Belfast: Queen's University, 1980).
Lamont, Peter, *The Rise of the Indian Rope Trick* (Abacus, 2005).
Lancashire Evening Post (Lancashire), 11 June 1902.
London Daily News (London), 30 December 1886.
Prediction, July 1965.
San Bernardino County Sun (San Bernardino, California),13 April 1912.
Stonehaven Journal (Stonehaven, Kincardineshire, Scotland), 7 September 1911.
Straits Times (Singapore), 1 February 1863.
Toronto Saturday Night (Toronto, Canada), 22 December 1900, p. 15.
Walsh Tom, 'The National System of Education, http://mural.maynoothuniversity.ie/9689/1/TW-National-2016.pdf [accessed May 2020].
Washington Post (Washington, District of Columbia), 8 May 1909.
Weekly Irish Times (Dublin), 18 August 1894.
Wichita Eagle (Wichita, Kansas), 28 August 1910.

CHAPTER 3

'Arrah-na-Pogue', *History Ireland*, Volume 19, Issue 2, (March/April 2011).
'Entertaining the poor people at Providence Row in April 1897', 31 March 2017, *Forgotten Victorians*, https://forgottenvictorians.com/tag/mlle-gratienne [accessed May 2010].
'Leather Apron—an account of his invention', *Casebook: Jack the Ripper*, https://forum.casebook.org/forum/ripper-discussions/suspects/general-suspect-discussion/1468-leather-Aprilon-an-account-of-his-invention [accessed June 2020].
'Princess's', *Theatres Trust*, 2017, https://database.theatrestrust.org.uk/resources/theatres/show/3271-princess-s-london [accessed February 2021].

SOURCES

'The Royal Princess's Theatre, 73 Oxford street, London', *Arthur Lloyd Music Hall and Theatre History Site*, http://www.arthurlloyd.co.uk/Princess.htm [accessed March 2021].

Begg, Paul and Fido Martin, *The Complete Jack The Ripper A-Z - The Ultimate Guide to The Ripper Mystery*, (London: Kings Road Publishing, 2015).

Blainey, Ann, *Marvelous Melba: The Extraordinary Life of a Great Diva* (Chicago: Ivan R Dee, Inc., 2009).

Capes, Bernard and Eglington, *Charles, The Theatre*, (London: Eglington and Co., 1891).

Chicago Tribune (Chicago, Illinois), 7 January 1909; 1 July 1909.

Clarion (London), 11 June 1892.

Daily Graphic (London), 11 June 1892.

Edinburgh Evening News (Edinburgh), 1 July 1892.

Era, The (London), 13 November 1864; 5 September 1891; 13 June 1891; 5 September 1891; 23 April 1892; 11 June 1892; 18 June 1892; 25 June 1892; 16 June 1892; 2 July 1892; 23 July 1892.

Freemason's Chronicle (London), 4 June 1892.

Gentlewoman (London), 20 February 1892.

Guardian (Manchester), 10 June 1892.

Hutchinson Gazette (Hutchinson, Kansas), 9 January 1909.

Jackson, Paul S. B., 'Fearing future epidemics: the cholera crisis of 1892', (University of Toronto), https://journals.sagepub.com/doi/pdf/10.1177/1474474012455017 [accessed May 2010].

London Evening Standard (London), 2 July 1892.

Loxton, Howard, 'After Dark; or, A Drama of London Life', *British Theatre Guide*, https://www.britishtheatreguide.info/reviews/after-dark-or-finborough-thea-17718 [accessed May 2010].

Morning Post (London), 4 October 1891; 3 November 1891.

Nicoll, Allardyce, *A History of Late Nineteenth Century Drama, 1850-1900*, Volume 1 (London: The University Press, 1949).

Pall Mall Gazette (London), 9 September 1891; 31 October 1891; 10 June 1892.

Payne, Ben Iden, *A Life in a Wooden O: Memoirs of the Theatre* (New Haven; London : Yale University Press, 1977).

People (London), 15 November 1891; 5 June 1892.

Referee (London), 10 June 1892; 19 June 1892; 24 June 1892; 25 June 1892;

Sartwell, Elissa, 'The other side of the tracks: railroads, race, and the performance of unity in nineteenth-century American entertainment' (unpublished doctoral thesis, Louisiana State University, 2006).

Schweik, Susan, 'Marshall P. Wilder and Disability Performance History', *Disability Studies Quarterly*, Vol. 30, No. 3/4 (Ohio State University Libraries in partnership with the Society for Disability Studies, 2010).

Sporting Life (London), 15 June 1892.

Stage, The (London), 24 December 1891.

Vancouver Daily World (Vancouver, Canada), 9 January 1897.

CHAPTER 4

Altoona Tribune (Altoona, Pennsylvania), 23 September 1910.

Blainey, Ann, *Marvelous Melba: The Extraordinary Life of a Great Diva* (Chicago: Ivan R. Dee, 2009).

Cheltenham Examiner (Cheltenham), 13 July 1892.

Cincinnati Enquirer (Cincinnati, Ohio), 11 January 1909; 11 June 1912.

Daily Gazette (London), 17 October 1892.

Derby Daily Telegraph (Derby), 17 June 1893.

Dibb, Geoff, 'Oscar Wilde and The Mystics. Thought Transference, The Detection of Crime and Finding a Pin', *The Wildean*, No. 42 (Oscar Wilde Society, January 2013), pp. 82-99, https://www.jstor.org/stable/45270250 [accessed May 2020].

Dover Express (Dover), 15 July 1892.

E. H. Mikhail (ed.), *Oscar Wilde: Interviews and Recollections*, Vol. 2 (New York: Barnes and Noble, 1979).

Era, The, 23 July 1892.

Evening Herald (Dublin), 5 June 1895.

Glasgow Evening Post (Glasgow), 26 August 1893.

Glen Innes Examiner and General Advertiser (New South Wales), 6 September 1892.

Hampshire Telegraph (Portsmouth), 7 October 1893.

Hansard PALMISTRY, HC Deb 16 June 1893 vol 13 c1188, https://api.parliament.uk/historic-hansard/commons/1893/jun/16/palmistry#column_1188 [accessed May 2020].

Hull Daily Mail (Hull), 15 November 1898.

Irish News and Belfast News (Belfast), 4 August 1893.

Irish Society (Dublin), 23 September 1893.

Marschall, Rebecca Fenning, 'Finding Aid for the Oscar Wilde and his Literary Circle Collection', *Online Archive of California*, https://oac.cdlib.org/findaid/ark:/13030/kt867nf36t/entire_text/ [accessed May 2020].

Morning Cheltenham Examiner (Cheltenham), 13 July 1892.

Morning Post (London), 13 April 1891; 20 April 1891; 22 May 1891; 24 November 1891.

Navarre, Joan, 'Oscar Wilde, Edward Heron-Allen, and the Palmistry Craze of the 1880s', *English Literature in Transition*, 1880-1920, Volume 54, Number 2, 2011, pp. 174-184.

North Eastern Gazette (Middlesbrough), 17 October 1892.

Northern Daily Telegraph (Blackburn), 17 October 1892.

Occult Review, June 1912.

Robinson, Bonnie J., 'The Other's Other: Neo-Victorian Depictions of Constance Lloyd Wilde Holland,' http://www.neovictorianstudies.com/past_issues/4-1%20 2011/NVS%204-1-2%20BJ-Robinson.pdf [accessed June 2020].

Rose, David Charles, *Oscar Wilde's Elegant Republic* (Cambridge: Cambridge Scholars Publishing, 2015).

Southern Echo (London), 20 October 1892.

Sphere (London), 18 May 1912.

Sporting Gazette (London), 11 June 1892.

Taylor, Kevin, 'Pardoning Harry: The Man Who Invented Jack the Ripper', *Aimée Crocker*, https://aimeecrocker.com/people/pardoning-harry-the-man-who-invented-jack-the-ripper/ [accessed February 2021].

Vancouver Sun (Vancouver, Canada) 25 November 1977.
Worthing Gazette (Worthing), 1 June 1892.

CHAPTER 5

'Dr. Henry Meyer & Mrs. Mary Meyer, American Serial Killer Team—1893', Unknown Gender History, 22 September 2011, http://unknownmisandry.blogspot.com/2011/09/mrs-h-w-meyer-champion-black-widow.html [accessed February 2021].
'Samuel Langhorne Clemens collection of papers 1856-1938', New York Public Library.
Akron Daily Democrat (Ohio) 21 July 1894.
Australian Star (Sydney, NSW), 23 July 1894.
Buffalo Enquirer (Buffalo, New York), 16 January 1896.
Buffalo Evening News (Buffalo, New York), 24 May 1894.
Daily Telegraph (Sydney) 16 May 1925; 18 July 1925; 1 August 1925; 8 August 1925; 12 Aug 1925.
Mysteries of the Unknown: Visions and Prophecies (Alexandria, Virginia: Time Life Books, n.d.).
Newcastle Courant (Newcastle), 13 January 1894.
Norway Heritage, http://www.norwayheritage.com/p_ship.asp?sh=cipa2 [accessed March 2021].
Parks, Ken, 'John Peurgini', *The Bright Stars of Yesterday*, http://www.starsofyesterday.org/john-perugini/ [accessed February 2021].
Red Lodge Picket (Red Lodge, Montana), 16 December 1893.
Scranton Republican (Scranton, Pennsylvania), 20 December 1893.
St. Albans Daily Messenger (Saint Albans, Vermont), 6 August 1910.
Sun, The (New York), 11 June 1894.
Times (Philadelphia, Pennsylvania) 26 August 1894.
Toronto Saturday Night, 22 December 1900.
Tribune (Scranton, Pennsylvania), 20 December 1893.
Whilhelm, Robert, 'Professional Poisoners', *Murder by Gaslight*, 4 March 2018, http://www.murderbygaslight.com/2018/03/professional-poisoners.html [accessed February 2021].
World, The (New York) 12 November 1893; 26 November 1893; 10 June 1894.

CHAPTER 6

'James B. Pond Lyceum Theatre Lecture Bureau & Agency collection', *Lord Durham*, https://www.ldrb.ca/pages/books/8225/james-burton-pond-james-b-pond-jr-pond-james-b-pond-jr-pond-major-pond-bim-pond/james-b-pond-lyceum-theatre-lecture-bureau-agency-collection [accessed December 2020].
'Student migrants: Cornelia Sorabji at Oxford', *University of Cambridge*, https://www.ourmigrationstory.org.uk/oms/cornelia-sorabji-at-oxford [accessed December 2020].
'Vivekananda Abroad A Postcard Pilgrimage', http://vivekanandaabroad.blogspot.com/2017/08/boston-ma-12-may-1895.html [accessed December 2020].
Alethian, 20 October 1916.
Altoona Mirror (Altoona, Pennsylvania), 8 January 1904.
Baltimore Sun (Baltimore, Maryland), 8 January 1909.
Borderland, Vol. 4, No. 4, October 1897.

SOURCES

Boston Globe (Boston, Massachusetts), 13 May 1895; 9 June 1895; 16 June 1895; 23 June 1895; 1 December 1895; 7 December 1895.
Boston Herald (Boston, Massachusetts), 19 April 1895.
Boston Post (Boston, Massachusetts), (Boston, Massachusetts), 12 May 1895; 14 May 1895.
Boston Weekly Globe (Boston, Massachussetts), 23 February *1887).*
Brooklyn Daily Eagle (Brooklyn, New York), 4 November 1896.
Buffalo Commercial (Buffalo, New York), 6 June 1901.
Buffalo Courier (Buffalo, New York), 20 January 1895; 1 January 1896; 8 January 1896.
Buffalo Enquirer (Buffalo, New York) 13 January 1896.
Chatterjee, Arup K., 'Suleman Noor in Shakespeare's times,' *The Hindu*, 4 August 2018.
Cheltenham Examiner, 16 June 1897.
Cole, G.et al., *Public Opinion*, Volumes 65-66, 189
D'Odiardi, E. Savary, 'Medical Electricity, what is it? and how does it cure?' *L'Académie des sciences*, tome 117, 1 January 1893.
Electrical Engineer, The, 1 January 1892 to 24 June 1892.
Era, The, 14 July 1888; 8 March 1891.
Evening Herald (Massachussetts), 6 May 1910; 14 February 1910; 5 July 1912.
Evening Star (Washington), 11 April 1896.
Evening World (New York), 16 September 1893.
Fall River Daily Evening News (Massachussetts), 11 May 1906.
Field, The, 13 September 1890.
Fincham, Johnny, 'Chirology in America', *Johnny Fincham Palmistry*, http://johnnyfincham.com/history/stgermain.htm [accessed December 2019].
Fisher, Michael H., Indian Travellers and Settlers in Britain, 1600-1857 (Permanent Black: 2004).
Ghosh, Durba, 'Empire Families: Britons and Late Imperial India, and Counterflows to Colonialism: Indian Travellers and Settlers in Britain, 1600-1857 (review)', *Journal of Interdisciplinary History*, Volume 38, Number 1 (Summer 2007), pp. 109-112.
Globe, The , 9 July 1888.
Gloucestershire Echo, 12 August 1886.
Harrisburg Telegraph (Pennsylvania), 27 October1903; 10 November 1903.
Hutchinson Gazette (Kansas), 9 January 1909.
Illustrated London News, 14 July 1888; 23 August 1890.
Inter Ocean (Chicago, Illinois), 3 August 1895.
Jersey Independent and Daily Telegraph, 17 April 1886; 8 May 1886; 31 July 1886.
Kilburn Times, 4 May 1888.
Koren, Yehuda and Negev Eliat, *First Lady of Fleet Street: The Life, Fortune and Tragedy of Rachel Beer* (New York: Bantam Books, 2013).
Lancaster Examiner (Pennsylvania), 24 December 1904.
Leavenworth Weekly Times (Leavenworth, Kansas), 24 February 1887.
London Standard, 4 February1904,
Los Angeles Herald (Los Angeles, California), 14 January 1898.
Morning Post, 15 July 1886.
Newcastle Courant, 16 May 1891.
Northern Echo, 12 April 1890.

Pall Mall Gazette, 15 January 1894,

Pandit, Hardik Bhalchandra, 'Decision support system for healthcare on the basis of medical palmistry through digital image processing and analysis' (unpublished thesis, Sardar Patel University, 2013).

Paul, Renu and Sharaf, Mitra, 'South Asians at the Inns of Court: Middle Temple, 1863-1944', https://dokumen.tips/documents/south-asians-at-the-inns-of-court-middle-temple-1863-1944.html [accessed January 2021].

Pond, Major J. B., *Eccentricities of Genius* (New York: G. W. Dillingham Company, 1900).

Register of Admissions to the Middle Temple, http://archive.middletemple.org.uk/Shared%20Documents/MTAR/updated/1886-1909.pdf [accessed December 2020].

Rider, Clare, 'The admission of overseas students to the Inner Temple in the 19th century', *The Inner Temple*, https://www.innertemple.org.uk/who-we-are/history/historical-articles/the-admission-of-overseas-students-to-the-inner-temple-in-the-19th-century/ [accessed April 2019].

Saint Paul Globe (Saint Paul, Minnesota), 18 January 1898.

Scranton Truth (Scranton, Pennsylvania), 11 May 1905.

Sporting Gazette, 4 April 1891.

St. Albans Daily Messenger (Vermont), 6 August 1910.

Stavig, Gopal, *Western Admirers of Ramakrishna and His Disciples* (India: Advaita Ashrama, 2010).

Tennessean (Nashville, Tennessee), 23 October 1897.

Times (Philadelphia), 26 April 1896.

CHAPTER 7

'Our History', Florida Chautauqua Assembly, https://floridachautauquaassembly.org/our-history [accessed March 2021].

'Vivekananda Abroad A Postcard Pilgrimage', http://vivekanandaabroad.blogspot.com/2017/08/boston-ma-12-may-1895.html [accessed December 2020].

Adams, Evangeline, *Bowl of Heaven* (New York: Dodd, Mead and Company, 1926).

Altoona Mirror (Pennsylvania) 8 January 1904.

Baltimore Sun (Maryland), 8 January 1909.

Beemer, Matthew Albert, 'The Florida Chautauqua as Text', (unpublished doctoral dissertation, Louisiana State University, 1997).

Belfast News-Letter (Belfast), 20 Jun 1896.

Boston Globe (Boston, Massachusetts), 16 June 1895; 1 December 1895; 7 December 1895; 9 February 1896; 3 April 1896; 25 October 1898.

Boston Post (Massachusetts), 14 May 1895; 1 December 1895; 15 December 1895; 18 May 1896.

Brooklyn Daily Eagle (New York), 13 June 1896; 4 November 1896.

Buffalo Commercial (New York), 4 January 1896; 8 January 1896; 11 January 96; 16 January 1896; 18 April 1896; 6 June 1901.

Buffalo Courier (Buffalo, New York), 20 January 1895; 29 December 1895; 1 January 1896; 3 January 1896; 4 January 1896; 8 January 1896; 11 January 1896; *Buffalo Enquirer* (New York), 9 January 1896.

Buffalo Evening News (New York), 2 January 1896; 4 January 1896; 8 January 1896.

Buffalo Morning Express and Illustrated Buffalo Express (New York), 10 January 1896.

Cheltenham Examiner, 16 June 1897.
Chicago Tribune (Illinois), 4 February 1896; 12 February 1896; 21 February 1896.
Daily Standard, 27 December 1895.
Des Moines Register (Des Moines, Iowa), 1 March 1896.
Detroit Free Press, 5 January 1896; 8 January 1896; 17 January 1896; 19 January 1896.
Direct Voice, The, Vol.1, No. 3 (New York, July 1930).
Evening Star (Washington), 8 April 1896; 11 April 1896; 24 April 1896; 27 April 1896.
Florida Chautauqua programme 1896, *University of Florida Digital Collections*, https://ufdc.ufl.edu/WF00000005/00002 [accessed March 2021].
Freeman's Journal (Dublin, Ireland), 15 Jun 1896.
Home News for India, China and the Colonies (London), 10 April 1891.
Indianapolis Journal (Indianapolis, Indiana), 20 June 1896.
Inter Ocean (Chicago, Illinois), 5 February 1896; 14 February 1896; 20 February 1896; 25 February 1896.
Kansas City Times (Kansas City, Missouri), 23 June 1896.
Lancaster Examiner (Pennsylvania), 24 December 1904.
Light, Vol. 24 (January 1904).
Liverpool Mercury, 20 June 1896.
Los Angeles Times, 5 January 1896.
Mahnich, Alison, 'A History of the Florida Chautauqua' (unpublished doctoral dissertation, University of Texas, 2014).
Pensacola News, 6 March 1896; 9 March 1896.
Rider, Claire, 'The admission of overseas students to the Inner Temple in the 19th century', Inner Temple, https://www.innertemple.org.uk/who-we-are/history/historical-articles/the-admission-of-overseas-students-to-the-inner-temple-in-the-19th-century/ [accessed March 2021].
Saint Paul Globe (Saint Paul, Minnesota), 18 January 1898.
San Francisco Call (California), 23 February 1896.
Schmidt, Leigh Eric, *Restless Souls: The Making of American Spirituality* (California: University of California Press, 2012).
Scranton Truth (Pennsylvania), 11 May 1905.
St. Albans Daily Messenger (Vermont), 6 August 1910.
Stavig, Gopal, *Western Admirers of Ramakrishna*.
Tampa Tribune (Florida), 14 March 1896.
Tennessean Nashville (Tennessee), 23 October 1897.
Times (Philadelphia), 26 April 1896.
Washington Times (Washington), 5 April 1896.
World, The (New York), 24 May 1896.
Young, Sue, 'The Smith name and homeopathy', https://www.sueyounghistories.com/2008-02-11-the-smith-surname-and-homeopathy/ [accessed March 2021].

CHAPTER 8

Borderland, October 1897.
Boston Globe (Boston, Massachusetts), 13 May 1897.
Boston Post (Boston, Massachusetts), 18 July 1896; 2 November 1896.
Boston Sunday Post (Boston, Massachusetts), 24 July 1898.

Brooklyn Standard (Brooklyn, New York), 15 May 1897.
Cheltenham Looker-On (Cheltenham), 10 July 1897.
Chicago Tribune (Chicago, Illinois), 22 December 1897; 25 December 1897; 6 March 1898; 10 March 1898.
Cochrane, Claire, *Twentieth-Century British Theatre: Industry, Art and Empire* (Cambridge: Cambridge University Press, 2011).
Dayton Herald (Ohio), 20 July 1897.
Eastbourne Gazette (Eastbourne, Sussex), 29 August 1894.
Edinburgh Gazette (Edinburgh), 2 September 1898.
Hegeler, Edward, *The Open Court*, March 1931.
Ingersoll, Anna Josephine, *Greenacre on the Piscataqua* (New York: Alliance Publishing Company, 1900).
Inter Ocean (Chicago, Illinois), 15 November 1896.
Kent and Sussex Courier (Tunbridge Wells), 28 October 1896.
Middletown Daily Argus (Middletown, New York), 3 August, 1898.
Morning Post (London), 17 July 1896; 18 July 1896; 20 July 1896.
New York Times (New York), 20 July 1898.
New York Tribune (New York), 29 May 1897.
Northern Echo, 1 November 1895.
Oshkosh North Western, 18 January 1898.
Pall Mall Gazette (London), 28 January 1898.
Saint Paul Globe (St Paul, Minnesota), Minnesota) 10 January 1898; 18 January 1898; 23 January 1898; 26 January 1898; 14 February 1898.
San Francisco Examiner, 9 October 1898.
Solomon Valley Democrat (Kansas), 3 February 1898.
Star Tribune (Minneapolis, Minnesota), 8 February 1898; 9 February 1898; 13 February 1998; 18 February 1898; 20 February 1898.
Stavig, Gopal, *Western Admirers of Ramakrishna*.
Sunday Times (London), *24 January 1897; 11 July 1897; 21 Feb. 1897; 8 May 1898.*
Tennessean (Nashville, Tennessee), 23 October 1897.
Wisconsin State Journal (Wisconsin), 17 January 1898.

CHAPTER 9

'Cecil Husk—Physical Medium,' *The Voice Box*, https://www.the-voicebox.com/huskcecil.htm [accessed April 2021].
'Proceedings of the Old Bailey', https://www.oldbaileyonline.org/browse.jsp?div=t19000402-279 [accessed April 2021].
Anaconda Standard (Anaconda, Montana), 13 Oct 1906.
Beauman, Fran, *Shapely Ankle Preferr'd: A History of the Lonely Hearts Ad* (London: Vintage Books, 2011).
Boston Sunday Post (Boston Massachussets), 24 July 1898.
Bridgnorth Journal and South Shropshire Advertiser (Shropshire), 25 February 1899.
Buffalo Evening News (Buffalo, New York), 24 August 1898.
Chicago Tribune (Chicago, Illinois), 4 March 1897; 31 July 1898.
Daily Mail, 12 May 1898; 17 August. 1898; 3 January 1899; 6 January 1899.
Daily Telegraph and Courier, 15 June 1899; 16 June 1899.

Davies, Owen, *Witchcraft, Magic and Culture*, 1736-1951, Manchester University Press, 1999, p.66.

Demarest, Marc, 'Not By Halves, But By Doubles: Some Notes On Cecil Husk (1847-1920)', *Chasing Down Emma*, http://ehbritten.blogspot.com/2018/04/not-by-halves-but-by-doubles-some-notes.html [accessed April 2021].

Divorce papers Walmisley v de Hamong and Walmisley, Divorce Court File: 548. Reference: J 77/676/548.

Dundee Evening Telegraph (Dundee), 2 June 1898.

Eastern Evening News (Norwich), 15 June 1899.

Evening Standard (London), 15 December 1897; 16 June 1899.

Halifax Courier (Halifax, Yorkshire), 22 April 1899.

Harris Hales, Brian and Laura, 'Other Mormon Leaders Practice Polygamy', *Joseph Smith's Polygamy*, https://josephsmithspolygamy.org/history/mormon-leaders-polygamy/ [accessed April 2021].

Ingram William, *Who's who in Paris Anglo-American colony, a biographical dictionary of the leading members of the Anglo-American colony of Paris*, 1905 (Paris: American Register, 1905).

Lancashire Evening Post (Preston, Lanashire), 15 December 1897.

Light, March 1899; 6 May 1899; 20 May 1899.

Mail (Adelaide), 3 March 1917.

Majoribanks, Edward, *Life Of Sir Edward Marshall Hall* (London: Victor Gollancz Ltd, 1929).

Malpas, Philip, 'Cagliostro, A Misunderstood Messenger, http://lodgeroomuk.net/intblog/download/count-cagliostro/Malpas%20P%20A%20-Cagliostro%20-%20A%20Misunderstood%20Messenger%201936.pdf [accessed April 2021].

Motion Picture News, September-October 1916.

New York Herald (New York), 16 January 1898.

New York Journal and Advertiser (New York),17 August 1898.

Owen, Alex, *The Place of Enchantment* (Chicago: University of Chicago Press, 2004).

Oxfordshire Weekly News (Oxford), 21 June 1899.

People (London), 4 August 1907.

Record-Journal (Meriden, Connecticut) 17 August 1898.

Roughhead, William, *Classic Crimes* (London: Cassell and Company, 1951).

San Francisco Examiner (San Francisco, California), 23 June 1927.

Trowbridge, William Rutherford Hayes, *Cagliostro: The Spendour and Misery of a Master of Magic* (London: Chapman and Hall, 1910).

Van Driel Kluit, Debra, 'Martha Brotherton 1824-1863 A Young Woman of Fortitude, Virtue and Courage', http://debrakluit.blogspot.com/2019/10/martha-brotherton-1824-1863-young-woman.html [accessed April 2021].

Victoria Daily Times (British Columbia, Canada), 11 September1893.

West Gippsland Gazette (Warragul, Victoria), 27 August 1901.

Western Mail (Cardiff, Wales), 15 June 1899.

Westminster Gazette (London), 14 June 1899.

CHAPTER 10

American Register (London), 26 January 1901.

Baltimore Sun (Baltimore, Maryland), 18 November 1899.

Boston Sunday Post (Boston, Massachusetts), 14 January 1900.

Brighton Gazette (Brighton), 19 September 1901.

Brooklyn Daily Eagle (Brooklyn, New York), 25 November 1899; 25 June 1906; 16 January 1943.

Buffalo Times (Buffalo, New York), 22 April 1900.

Chandler, Arthur, 'The Paris Exposition Universelle of 1900', http://www.arthurchandler.com/paris-1900-exposition [accessed April 2021].Chicago *Tribune* (Chicago, Illinois), 3 August 1900.

Daily News (New York), 4 October 1942.

Daily Telegraph (Sydney) 20 May 1925; 27 May 1925.

Democrat and Chronicle (Rochester, New York) 11 April 1900.

Deseret News (Utah), 7 March 1899.

El Paso Herald (El Paso, Texas), 15 September 1899; 26 September 1899; 2 October 1899; 6 October 1899.

El Paso Times (El Paso, Texas), 3 September 1899; 9 January 1902.

Evening Sentinel (Stoke-on-Trent), 4 March 1899.

Hartford Courant (Hartford, Connecticut), 29 May 1900.

Howard, Victoria, 'The American Heiresses Who Saved the Bristish Aristocracy—Jennie Jerome, Lady Randolph Chuchill', *The Crown Chronicles,* https://thecrownchronicles.co.uk/history/history-posts/american-heiresses-saved-british-aristocracy-jennie-jerome-lady-randolph-churchill/ [accessed April 2021].

Idaho Statesman (Boise), 22 July 1899.

Indianapolis Journal (Indianapolis, Indiana), 16 June 1901; 13 May 1902;

International Herald Tribune (Paris), 13 June 1900.

New York Times (New York), 10 April 1900; 13 July 1902.

Salt Lake City Herald (Salt Lake, Utah), 11 March 1899.

Salt Lake Telegram (Salt Lake, Utah), 5 January 1903.

Salt Lake Tribune (Salt Lake, Utah), 25 October 1902.

San Francisco Call (San Francisco, California) 15 January 1899.

Santa Cruz Sentinel (Santa Cruz, California), 19 March 1899.

Santa Cruz Surf (Santa Cruz, California), 25 March 1899.

Seattle Post-Intelligencer (Seattle, Washington), 20 November 1900.

South Bend Tribune (Indiana),08 May 1901; 15 August 1901.

Spokane Chronicle (Spokane, Washington), 10 June 1899.

Temel Paso Herald (El Paso, Texas). 10 October 1899.

Times (Philadelphia, Pennsylvania), 13 July 1902.

Times (Shreveport, Louisiana(, 13 March 1904.

Warder and Dublin Weekly Mail (Dublin), 22 June 1901; 31 May 1902.

Woodstock Sentinel (Woodstock, Illinois), 9 August 1900.

CHAPTER 11

'Annie Kershaw DeMontaigue', Find a Grave, https://www.findagrave.com/memorial/47025518/annie-demontaigue [accessed September 2020].

'Coriolanus', Ellen Terry Archive, https://ellenterryarchive.essex.ac.uk/shakespeare/event/260/coriolanus [accessed September 2020].

'Documents de la session de la Puissance du Canada—1916, (Volume 51, no.3, Documents de la session 6)', https://archive.org/stream/documents6s1916cana/documents6s1916cana_djvu.txt [accessed September 2020].

American Register (London), 7 November 1903; 16 January 1904; 23 April 1904; 7 May 1904; 9 September 1904; 15 January 1905; 2 April 1905; 9 April 1905; 25 April 1905; 22 May 1905; 18 June 1905.

Austin American Statesman (Texas), 18 November 1905.

Baltimore Sun (Maryland), 27 June 1904.

Brereton, Austin, *The Life of Henry Irving*, vol. 2 (London: Longman, Green and Co., 1908).

Bricaud, J, Le Maitre Philippe, 'The Last Duchess D'Avaray', *New York Life—Day by Day*, 4 May 2017, http://newyorkdaybyday.blogspot.com/2017/05/the-last-duchess-davaray-second-episode.html [accessed December 2020].

Brooklyn Citizen (New York), 13 May 1905.

Cambridge Daily News (Cambridgeshire), 17 August 1903.

Cumberland Evening Times (Maryland), 27 June 1905.

Figaro, Le (Paris), November 1903; 29 May 1905.

Folkestone Observer (Folkestone), 17 September 1905.

Globe, The (London), 26 January 1904.

Greenhouse, Herbert, 'Cheiro—Prophesies the demise of Grigori Rasputin, the Mad Monk of Russia', 1971, https://allaboutheaven.org/observations/cheiro-prophesies-the-demise-of-grigori-rasputin-the-mad-monk-of-russia-025825/221 [accessed September 2020].

Hollway, Don, 'Mata Hari', *History Magazine*, 2016, http://donhollway.com/matahari/[accessed September 2020].

Hume Ford, Alexander, 'The Americanization of Paris, *The Busy Man's Magazine*, 1 February 1906, https://archive.macleans.ca/article/1906/2/1/the-americanization-of-paris [accessed September 2020].

Indianapolis Journal (Indianapolis, Indiana), 12 May 1902; 9 September 1903; 21 November 1903.

Inter Ocean (Chicago, Illinois), 7 August 1904.

Jones, Nigel, 'Ceremonies of Bravery: Oscar Wilde, Carlos Blacker, and the Dreyfus Affair by J. Robert Maguire—review', *Spectator*, 24 April 2013.

Lead Daily Call (Lead, South Dakota), 5 November 1903.

Leonard, M C, 'Death of a Princess', *Sunland Tribune*: Vol. 10 (1984), https://scholarcommons.usf.edu/sunlandtribune/vol10/iss1/8 [accessed September 2020].

Light, May 1903.

London Daily News (London), 1 September 1904.

Long, James William. 'Russian Manipulation of the French Press, 1904-1906', *Slavic Review*, vol. 31, no. 2, 1972, pp. 343–354. JSTOR, www.jstor.org/stable/2494338 [accessed September 2020].

Maurice Paleologue (tr. F A Holt), *An Ambassador's Memoirs*, vol. 3 (London: Hutchinson, 1924).

Melton, J Gordon, *Encyclopedia of Occultism and Parapsychology* Vol. 2 (Michigan: Gale Group, 2001.

Muscaline News Tribune (Iowa), 24 January 1904.

New Castle Herald (New Castle, Pennsylvania), 28 March 1906.

New York Times (New York), 7 February 1897; 15 February 1903; 24 September 1911.

Northern Chronicle and General Advertiser for the North of Scotland (Inverness, Scotland), 13 January 1909.

Occult Review, October 1912.

Rocco, Lucio, 'The Sad Story of the Princess de Montglyon', 8 August 2015, http://www.pastorescozzese.com/2015/rose_e.htm [accessed September 2020].

Santa Cruz Sentinel (California), 28 February 1903.

Spokane Chronicle (Washington), 6 July 1905; 9 July 1905.

St. Louis Post-Dispatch (Missouri), 12 Jul 1931.

Sun, The (New York), 1 August 1904.

Times, The (London), 8 October 1904.

Times Despatch (Virginia) 27 June 1905.

West Gippsland Gazette (Warragul, Victoria), 6 September1904.

Williams, Valentine, *The World of Action:The Autobiography of Valentine Williams* (Guernsey: Star and Gazette, 1908).

Yadav, Shivani, 'Captain John Bonavita: the One-armed Lion Whisperer', *STSTW Media,* 13 December 2018, https://www.ststworld.com/captain-jack-bonavita/ [accessed September 2020].

CHAPTER 12

'America's Dollar Princesses & the British Aristocracy', Nobility Titles, 28 August 2020, https://nobilitytitles.net/nobility-articles/americas-dollar-princesses-and-the-british-aristocracy.html [accessed September 2020].

'How American Dollar Princesses Changed Nobility', *Ancestry*, 25 January 2016, https://blogs.ancestry.com/cm/how-american-dollar-princesses-changed-british-nobility/[accessed September 2020].

'Hugo Loewy and Martha Loewy', *Claims Resolution Tribunal*, https://crt-ii.org/_awards/_denials/_apdfs/Loewy_Hugo_den.pdf [accessed September 2020].

'Reginald Henshaw Ward ('Men of the Day. No. 754.')', *National Portrait Gallery*, https://www.npg.org.uk/collections/search/portrait/mw258712/Reginald-Henshaw-Ward-Men-of-the-Day-No-754 [accessed September 2020].

American Register (London), 12 June 1904; 14 May 1905; 17 December 1905; 27 January 1906; 12 May 1906; 14 May 1906; 20 October 1906; 15 December 1906; 22 December 1906; 29 December 1906; 30 March 1907; 24 August 1907; 18 January 1908; 21 March 1908; 2 May 1908; 9 May 1908; 30 May 1908; 25 September 1909.

Archives commerciales de la France, 6 May 1886.

Argus (Melbourne), 28 November 1891.

Atchison Daily Champion (Kansas), 13 November 1914.

Boston Globe (Massachusetts), 1 February 1892.

Brooklyn Daily Eagle (New York) 30 October 1942.

Burlington Daily News (Vermont), 16 September 1911.

Chicago Tribune (Illinois), 7 January 1909.

Cincinnati Enquirer (Ohio), 7 January 1909.

Daily News (Lebanon, Pennsylvania), 1 February 1892.

Daily News (London), 29 July 1905; 4 August 1905; 9 January 1909.

Daily Telegraph (Sydney), 13 June 1925.

*Daily Telegraph and Courier (*London) 1 August 1902.

Darby, Nell, Life on the Victorian Stage Theatrical Gossip (Pen and Sword History, 2017).

Dimanche, Le (Paris), 19 December 1891. *Edina Sentinel* (Missouri), 2 February 1906.

Evening News and Post (London), 7 October 1892.

Evening Standard (London), 19 April 1901.

Evening Star (London), 8 January 1909.

Examiner, Vol VIII, no. 808 (Woodville, New Zealand), 28 November 1891.

Express and Telegraph (Adelaide), 8 October 1892.

Fitzsimons, Eleanor, *Wilde's Women: How Oscar Wilde was Shaped by the Women he Knew* (Gerald Duckworth & Co Ltd., 2015).

Forres Elgin and Nairn Gazette, Northern Review and Advertiser (Morray, Scotland), 30 June 1909.

Green, Nancy L, *The Other Americans in Paris* (Chicago: University of Chicago Press, 2014).

Herald Journal (Logan, Utah) 9 December 1919.

Howard, Victoria, 'The American Heiress Who Saved the British Aristocracy—Jennie Jerome, Lady Randolph Churchill,' *Crown Chronicles*, 30 December 1015, https://thecrownchronicles.co.uk/history/history-posts/american-heiresses-saved-british-aristocracy-jennie-jerome-lady-randolph-churchill/ [accessed September 2020].

Hugelmann, Gabriel, *Les Ecuries d'Augustias* (Paris: Lalouette-Doucé, 1889).

Hume Ford, Alexander, 'The Americanization of Paris, *The Busy Man's Magazine*, 1 February 1906, https://archive.macleans.ca/article/1906/2/1/the-americanization-of-paris [accessed September 2020].

Hutchinson Gazette (Hutchinson, Kansas), 9 January 1909.

Larne Times (Northern Ireland), 1 May 1926.

Leeds Mercury (Leeds), 9 January 1909.

Liberte, La (Paris), 9 January 1909.

Lisburn Standard (Northern Ireland), 4 November 1905.

London Standard (London), 14 May 1906.

Manchester Courier and Lancashire General Advertiser (Manchester), 24 May 1902.

Moore, Larry, 'Musical of the Month: Babes in Toyland,' *New York Public Library*, 25 January 2012, https://www.nypl.org/blog/2012/01/24/musical-month-babes-toyland [accessed September 2020].

Morning Post (London), 14 May 1906.

New York Herald (New York), 5 October 1892.

New York Times (New York), 19 October 1894; 24 January 1901; 9 September 1909; 23 September 1909; 15 September 1911; 16 September 1911.

Newark Advocate (New York), 26 August 1903.

North Otago Times (New Zealand), 1 August 1903.

Northern Chronicle and General Advertiser for the North of Scotland, 13 January 1909.
Oklahoman (Oklahoma) 17 January 1909,
Old Bailey Proceedings, '28th January 1907,' https://www.oldbaileyonline.org/browse.jsp?name=19070128 [accessed September 2020].
Omaha Daily Bee (Nebraska) 26 March 1893.
Pall Mall Gazette (London) 3 June 1905.
Parsons, E Bryham, *Pot-Pourri Parisien* (New York: Broadway, 1912).
Pittsburgh Press (Pennsylvania) 4 May 1902.
Poole, David, 'Fulwell Park, House and Heritage, 24 January 2019, https://houseandheritage.org/2019/01/24/fulwell-park/ [accessed September 2020].
Salem News (Massachusetts), 7 January 1909.
St Louis Post Despatch (Missouri), 10 January 1909.
St Albans Daily Messenger (Vermont), 6 August 1910.
Sun, The (New York), 8 January 1909; 7 August 1915.
Telegraph, The (Brisbane, QLD), 21 December 1905.
Times, The (London), 21 September 1910.
Times Democrat (New Orleans), 7 January 1909.
Toronto Daily Mail (Toronto), 1 February 1892.
Washington Herald (Washington), 23 August 1915.
Washington Post (Washington), 8 May 1909.
Weekly Mail (London), 31 May 1902.
Westminster Gazette (London), 27 July 1905.
Winnipeg Tribune (Canada), 8 January 1909.
Worthing Herald (Worthing), 30 August 1924.
Yorkshire Evening Post (Yorkshire), 2 October 1909.

CHAPTER 13

'Cheiro—W T Stead perished because of insufficient lifeboats on the Titanic,' *All About Heaven*, https://allaboutheaven.org/observations/cheiro-w-t-stead-perished-because-of-insufficient-lifeboats-on-the-titanic-025827/221 [accessed October 2020].
'Etta Wriedt,' *Psi Encyclopedia*, https://psi-encyclopedia.spr.ac.uk/articles/etta-wriedt [accessed October 2020].
'Flora Matilda Hayter,' *At the Circulating Library:A database of Victorian fiction*, https://www.victorianresearch.org/atcl/show_author.php?aid=348 [accessed October 2020].
'Hugo Ames,' *At the Circulating Library:A database of Victorian fiction*, https://www.victorianresearch.org/atcl/show_author.php?aid=348 [accessed October 2020].
'The slumps that created modern finance,' *The Economist*, https://www.economist.com/news/essays/21600451-finance-not-merely-prone-crises-it-shaped-them-five-historical-crises-show-how-aspects-today-s-fina [accessed October 2020].
Altoona Tribune (Pennsylvania), 23 September 1910.
American Register (London) 30 March 1907; 4 May 1907; 15 June 1907; 18 January 1908; 29 February 1908; 21 March 1908; 9 May 1908; 30 May 1908; 12 December 1908; 31 July 1909; 25 September 1909; 15 January 1911; 23 July 1911; 29 January 1911; 7 May 1911; 5 February 1912; 21 December 1913.
Ames, Flora Hayter and Ames Hugo, *Book of the Golden Key* (London: K Paul, Treach, Trubner 1909).

Bay Herald (New Zealand), 23 March 1920; 3 April 1920.

Belfast Telegraph (Belfast), 5 June 1909; 24 May 1911.

Boston Globe (Boston, Massachusetts), 3 August 1910.

Briefel, Aviva, *The Racial Hand in the Victorian Imagination* (Cambridge: Cambridge University Press, 2015).

Bruner, Robert F and Carr, Sean D, 'The panic of 1907', https://www.moaf.org/publications-collections/financial-history-magazine/89/_res/id=Attachments/index=0/Article_89.pdf [accessed October 2020].

Butte Daily Post (Montana), 7 January 1909.

Chicago Examiner (Illinois), 7 May 1909; 21 September 1910.

Chicago Tribune (Illinois), 7 January 1909.

Cincinnati Commercial Tribune (Ohio), 7 January 1909.

Cincinnati Enquirer (Ohio), 7 January 1909.

Civil & Military Gazette (Lahore), 22 March 1912.

Common Cause (London), 23 November 1911.

Connor, Steven, *Dumbstruck: A Cultural History of Ventriloquism* (Oxford: Oxford University Press, 2000).

Daily Gazette (Middlesbrough), 16 January 1911.

Daily Herald (London), 21 June 1933.

Daily Mail (London) 21 September 1912; 5 January 1926.

Daily Mirror (London), 23 March 1911.

Daily News (London), 9 January 1909.

Daily Telegraph (London), 16 October 1909; 27 May 1911.

Daily Telegraph (Sydney,) 3 June 1925.

Daily Telegraph and Courier (London), 14 May 1909.

Demarest, Marc, 'Plainsong, by Post: More on A. F. Tindall', *Chasing Down Emma*, 25 October 2014, http://ehbritten.blogspot.com/2014/10/plainsong-by-post-more-on-f-tindall.html [accessed October 2020].

Dos Passos, John, 'Introduction' in Harris, Frank, *The Bomb* (Portland, Oregon: Feral House, 1996).

Dundee Courier (Dundee), 27 May 1911.

Dundee Evening Telegraph (Dundee), 27 September 1909.

East Anglian Daily Times (Suffolk), 16 October 1909.

Edinburgh Gazette (Edinburgh), 22 July 1910; 1 May 1913.

Evening News (Sydney), 17 April 1909

Evening Standard (London), 16 October 1909.

Evening Star (London), 8 January 1909.

Evening Statesman (Washington), 11 November 1909.

Express (Wales) 24 September 1909.

Figaro, Le (Paris), 7 January 1909.

Fletcher, Anne, *From the Mill to Monte Carlo* (Amberley, 2018).

Folkestone, Hythe, Sandgate and Cheriton Herald (Folkestone), 27 July 1912; 3 August 1912.

Gilbert, R A, *A E Waite: A Magician of Many Parts* (Wellingborough: Crucible, 1987).

Globe, The (London), 20 September 1910; 19 January 1915.

Guardian, The (Manchester), 24 September 1909.

Harrisburg Daily Independent (Pennsylvania), 9 January 1909.

SOURCES

Hendon and Finchley Times (London), 13 January 1911.
Hull Daily Mail (Hull), 2 August 1910.
Hutchinson Gazette (Kansas), 9 January 1909.
Inter Ocean (Chicago, Illinois), 26 October 1909
Lachman, Gary, *Aleister Crowley: Magick, Rock and Roll, and the Wickedest Man in the World* (London: Tarcher, 2014).
Lawrence, David Russell, *The Naturalist and His 'beautiful Islands': Charles Morris Woodford in the Western Pacific* (ANU Press, 2014).
Lakes Herald (Westmoreland), 15 May 1908; 1 October 1909.
Lancashire General Advertiser, 28 September 1909; 16 October 1909.
Leeds Mercury (Leeds), 15 April 1893; 9 January 1909 11 October 1909; 30 December 1911.
Le Petit Parisien (Paris), 6 January 1909.
Liberté, La (Paris), 9 January 1909; 16 January 1909. Manchester Courier and Lloyd's Weekly, (London), 23 April 1911.
London Gazette (London), 19 July 1910; 22 July 1910; 12 January 1911; 14 February 1911.
Los Angeles Herald (California), 25 February 1892; 9 January 1909.
Los Angeles Post Record (California), 28 July 1908.
Los Angeles Times (California), 9 January 1909.
Manchester Courier and Lancashire General Advertiser (Manchester), 28 September 1909; 16 October 1909.
Manchester Evening News (Manchester), 25 September 1909.
Marshall, William, The creation of Yorkshireness: Cultural identities in Yorkshire c.1850-1918 (Doctoral thesis, University of Huddersfield, 2011).
Mercury (London), 15 April 1893.
Moore, W Usborne, *The Voices* (London: Watts and Co,. 1913).
Morning Union (California), 28 February 1909.
New Brunswick Daily Times (Canada), 7 January 1909.
New York Sun (New York), 8 January 1909.
New York Times (New York), 9 January 1909.
Northampton Mercury (Northampton) 21 June 1907; 24 March 1911; 05 February 1943.
Northern Chronicle and General Advertiser for the North of Scotland (Inverness), 13 January 1909.
Oakland Tribune (California), 11 February 1912.
Pall Mall Gazette (London), 1 May 1913.
*Parsons Daily Eclipse (*Kansas), 12 February 1908.
Radical, Le (Paris), 7 January 1909.
Reynolds Newspaper (London), 16 March 1913.
Richmond Palladium (Indiana), 8 January 1909.
Rugby Advertiser (Rugby), 16 May 1908.
Sacramento Union (California), 7 January 1909.
Saint Paul Globe (Minnesota), 10 January 1909.
Salem News (Massachusetts), 7 January 1909.
Salt Lake Herald (Utah), 8 January 1909.
San Francisco Call (California), 10 March 1912.
Scotsman (Edinburgh), 15 October 1909.

SOURCES

Scranton Truth (Pennsylvania), 24 September 1910.
Sheffield Daily Telegraph (Sheffield), 11 October 1909; 16 October 1909.
Smith, Andrew, *The ghost story 1840–1920: A cultural history* (Manchester: Manchester University Press, 2013).
South Bend News-Times (Indiana), 30 November 1919.
South Bend Tribune (Indiana), 7 March 1935.
Southern Echo (Hampshire), 25 September 1909.
Sporting Life (London), 12 October 1909.
St. Albans Daily Messenger (Vermont), 6 August 1910.
St. Louis Post-Dispatch (Missouri), 10 January 1909.
Staffordshire Sentinel (Staffordshire), 19 October 1909.
Standard Union (New York) 8 January 1909.
Star Tribune (Minnesota), 16 June 1912.
Stockton Independent (Teeside), 8 January 1909.
Straits Times (Singapore), 8 March 1901.
Swindon Advertiser and North Wilts Chronicle (Wiltshire), 22 October 1909.
Symonds, John, *The Great Beast: The Life and Magick of Aleister Crowley* (McDonald, 1971).
Tatler (London), 9 February 1918.
Times, The (London), 16 October 1909; 3 August 1910; 21 September 1910.
Times Democrat (New Orleans), 7 January 1909.
Times Union (New York), 7 January 1909.
Vancouver Daily World (Vancouver), 14 October 1909.
Warren Times Mirror (Pennsylvania), 27 May 1911.
Washington Post (Washington), 9 January 1909; 8 May 1909; 11November 1909; 27 May 1911.
Whiting, Lilian, *The Lure of London* (Boston: Little Brown and Co., 1914).

CHAPTER 14

'The beauty, the journalist, and the Titanic,' *BBC News*, 28 December 2014, https://www.bbc.co.uk/news/magazine-30588404 [accessed September 2020].
Bradford Daily Telegraph (Bradford), 4 December 1907.
Everett, William, Musical of the Month: "The Prince of Pilsen", *New York Public Library*, https://www.nypl.org/blog/2011/10/31/musical-month-prince-pilsen [accessed September 2020].
Larne Times (Northern Ireland), 1 May 1926.

CHAPTER 15

'Application no: F/2014/2784 – Green Isle, Wargrave Road, Remenham,' https://wokingham.moderngov.co.uk/mgAi.aspx?ID=2146 [accessed August 2020].
Bath Chronicle and Weekly Gazette (Bath), 18 February 1928.
Brooklyn Daily Eagle (New York), 4 October 1942; 19 January 1943.
Buckinghamshire Examiner (Buckinghamshire), 16 November 1917; 14 December 1917; 18 January 1918.
Bucks Herald (Buckinghamshire), 16 February 1918.
Buffalo Times (New York) July 25, 1917

SOURCES

Bystander, The (London), 8 August 1917.
Carrington, Hereward, *Psychical Phenomena and the War* (London: Dodd, Mead, 1918).
Daily News (New York), 29 October 1942; 16 January 1943; 19 October 1951.
Forbes, Lady Angela, *Memories and Base Details* (London: Hutchinson and Co., 1920).
Globe, The (London), 14 February 1917.
Graphic, The (London), 25 December 1915.
Jong, K H, 'The Trumpet Medium Mrs. Harris', *Journal of the Society for Psychical Society for Psychical Research 16* (1914).
Larne Times (Northern Ireland), 1 May 1926.
Leeds Mercury (Leeds), 3 August 1916.
Light, July 1917.
London Gazette (London), 21 April 1916.
National Post (Ontario), 10 February 1917.
New York Times (New York), 30 May 1914.
Pall Mall Gazette (London), 30 May 1916.
Portsmouth Evening News (Portsmouth), 23 March 1914.
Post Office London Directory 1914, Part 5.
Province (Vancouver, British Columbia, Canada), 6 August 1910.
Richet, Charles, *Thirty Years of Psychical Research*, (New York: Macmillan, 1923).
Sacramento Union (California), 18 December 1916.
Schippers, Mishqah, 'The Golden Era returns to Kruger', *Getaway*, 13 January 2021, https://www.getaway.co.za/accommodation/the-golden-era-returns-to-kruger/ [accessed February 2021].
Times, The (London), 24 November 1915; 9 January 1917; 15 February 1917.
Truth (London), 13 January 1915.
Victoria Daily Times (Victoria, British Columbia, Canada) 14 July 1914.
Westminster Gazette (London), 14 February 1917; 19 June 1917.
Yorkshire Post and Leeds Intelligencer (Yorkshire), 26 March 1932.

CHAPTER 16

Abstracts (1919) Vol. 38, No. 1-12, https://archive.org/stream/in.ernet.dli.2015.45483/2015.45483, [accessed October 2020].
Abstracts issued by the Bureau of Chemical Abstracts, 3 July 1925, https://onlinelibrary.wiley.com/doi/pdf/10.1002/jctb.5000442713 [accessed October 2020].
Albany-Decatur Daily (Alabama), 26 February 1924.
Belfast Telegraph (Belfast), 26 April 1926.
Benyon, Mark, *London's Curse: Black Magic and Tutankhamun in the 1920s* (History Press, 2011).
British Chemical Abstracts 1926, January 1926, https://archive.org/stream/1926A/1926_auth_index_djvu.txt [accessed October 2020].
Bucks Herald (Buckinghamshire), 29 November 1919.
Coniam, Matthew, *Egyptomania Goes to the Movies* (McFarland & Co Inc; 2917).
Coppens, Philip, 'Found: One Ark of the Covenant?' https://www.eyeofthepsychic.com/juvelius/ [accessed October 2020].
Daily Commercial News and Shipping List (Sydney, NSW), 15 August 1923.
Daily Mail (London), 5 January 1926.

Daily Mail Atlantic Edition (London), 8 November 1923.

Daily Telegraph (London), 8 January 1926.

Drogheda Argus and Leinster Journal (Northern Ireland), 13 November 1926.

Dundee Courier (Dundee), 5 January 1926.

Evening Herald (Dublin), 24 April 1926; 26 June 1926.

Evesham Standard & West Midland Observer (Worcestershire), 19 May 1926.

Franklin Times (Pukekohe, New Zealand), 5 May 1924.

Hartlepool Northern Daily Mail (Hartlepool), 16 May 1911.

Haynes, Marc, 'The British Museum's Cursed Mummy,' Darkest London, 20 February 2012, https://darkestlondon.com/tag/thomas-douglas-murray/ [accessed October 2020].

Illustrated Police News (London), 22 July 1922.

Irish Independent (Dublin), 27 April 26; 28 June 1926; 4 February 1927; 5 February 1927.

Irish Times (Dublin), 3 July 1926.

Jersey Financial Services Commission, https://www.jerseyfsc.org/registry/ [accessed October 2020].

Kinematograph Weekly (London), 3 September 1925.

Larne Times (Northern Ireland), 19 May 1926.

Leeds Mercury (Leeds), 6 January 1926.

Leinster Reporter (Northern Ireland), 26 August 1922; 11 February 1928.

Londonderry Sentinel (Northern Ireland), 5 February 1927.

Luckhurst, Roger, 'Unwrapping the Mummy's Curse,' *New Humanist*, 10 September 2012.

Northern Whig (Northern Ireland), 28 June 1926.

Offaly Independent (Offaly, Ireland), 1 May 1926.

People (London), 10 June 1928.

Portsmouth Evening News (Portsmouth), 8 February 1924.

Rosenberg Stephen Gabriel, 'Guest Columnist: Mission impossible,' *Jerusalem Post*, 15 November 2012, https://www.jpost.com/opinion/op-ed-contributors/guest-columnist-mission-impossible [accessed October 2020].

Saturday Herald (Dublin), 26 June 1926.

Sheffield Daily Telegraph (Sheffield), 22 January 1926.

Sunday Despatch (London), 4 December 1932.

Sunday Independent (Dublin), 25 April 1926.

Targett, Kate (transcriber), *1926 Diary of Sir Horace Curzon Plunkett* (1854–1932), 2012, http://www.nli.ie/pdfs/diaries_of_sir_horace_curzon_plunkett/1926_diary_of_sir_horace_curzon_plunkett.pdf [accessed October 2020].

Times, The (London), 1 May 1926.

Western Morning News (Cornwall), 5 January 1926.

Westmeath Independent (Westmeath), 31 March 1923.

Wicklow People (Dublin), 1 May 1926.

CHAPTER 17

'Field Marshal Lord Horatio Herbert KITCHENER,' Masonic Great War Project, https://www.masonicgreatwarproject.org.uk/legend.php?id=1797 [accessed July 2020].

Age, The (Melbourne) 22 February 1924,

Brisbane Courier (Queensland), 22 October 1932.

Cheiro, 'What I read in Lord Kitcheners Hand,' *Strand Magazine*, https://archive.org/stream/TheStrandMagazineAnIllustratedMonthly/TheStrandMagazine1916bVol.LiiJul-dec_djvu.txt [accessed July 2020].
Dundee Courier (Dundee), 1 September 1932.
England, United Grand Lodge of England Freemason Membership Registers, 1751-1921.
International Psychic Gazette, August 1919.
Los Angeles Times (California), 10 March 1927.
Mid Sussex Times (Sussex), 8 May 1928.
Occult Review, August 1918; July 1922.
People, The (London), 5 September 26; 10 October 1926; 22 August 1927; 24 June 1928.
Stage, The (London), 13 October 1927; 15 November 1928.
Tampa Tribune (Florida), 15 May 1927.

CHAPTER 18

'[Letter] 1935 November 30, Hollywood [to] Louis Hamon/Secretary [Catherine Hunter]', *Charlie Chaplin Archive*, http://www.charliechaplinarchive.org/en/collection/cerca/lettera-1935-november-30-hollywood-a-louis-hamon-secretary-catherine-hunter [accessed August 2020].
Argus (New Mexico), 24 September 1929.
Boston Globe (Massachusetts), 12 December 1935.
Campbell, Neal, 'Obituary: Edouard Nies-Berger,' *Neal Campbell—Words and Pictures*, 2002 [accessed August 2020].
Catalog of Copyright Entries 1934 Dramatic Compositions Motion Pictures Vol 7 Pt 1 For the Year 1934, https://archive.org/stream/catalogofcopyrig71libr/catalogofcopyrig71libr_djvu.txt [accessed August 2020].
Direct Voice, The, July 1930. Harrison *Daily Times* (Arkansas), 23 September 1929.
Forum of Psychic and Scientific Research, August 1932; January 1933.
Lincoln Journal Star (Nebraska), 25 August 1918; 14 February 1931.
Los Angeles Evening Citizen News (California), 18 September 1929; 1 June 1932; 21 November 1932.
Los Angeles Evening Express (California), 12 March 1931; 13 March 1931; 11 July 31; 20 July 1931 10 August 1931; 11 October 1931; 3 November 1931; 11 February 1932; 16 May 1936.
Los Angeles Evening Express (California), 2 May 1931.
Los Angeles Evening News (California), 9 July 1932.
Los Angeles Evening Post (California), 30 September 1933.
Los Angeles Times (California), 5 August 1929; 18 September 1929; 20 October 1929; 17 November 1929; 4 January 1931; 29 February 1931; 8 June 1931; 15 June 1932; 16 July 1932; 7 June 1936.
MacKay, Alex, *Tibet and the British Raj: British Raj: The Frontier Cadre, 1904-1947* (SOAS, London Studies on East Asia, 1997).
Mill Valley Record (California), 29 January 1932.
Morning Post (Camden, New Jersey), 24 April 1933.
Nashville Banner (Tennessee), 20 February 1931.
New York Times, 28 January 2002.
Oakland Tribune (California), 13 March 1931.

Observer (London), 13 March 1932.

San Bernadino County Sun (California), 28 March 1924; 3 October 1928; 3 February 1930; 16 February 1930; 23 April 1930.

San Francisco Examiner (California), 26 December 1929. Chichester Observer (Chichester), 10 December 1938.

San Pedro News-Pilot (California), 30 January 1932; 1929 May 1933; 23 October 1934.

St. Feather River Bulletin (California), 6 November 1930.

Starr, Martin P, *The Unknown God: W.T. Smith and the Thelemites* (Teitan Press, 2003).

Times Colonist (Victoria, Canada), 21 July 1932.

Winnipeg Tribune (Manitoba, Canada), 11 January 1937.

CHAPTER 19 AND POSTSCRIPT

American Register (London), 15 March 1902.

Brooklyn Daily Eagle (New York), 29 October 1942, 16 January 1943.

Chichester Observer (Chichester), 10 December 1938; 11 November 1939.

Crown Colonist, volume 7, 1937.·

Daily Gleaner (Jamaica), 16 January 1937; 1 February 1937; 11 February 1937; 12 March 1937; 9 April 1937.

Daily Mirror (London), 4 August 1945.

Daily News (New York), 28 October 1942; 29 October 1942; 16 January 1943.

Hollywood Citizen-News (California), 13 November 1934.

Ironwood Daily Globe (Michigan), 9 October 1936.

Light of Egypt: Church of Light Quarterly, March 1935.

Los Angeles Daily News (California), 10 October 1936.

Los Angeles Evening Citizen News (California), 13 November 1934; 8 October 1936.

Los Angeles Times (California), 9 October 1936; 10 October 1936.

Mail, The (Adelaide), 4 August 1945.

Nottingham Journal (Nottingham), 11 December 1937.

Salt Lake Tribune (Utah), 11 October 1936.

San Bernardino Sun (California), 5 February 1938.

Spokane Review (Washington), 3 February 38.

Time Magazine (New York), 19 October 1936.

West London Observer (London), 28 August 1936.

Western Gazette (Somerset), 17 December 1937.

Yorkshire Mail (Adelaide, SA) 4 August 1945.

INDEX

INDEX

www.ingramcontent.com/pod-product-compliance
Lightning Source LLC
Chambersburg PA
CBHW030917140626
46545CB00016B/1388